**Popular Entertainment,
Class, and Politics
in Munich, 1900–1923**

Popular Entertainment, Class, and Politics in Munich, 1900–1923

Robert Eben Sackett

Harvard University Press
Cambridge, Massachusetts
London, England   1982

Publication of this book has been aided by a grant
from the Andrew W. Mellon Foundation

Library of Congress Cataloging in Publication Data
Sackett, Robert Eben, 1951–

    Popular entertainment, class, and politics in
Munich, 1900–1923.

    Bibliography: p.
    Includes index.
    1. Folk singers—Germany—Munich—Biography.
2. Entertainers—Germany—Munich—Biography. 3. Theater
—Germany—Munich—Political aspects. 4. Theater and
society—Germany—Munich. 5. Munich (Germany)—Popular
culture. 6. Germany—Politics and government—1918–1933.
7. National socialism. I. Title.
ML400.S16   784.5′00943′36   82-2919
ISBN 0-674-68985-2   AACR2

For my father,
for my mother,
and for my brother John

Preface

This book began as an exploration in cultural history. Its topic was the Munich folksingers, a group of stage entertainers who performed for largely middle-class audiences in the late nineteenth and early twentieth centuries. The political, social, and economic developments of the period formed a context within which these artists' routines could be interpreted and understood.

Gradually, I concluded that the folksingers were not only reacting to historical situations like industrialization, World War I, and the Weimar Republic; they were also expressing their public's reactions. Aside from being interesting in themselves, therefore, their acts contain valuable information about the middle class's outlook during these years.

The study's background and foreground had switched places. Although I had been familiarizing myself with the basic history of the period in order to assess the entertainers' statements, I was now using those statements in an attempt to describe the place of a particular social group in that same history. A sense of dual focus remains. The folksingers appear to be the center of attention in sections of this book, but the most important arguments involve their customers, Munich's tradesmen, shopkeepers, office employees, salespersons, lower-level officials, and their families.

My first word of thanks is for Professor Robert C. Williams of Washington University, Saint Louis. He guided the dissertation out of which this book has emerged. I have benefited more than I can possibly say from his scholarly advice and personal concern. It would be highly satisfying if this study reflects any of the passion for history and the openness to new ideas that he conveys to his students.

The Department of History at Washington University treated me very well during my graduate career. Professors Solon Beinfeld, Richard W. Davis, Gerald Izenberg, and Max Okenfuss helped me considerably, and I am grateful to all of them. Venita Lake, the department secretary, gave me her assistance on countless occasions.

The archival research was funded by a fellowship from the German Academic Exchange Service (DAAD). I thank the people of the DAAD and the staffs of the following archives: Stadtmuseum München, in particular Erich Lang and Manfred Hackl; Bayerisches Hauptstaatsarchiv München; Münchner Staatsarchiv; Stadtbibliothek München—Monacensia Sammlung, in particular Richard Lemp, Ludwig Hollweck, and the library's friendly and helpful staff; Bundesarchiv Koblenz; Institut für Theaterwissenschaft der Universität Köln; and Theatermuseum München, in particular Georg R. Laub and Rainer Theobald.

Frau Weiss Ferdl was extremely generous in sharing her memories of her husband with me and in providing me with valuable documents.

Several persons in my new homeland, the Federal Republic of Germany, have helped to broaden my understanding of German culture: Werner Goebel; Karl-Heinz Kraus and Marga Kraus; Christian Enzensberger, who would no doubt be surprised to learn that much of this study was written in a kind of dialogue with him; and my parents-in-law, Wilhelm and Anneliese Gröne.

My editors at the Harvard University Press have been extremely helpful throughout the process of publishing this book. I am particularly grateful to Aida D. Donald.

My employer, Klaus Janssen of Stern Verlag in Düsseldorf, has been very sympathetic to my needs for time off from the job to complete this study, as has my immediate superior, Hermann Bollen. Two colleagues, Irmgard Hachmeister and F. Ulrich Cramer, were helpful in supplying me with needed materials.

Robert Leventhal listened while I was attempting to give final expression to my book's main concepts. He may not realize how important that was. I have enjoyed Bernard R. Davidson's hospitality on visits to Saint Louis over the past several years.

Edith Grunewald, the typist, has added her enthusiasm and support to this project, for which I thank her. Jutta Scholl of the Düsseldorf City Music Library helped me to identify certain songwriters, and I appreciate her efforts.

My last and fondest thanks go to my wife, Christiane, who has backed me in so many ways, who has come to accept my work very deeply, and whom I treasure.

Contents

**Popular Entertainment,
Class, and Politics
in Munich, 1900–1923**

1

A City of Entertainment and a Sense of Decline

At the close of a performance before his usual Munich audience one evening in April 1924, nearly five months after the city had been jolted by the unsuccessful putsch of Adolf Hitler's National Socialist German Workers' Party (NSDAP), Weiss Ferdl (1883–1949) sang a round of patriotic songs. His fists clenched, the folksinger *(Volkssänger)* was in a mood of impassioned conviction. "One could see," a local newspaper reported, "that he feels with body and soul for his fatherland." As soon as he had finished singing, the article continued, the house rang with "thunderous applause." From what followed, it is clear that this part of Weiss Ferdl's show amounted to no less than a public demonstration of sympathy for the National Socialists. Some of his admirers presented him with two laurel wreaths, each with a long ribbon tied to it: "On the first ribbon were the signatures of all the defendants in the Hitler trial, and on the second those of their attorneys." Although there is no record that the Munich entertainer voiced specific approval of the Nazis before the putsch, it is not surprising that so staunch an opponent of the Weimar Republic would gravitate to the radical right. The colors of the ribbons on his laurel wreaths, it is important to note, were black, white, and red, the Empire's colors.[1] By accepting them, the folksinger expressed both his allegiance to the Imperial state that had ceased to exist at the end of World War I and his disdain for the successor state that had signed the notorious Treaty of Versailles in 1919. Hitler had pledged to destroy the Republic. His bold attempt to seize power in the Bavarian capital was the first step of a larger plan to assume national control and restore German might. This was all to his credit in Weiss Ferdl's eyes.

By mentioning the "thunderous applause" that rewarded Weiss Ferdl for his nationalistic fervor, the newspaper account of his performance touches upon this book's central methodological argument: that popular entertainment in early twentieth-century Munich reflected the political and social attitudes, ideas, and sentiments of its audience. Weiss Ferdl—this stage name means "little white horse" in the Bavarian dialect—once wrote that the typical folksinger "came from the common people. He lived among them and knew what troubled their hearts, and what did not suit them. And so, he always found the right tone for his listeners."[2] Treating entertainment as an indicator of its audience's views, however, requires a clearer idea of who was in the audience than the phrase "the common people" affords. Is it possible to be more exact than Weiss Ferdl about the social groups that were most represented in the folksingers' public? The one other historian who has dealt with this stage tradition, Ludwig M. Schneider, has concluded that this was a "largely middle-class to lower middle-class audience."[3] I agree that Munich's popular entertainers drew most of their customers from the city's "traditional" or "lower" middle class of tradesmen and shopkeepers, and from the "new" or "white-collar" middle class of office employees, salespersons, and minor government officials. There is already considerable historical interest in these groups; many scholars have argued that they formed the base of popular support for the early Nazi movement.[4] Information about Munich middle-class attitudes toward political and social issues, therefore, adds to knowledge of the setting within which the NSDAP rose.

Since before 1914, a sense of economic and social decline pervaded these middle reaches of society in the Bavarian capital. Industrialization had brought serious problems for tradesmen and shopkeepers in its wake, until the future of these occupations appeared uncertain. Factories were mass-producing goods that could be sold at lower prices than those that came from traditional workshops, while department stores were luring customers away from small retailers. The working-class movement, in the form of unions, was at the same time gradually raising the living standards of industrial workers to the middle class's level. Pessimistically, tradesmen and shopkeepers faced slow impoverishment, which in the end could force them to quit their businesses, to enter the proletariat, and to suffer the accompanying loss of social status. Munich, it is true, was not among the areas of Germany most shaken by industrialization. But to label its economy of the early twentieth century "middle-class," as historian Karl Bosl has done, is not to suggest that owners of small businesses lived free of the pressures that affected their counterparts in more industrialized regions of the country, like the Ruhr Valley and parts of Saxony. Factories and other enterprises of large-scale production—for example, some world-famous breweries—had in fact broken ground in the city during the late nineteenth century. Of course, they impinged upon the traditional middle class's sphere of buying and selling. Small firms also competed among themselves; the most successful enlarged their operations, employing more journeymen and apprentices or more shop assistants, and even introducing new machines to the extent that it was profitable. Nor did Munich exist in isolation from the larger German and European markets. Indeed, although it was not a leading industrial center, the volume of its commerce had expanded greatly in the second half of the nineteenth century. Linked by rail to other cities' and areas' factories, Munich daily received their finished goods, which were promptly displayed in department stores. Under these conditions, Munich's traditional middle class lived on, not as hard-pressed as many tradesmen and shopkeepers had been where industrialization was fully under way, yet wondering uneasily how long it would be before the forces of the new economy advanced to their own already weakened positions.[5]

Also well represented in the folksingers' clientele, the men and women of Munich's white-collar middle class had problems similar to those of the city's tradesmen and shopkeepers. On the surface, these two groups appear quite divided, above all, as regards economic change. Industrialization threatened the traditional middle class, while the sheer complexities of its private operation and public administration created jobs for sales and office personnel and lower-level officials. By enlarging and thus strengthening the working class, however, it alarmed the two middle classes equally. This was the most important point of connection between them: their common fear of losing income and status until nothing distinguished them from the proletariat. White-collar employees in Munich viewed the first signs of labor agitation, even from the city's relatively small working class, with concern. They envisaged a future in which their standard of living would drop, while that of workers would rise because of the success of unions in negotiating better wage contracts. In the end, there would be an immense new mass of social equals. Particularly injurious to office employees, salespersons, and minor officials prior to World War I were their own scruples against taking the step that would have been most effective in self-defense: unionization. They disavowed organizing because of its association with the working class and thereby waived the salary increases that certainly would have followed. Apparently, they believed that they could somehow maintain their superior social status by grandly refusing the additional income upon which their status would have to rest.[6]

In the decade that followed the outbreak of World War I, middle-class problems turned into hardships. The economic situation of many Munich tradesmen and shopkeepers worsened during the four years of war. Despairing, these owners of small businesses watched as raw materials and finished goods that they needed went to large firms with military contracts. Moreover, the war was having a direct social leveling effect to their disadvantage. Resentment ran high among men and women from this social stratum over the extra pay and food that unions had won for manual workers, especially for those in the armaments industry, while they themselves hungered under wartime rationing. The white-collar middle class did not fare any better. Forced to work additional hours without salary raises that even kept pace with wartime inflation, many office employees, salespersons, and minor officials reached the point where they began to look for help. They recognized that the unions were protecting many workers from a similar decline of living standards, and their readiness to join and back their own organizations grew. In general, the living conditions of Munich's middle class had become so dismal by 1918 that support for the war effort—and even for the Empire—sagged. After the defeat, the Weimar Republic's failure to restore economic order added to its difficulties at gaining the loyalty of tradesmen, shopkeepers, and white-collar workers. The exorbitant inflation of the early 1920s stifled the postwar recovery. While the real incomes of office and sales personnel and of lower-echelon bureaucrats deteriorated even further, the operations of small companies were disrupted by the utter lack of solid money.[7] It was in this climate of middle-class pessimism and uncertainty that Adolf Hitler's Nazi party thrived in the Bavarian capital.

IN INVESTIGATING the political and social contents of Munich popular entertainment up to the 1923 Hitler putsch, this study does not begin with 1919, the first year of both the Weimar Constitution and the NSDAP, but instead returns to about 1900, when industrialization was already transforming the city's economic life. It traces the continuity of middle-class attitudes, concepts, and moods between the prewar and postwar eras. It demonstrates that opposition to the Republic emerged out of sentiments that had permeated the world of tradesmen, shopkeepers, white-collar workers, and their families since the turn of the century. Thus, it contradicts a time-honored myth, according to which prewar Munich was too cultural and harmonious a city to have been the scene of any real unpleasantness. One who propagated the myth was Thomas Mann: in a 1926 speech he maintained that before 1914 Munich had had a "popular character [*Volkstümlichkeit*], on the healthy, rich topsoil of which the most peculiar, tender, and audacious things, and sometimes exotic plants, could thrive under truly favorable conditions." Taken as a whole, Munich was "artistic," unlike Berlin, which was "political and economic."[8] Clearly, Mann was generalizing from the Munich he knew, a place of galleries, artists' cafes, and beautiful parks. There was another Munich, however, a city plagued by industrial change, experiencing the ill effects of rapid urbanization. Because of the work opportunities that a growing economy provided, this city drew in tens of thousands of new inhabitants—many from rural areas of Bavaria—in the late nineteenth and early twentieth centuries. Its population increased dramatically, until the provincial capital of thirty thousand in 1800 had grown to nearly half a million in 1900. Urban problems followed: overcrowding; food price inflation; noise; inadequate sanitation; heavy traffic; and not the least, conflict among different ethnic and national groups.[9] It is important to consider that the men and women of Munich's middle class were having to adjust to the requirements of modern city life at the same time that they were having to cope with their economic difficulties.

Reflected in the popular entertainment of early twentieth-century Munich, particularly in Weiss Ferdl's routines, was a structure of middle-class views on political and social questions. Its main parts included yearning for a preindustrial community, disdain for Jews, patriotism, and especially after World War I, anti-Marxism. This structure arose in the late nineteenth century, grew firm before the war, and kept large parts of the middle class from accepting the spirit and institutions of the Weimar Republic after 1918. Why was it built? Tradesmen, shopkeepers, and white-collar workers in prewar Munich lived in fear of the day when they would have to relinquish their last advantages of status and income after a humiliating decline into the working class, that is, of the day when they would no longer belong to their own class. Regarding social and political issues, they formed their attitudes, developed their concepts, and withdrew into their moods all in an effort to compensate for this deep-seated fear of not belonging. In effect, they constructed an edifice that was held together by their own widespread need for assurance. Within its walls and underneath its roof, everyone belonged; everyone felt like an "insider" and looked out at the rest of the world as though it were composed of "outsiders."

Near the base of this structure was the middle class's nostalgia for a harmonious, rural, preindustrial community to which each individual belonged from birth onward, in which no one had to worry about becoming an "outsider," and in which there were no social divisions between classes. Nor did uncertainty over relations between the sexes arise in this haven of old-fashioned values: in contrast to the city, traditional rules of courtship were observed; divorce was virtually unknown. People from the middle reaches of society dreamed of being in such a community, but the hard reality of their lives constantly awakened them, forcing them to require other, less fantastic assurances. Resentment of Jews helped to satisfy this requirement. Jews, as the occupants of many of the economic positions from which the non-Jewish middle class felt threatened, were the objects of considerable ill feeling. Moreover, because they had a different religious and cultural tradition, often bore distinguishable physical characteristics, and had been recently and only partially integrated into German society, they were natural "outsiders." Those who desired a sense of membership in a special group excluded the Jews.

Loyalty to the Empire, pride in the Imperial military, and satisfaction over Germany's "place in the sun" crowned the structure of middle-class attitudes before World War I. By comparison, grievances over taxes and freedom of trade appear insignificant; they never opened the regime's legitimacy to doubt. Close identification with the Empire and with its deeds remained quite widespread. Thousands of Munich's men, including many at the outset of middle-class work lives, had internalized the habits of devotion to the state while on terms of duty in the Imperial army or navy. These "schools of the nation" had accustomed them to executing commands, and more important, had impressed them with a lifelong sense of participation in a grand and glorious national enterprise.

Thus, as tradesmen, shopkeepers, and white-collar workers faced the economic problems that spread fear in their class, many of them were able to take comfort in idealized memories of a time when they had belonged to a truly purposeful organization. More generally, they found "insider" status in the Empire, as long as they obeyed its laws and uncritically believed that their interests were being served by its accomplishments.

Portraying the attitudes, sentiments, and ideas of Munich's middle class as parts of a structure is valid only if one recognizes that "the structure" is a metaphor that has uses but also definite limits. For example, some allowance must be made for historical change. To demonstrate that a certain attitude was widespread in 1923, 1915, and 1900 is not to suggest that it existed with unwavering force throughout the twenty-three years under consideration. Nonetheless, a continuity of views is evident, based in the problems of industrialization and revealing itself in the acts of the Munich folksingers. "The structure" is meant to express this continuity. Another of the metaphor's limits is imposed by the sheer variety within the middle class. Certainly, many tradesmen, shopkeepers, and employees supported the Empire, shunned the Jews, and fantasized about a lost community. These were the structure's permanent inhabitants. It should not be surprising, however, that other middle-class men and women only came to visit, experiencing—at least partially—the security that the structure provided, but then carrying their quest for social assurance elsewhere. Undoubtedly, some did not come at all. In this study I offer some general theses about the political and social orientation of a relatively broad portion of society. My conclusions are not designed to include everyone who could be seen as "middle-class."

After World War I, the intensification of economic difficulties and the survival of social and political attitudes from the Empire underlay the antipathy that large sections of Munich's middle class felt toward the Revolution, and toward the Revolution's political offspring, the Weimar Republic. For a few months after its proclamation on 7 November 1918 in the Bavarian capital, the new state enjoyed a period of grace with many tradesmen, shopkeepers, white-collar workers, and their families. Mourning for their dead sons and brothers, and living in the misery that wartime food and coal shortages had created, these people accepted the Revolution because it had brought them peace. Shortly, however, they sensed that they were being drawn into a working-class state, one that would strip them of their last advantages of property and social status. Horrified and angered, they quickly repaired the structure of anti-industrial, anti-Jewish, and patriotic attitudes that had made them feel safe during the Empire, and added a large, antisocialist watchtower to it.

Throughout Germany, the middle class tended to see the Republic as the Empire's unholy and unwanted successor, a dangerous mixture of Marxist communism, Jewish materialism, and disgraceful internationalism. Many Germans from this part of society never forgot the spirit of proletarian upheaval that the Revolution had exuded and passed on to Weimar. Nor did they forget the prominence of several radical left-wing Jews—Rosa Luxemburg in Berlin, Kurt Eisner and Ernst Toller in Munich—at the Revolution's beginning. Regarding foreign policy, they resented the Republic for signing the "dictated peace" (*Diktat*) at Versailles in June 1919. The state that arose in late 1919 and early 1920, however, did not actually fulfill the middle class's worst expectations. Under the leadership of the moderate Social Democratic Party (SPD), its socialism halted after the establishment of the eight-hour workday, and its internationalism collapsed under the weight of Versailles. Many of its leading Jews had departed, having either been jailed for their radicalism or fallen victim to assassination. However, the Republic failed to overcome its stigma as a Marxist-pacifist-Jewish conspiracy. Had it been given the chance to establish its legitimacy under conditions of economic calm, it might still have succeeded. Opposition to it became much less vigorous, in fact, during the years of relative prosperity, 1924–1929. Economic hardships marked the period 1919–1923, however, and contributed immeasurably to the spread of antirepublican views, particularly among the middle class.

Concentrating here upon the relationship of popular entertainment to popular attitudes in Munich, this book stops short of answering the question of how opposition to the Weimar Republic developed into support for National Socialism in the crucial months before the putsch. Obviously, the NSDAP preyed upon this opposition. But prior to the Nazis' attempt to seize power, there is little indication of direct sympathy for them in the Munich folksingers' acts. What middle-class audiences thought about National Socialism in the period leading up to its sensational deed is not clear. There is no justification for assuming that tradesmen, shopkeepers, and employees who despised the Republic for signing the Versailles *Diktat,* for advancing the Jews, and for exhibiting socialist tendencies were Nazi backers, even if many leaned in that direction. Hostility to Weimar certainly lies in the background of popular support for Hitler. It is nonetheless a historical topic in itself, a topic that warrants investigation.

Weiss Ferdl's entertainment mirrored the yearning for a preindustrial way of life, the resentment of Jews, and the patriotism of Munich's middle class. The city's one other great folksinger of the early twentieth century, Karl Valentin (1882–1948), expressed none of these views. In his performances, one directly encounters the audience's fear of social decline. A starting point for understanding the relationship between Valentin's acts and popular sentiments is to recognize that he was almost invariably funny; portraying his own bewilderment, inadequacy, and misfortune, he generated laughter.[10] What does this reveal about his public? In answering this question, it is extremely useful to turn to the works of philosophers, psychologists, and sociologists on the function of laughter, or humor, in society. Specifically, the French philosopher Henri Bergson and, more recently, the Dutch sociologist Anton C. Zijderveld have advanced arguments that put Valentin and his early twentieth-century Munich following in a very interesting perspective. Bergson and Zijderveld have diametrically opposed concepts of laughter's place in human existence: Bergson defined humor as "something mechanical in something living," that is, as the result of someone's machinelike failure to act with the spontaneity that society demands from all its members at all times; Zijderveld, by contrast, regards society—with its network of behavioral norms—as a machine, and humor as an essential and harmless outlet for natural, unregulated feelings, that is, for spontaneity.

Bergson and Zijderveld agree, however, that the person who is the object of humor becomes a social outcast, or in the language of the present study, an "outsider." Bergson described laughter at one point as the "punishment" that society imposes upon someone whose awkwardness has suddenly become noticeable. He also wrote that "the laugher considers himself, and more or less proudly says yes to himself, while he sees the other as a marionette." Zijderveld, analyzing the role of the "ceremonial clown" in tribal societies, reaches the conclusion that this outlandish prankster in effect forces his amused onlookers to draw together in recognition of their common bond to social values and habits. His uncontrolled sexual antics, above all, "are clever means to the end of [social] integration and conformity." He confronts other members of society with an image of the chaos that would engulf their lives if they no longer observed social restrictions; laughing because the "clown" is not a serious threat to society, they also keep their distance from him, inwardly frightened and at the same time convinced of their superiority.[11] Valentin, of course, was far from a "ceremonial clown." His entertainment was not as wildly impulsive, and his integrative function would not seem to have been as great. Still, he did make a career out of representing chaos for those in his audience, and whether he was aware of it or not, thereby gave them feelings of superiority. As Bergson would have put it, he allowed them "to say yes to themselves." For Munich's hard-pressed tradesmen, shopkeepers, and white-collar workers, this was a highly desired effect. Worried that they were caught on a ladder of social decline, it reassured them to see Valentin on a much lower rung. They would continue to belong to the middle class, they felt, as long as their physical and mental powers so obviously distinguished them from someone who did not belong. By laughing, they "punished" Valentin for his failures; grateful for the chance to do so, they rewarded him by coming again and again to watch him fail.

Both Karl Valentin and Weiss Ferdl soothed the "insider" and "outsider" anxieties of their public. Their styles could hardly have been more different. Weiss Ferdl's songs and one-act plays lovingly recreated the atmosphere of a traditional rural community and invited the men and women of the audience to simply dream of all the happiness they had been forced to abandon. It amused people when Weiss Ferdl pointed his finger at the Jews, and it made them solemn when he raised his full-throated voice to honor the German fatherland. Valentin had little to do with any of this. The trademark of his outrageous comedy was that it made people laugh over his misfortunes; finally, they could not help but conclude that their positions in society were not half as bad as his. Both folksingers assured their middle-class customers that they belonged to a greater social whole.

* * *

THE MUNICH FOLKSINGERS date from the middle of the nineteenth century, and probably drew their largest crowds in the 1880s
and 1890s. From the beginning, they vigorously articulated popular
views on a great range of social and political issues. This entertainment tradition died out gradually during the first third of the twentieth century, as new forms of amusement, such as jazz, dancing,
and the cinema, started winning the public's favor. Karl Valentin
and Weiss Ferdl, both of whom began their careers after the turn of
the century, represent a last surge of the folksinger movement. Both
enjoyed great popular affection. Like their most successful nineteenth-century predecessors, they had their acts printed into book or
booklet form and sold. For this reason, there is a wealth of revealing
material on how middle-class people in Munich regarded the social
and political developments that lined the way to the Weimar Republic.

By unofficial estimate, nearly four hundred folksingers were performing in Munich around 1900. A few of the most versatile appeared as one-man shows, but the great majority belonged to folksinger troupes. Their name creates the mistaken impression that
they were solely musical artists. Although they did sing, accompanying themselves on stringed instruments or with a piano in the
background, they were usually also actors and comedians. Moreover, these generally Bavarian-born and -raised entertainers wrote
most of their own routines: songs, one-act plays, monologues, and
dialogues. As a result, their performances exuded a genuinely local
air. Certain acts took this to an extreme; delivered in thick Bavarian
dialect, they were incomprehensible to anyone from outside the
province.[12]

Entertainment in Munich was tied to the popular beer-drinking
culture that had already given the city a worldwide reputation: taverns housed the folksinger performances; men and women swigging
tall glasses of the local brews made up the audiences. The physical
appearance of these taverns is described in the following recollection: "At one corner of the tavern stood a small platform, a rough
canvas with a pastoral cottage painted on it as a background, and
next to the platform, a piano. There was no curtain. Often there
were not even dressing rooms for those performing, so they had to
change clothes and put on makeup in the kitchen. For their en-

trance, they had to go through the rows of tables to the platform."[13] It is surely an irony that the owners of these common taverns used high-sounding French titles to label their houses "cabarets" (sometimes Germanized to *Kabaretts*), or "*varietés*," when they did not call them "music halls" (*Singspielhallen*). None of these terms carried much precision, but they do appear to have had different connotations. Whereas the folksingers had an evening on a cabaret stage to themselves, a *varieté* was likely to engage other kinds of acts as well—for example, magical, acrobatic, or juggling acts. Music halls seem to have been distinguished by their large size and by group singing during the performances. Thus, the terms "cabaret," "*varieté*," and "music hall" are not interchangeable.[14] Their meanings are, however, similar enough that another term—"small stage" (*Kleinbühne*)—can be applied for most generalizations. The small stages did not constitute the only setting of Munich's popular entertainment. Often, the folksingers appeared at private gatherings or at the city's breweries, which gave enormous festivals on certain holidays. Still, it is from Munich's cabarets, *varietés*, and music halls that these local performers are most often remembered.

Three kinds of evidence make it clear that the folksinger audience was largely middle-class: memoirs of the folksingers themselves; memoirs of people who had attended performances; and police files on the small stages, often relating to censorship, but also recording quite useful observations about the clientele.[15] Of course, it would be desirable to further characterize the audience in terms of occupation, neighborhood, religion, age, and place of birth. But this would require more and better evidence than is available. For the purposes of this study, the general information suffices. From the entertainment that the folksingers delivered to their public, it is possible to glean an understanding of the deep-seated "insider" and "outsider" worries that ultimately alienated thousands of Munich tradesmen, shopkeepers, and white-collar workers from the Weimar Republic.

The folksinger audience was mostly but not exclusively middle-class. Some manual workers, for example, also visited the small stages. Ludwig M. Schneider has explained this with reference to Munich's overall economic and social conditions. Although the city expanded into a major commercial center in the late nineteenth century, it did not heavily industrialize. Production increases tended to occur in enlarged tradesmen's workshops, not in factories. This retarded the development "of a modern, closed industrial working

class; the workers were far too colored by the lower middle class."
Strikes, it is true, grew more frequent in Munich during this period,
but they lacked the scale, the organization, and the ideology that
marked labor unrest in more industrialized regions of Germany. Politically, the domination of the working class by tradesmen made the
Bavarian section of the SPD resistant to hard-line socialism. Cul-
turally, it stifled the rise of proletarian art and amusement forms.
Workers in Munich had not reached the state of class consciousness
where they would have rejected a folksinger for his middle-class orientation and demanded their own entertainment.[16]

Contending that this largely middle-class audience saw its own
structure of yearnings, resentments, loyalties, and fears reflected in
the entertainment is not meant to trivialize the folksinger's extremely important role in giving these attitudes a voice. On the contrary, people went to a tavern cabaret in order to hear something
that they themselves were unable to say—at least not fluently. In-
tently, they listened for the entertainer to transmit his message of assurance: that they occupied unassailable positions in a larger social
body; that they were "insiders." Original as the folksinger may have
been in wording and in presenting this message, he nonetheless had
taken its basic content out of the store of common popular attitudes.
In the case of Weiss Ferdl, his songs and plays so alluringly portrayed a preindustrial community that the audience felt a sense of
belonging among its good-hearted and solid inhabitants. At other
times, he joked about "outsiders" like the Jews, or called upon his
listeners to revel in their pride at being part of the glorious German
Empire. Karl Valentin, by contrast, made his own worries and
problems the center of attention until people forgot theirs, that is,
until he himself became the "outsider." Both entertainers had the
public's implicit trust. Upper-class observers had trouble appreciat-
ing this. So unrefined a public, they assumed, was only looking for
something frivolous to roar over in a state of mindless, rowdy inebri-
ation. Naturally, there was more than the folksinger's message at a
cabaret, varieté, or music hall. Men and women from the middle
layers of Munich society wanted to leave their private cares at the
front door and enter a brightly lit, smoke-filled hall of plentiful beer,
rousing music, and thunderous laughter.[17] Many also wanted to
hear the folksinger's views on the enormous social and political
changes that the times had brought.

Middle-class people at the tavern cabarets derived their sense of "insider" status not only from the entertainment but also from the mere fact of being in the audience. Ordering mugs of the house brew, tapping their feet to the music, and exchanging words with their friends, they felt like members of a large, close-knit group. Often reinforcing this feeling was the presence of "outsiders." Aristocrats, professional people, intellectuals, students, and even tourists saw the Munich folksingers perform. Curiosity led some of them to the small stages; some felt the desire to experience a coarse, yet amusing popular diversion. Some may even have been influenced by the attitudes they heard, at least for the evening. But their social backgrounds established a distance between them and the regular, largely middle-class clientele.[18]

BECAUSE MUNICH'S FOLKSINGER entertainment was so distinctive, many writers have assumed that its origins lay in age-old city traditions of popular amusement, or at least no farther away than the nearby Bavarian Alps, where a mountain people had supposedly always shown an instinct for clowning. Actually, there is more romance here than historical insight. When the Munich folksingers began performing on their small stages in the 1860s, they drew quite heavily from outside sources, especially from the popular entertainment of another city of the southern German-speaking world, the Austrian capital of Vienna. As early as the 1820s, some Vienna taverns were featuring native singers and actors, who presented original songs and short plays. To the small degree that the Metternichian system permitted, these small-stage acts expressed social and political attitudes. Frequently, the early Munich folksingers adapted the Viennese songs to the Bavarian dialect or used them as models for their own creations.

Another line of influence from Vienna to Munich begins in the former's mid-nineteenth-century popular theaters (*Volkstheater*), where ticket prices were kept low enough that not only tradesmen and shopkeepers but also manual workers could afford to join upper-class people in the audiences. Normally these theaters offered a form of comic musical play (known as a *Posse*) in which stock Vienna characters—masters and apprentices, servants, farmers in from the country—strove to attain happiness and to avoid ruin, often unaware that their destinies were being influenced by supernatural beings and occurrences. Although there was some attempt to realistically depict the hardships that these common social types endured, the presence of such otherworldly forces helped convince the public that a change of mere human social and political arrangements would bring no improvement. Likewise, the happy endings that were a part of this theatrical form soothed those in the house who might have been on the verge of drawing radical conclusions. The most famous person in the Viennese popular theaters was Johann Nestroy (1801–1862), who wrote, staged, and acted in plays at the Theater an der Wien (Theater on the Vienna). Over time, Nestroy dropped the supernatural elements from his works and let his characters simply fight the social odds with which they were confronted. There was a certain bitterness in his humor, and his happy endings often ironically resolved what had seemed to be truly hopeless situations.

Plays by Nestroy and by other Vienna dramatists appeared in Munich from about 1830 through the 1860s at theaters that had been newly opened on the example of those in the Austrian capital. Just as the Munich folksingers later reworked Viennese tavern songs, the directors of Munich's popular theaters had the Viennese plays either changed into the Bavarian dialect or imitated with Bavarian themes and characters, often pastoral in nature. Generally, when financial troubles began to close these Munich theaters in the 1860s, the cabarets and music halls that replaced them for much of the popular audience took over song and play forms that had already—in Vienna and then locally—been used to portray social conditions in a humorous but at times searching light.[19]

Popular entertainment in Vienna slowly declined during the late nineteenth century, for which historians have held a mid-century split of its audience into middle- and working-class parts responsible. In one older account, the Revolution of 1848 is seen as playing an instrumental role in this process by freeing the peasants from serfdom and thus bringing many of them into the cities as wage laborers; in Vienna, the newcomers, often of the Empire's non-German nationalities, took no interest in the existing popular culture.[20] According to a more recent Marxist study, the division of the audience into middle-class and proletarian groups had occurred a few years before the Revolution, as the two began to recognize their fundamental conflict over private property.[21] Either way, the popular theaters began to raise their prices in order to keep the workers out, and more important, the social harmony out of which the entertainment had grown was destroyed.

Similar attempts to explain the Munich folksingers' rise in terms of social and economic development result in a series of interesting but partial hypotheses. In 1935 one writer suggested that "the prosperity of [Munich's] people grew, and with it, a sense of humor."[22] With regard to the working class, there may be a kernel of truth in this. Essentially, the late nineteenth century did improve the German working class's standard of living, both in real wages and through the ameliorative social programs of Bismarck. Perhaps more Munich workers came to the small stages to drink beer and be entertained because they had more money to spend on their own amusements. Still, this cannot be offered as an explanation of the folksinger movement as a whole. Workers may have experienced increasing prosperity in late nineteenth-century Munich, but the tradesmen and shopkeepers who were more numerous in the audience did not.

Another, even more general line to take is that popular entertainment in Munich was a cultural response to economic growth: people had come into the city from small towns and farm villages and had given up the occupations of their ancestors for new kinds of work in commerce and industry; having left the environment in which religion and religious celebrations had dominated cultural life, they needed new forms of free-time diversion, secular and wholly modern. Put so broadly, there can be little objection to this. It too, however, ignores that it was precisely the least modern members of Munich society—the owners of small businesses—who formed the center of the folksinger audience. Indeed, in terms of both the social basis of the audience and the social perspective of the acts, Munich's folksinger entertainment seems more related to the embattled survival of old groups than to the sudden appearance of new ones. Moreover, with reference to what has been written about Vienna, one wonders if the predominance of Munich's tradesmen and shopkeeper class did not in effect create a "social harmony" from which the city's entertainment drew sustenance. This may seem plausible, but doubts remain. These doubts arise in reducing a cultural phenomenon as unique as the Munich folksingers to social conditions that were much less unique themselves. If class relationships supported certain forms of popular culture in Munich, why did similar forms not emerge in other cities with similar class relationships? What distinguishes Munich? Inevitably, these questions raise complex issues of historical causation, issues that cannot be dealt with here.

REGARDING THE METHODOLOGY used in this study of middle-class social and political attitudes in Munich, it is important to consider the problem of documenting popular attitudes in general. Historians dealing with the views of ruling elites, of the aristocracy, or of the educated upper middle class in modern Germany, for example, often have whole archives of literary evidence to peruse. It is quite different for scholars interested in lower levels of German society. Tradesmen, shopkeepers, white-collar employees, and workers wrote fewer memoirs and kept fewer diaries than did their social superiors. If there were prodigious correspondents among them, the letters have not usually been preserved. Even in the age of mass literacy, it is not always clear which books influenced or expressed the thinking of men and women from these parts of society. Better literary testimony can certainly be found in widely circulated magazines and newspapers. Recently, historians of popular attitudes have sought other kinds of material. Werner K. Blessing, for instance, has argued that researchers must be prepared to look for evidence beyond the sphere of the conventional written word. Popular culture offers a great variety of sources, he continues; among the most valuable are traditions of popular entertainment, which often quite clearly reflect the sentiments of their audiences.[23]

Gregory H. Singleton has stated this argument in the following terms: "Those forms and themes which achieve popularity are those which accurately reflect the psychic will of the people." He proceeds to object: "The problem is that the people choose their entertainment forms from a relatively limited range of options, and within the context of patterns of daily life which inform that selection . . . Perhaps a safer premise would be that no form which is absolutely contrary to widely shared values will achieve popularity."[24] Concerning this study, Singleton would maintain that Munich folksingers Karl Valentin and Weiss Ferdl may not have reflected the attitudes of their middle-class audience; all that can be claimed is that they did not offend those attitudes. Two sets of circumstances reduce the force of such doubts. First, Valentin and Weiss Ferdl rose out of a field of hundreds of popular entertainers to win widespread, lasting acclaim. Perhaps their customers would have gone to the small stages in any case. The point is, however, that they chose to go where Valentin and Weiss Ferdl were appearing—out of dozens of alternatives on any given night. It is difficult to imagine that they would have done so while remaining neutral toward the two artists' pronounced and often blatant social and political views.

Second, like most Munich folksingers, Valentin and Weiss Ferdl began their working lives in the lower middle-class milieu of much of their audience: Valentin had been a cabinetmaker; Weiss Ferdl was a former printer who once declared that the performers in his troupe had all the skills necessary to open a press. Both had turned to entertainment only after failing to gain secure positions in their trades, which were declining because of industrialization. Both understood the problems that beset those whose livings depended upon a small business. Naturally, they identified on stage with their middle-class public. Valentin became a master of portraying the living conditions of people at this level of society through comic exaggeration. His daughter later described how he found inspiration for many of his routines: "With half an ear and half an eye open, he was always somewhere on a street corner, in a streetcar, in a bar or in a stairway, snatching up bits of conversation and other proceedings . . . which developed immediately inside his mind into a scene or dialogue."[25] To the extent that Valentin mixed socially, it was with Munich's common people: "Small tradesmen from the neighborhood," as one of Valentin's friends later wrote, formed most of his inner circle. "These gatherings offered him inspiration and models. Above all, they explain his comedy."[26] Weiss Ferdl's entertainment also reflected the concerns of his public. An admirer understood this, and wrote: "What a person laughs about is his best mirror."[27] Valentin and Weiss Ferdl both fit the following description by a folksinger enthusiast: the performers "had a sense of humor and appeared before people receptive to humor, from whom they were distinguished by nothing but talent and their lower middle-class audacity to want to prove themselves on stage."[28]

Naturally, more went into Karl Valentin's and Weiss Ferdl's acts than the social and political attitudes of the audience. Both folksingers had strong personalities that affected their outlooks and styles. How is a question with which this study will have to deal. The result is not to divide their entertainment into "personal" and "public" components, but rather to indicate why they were able to voice this or that popular feeling with such sincerity and conviction. Although evidence of their psychological makeups is scarce, it is generally clear that both Valentin and Weiss Ferdl projected their inner selves into the social spirit of their performances.

As entertainers, Valentin and Weiss Ferdl were members of a profession that was heavily influenced by economic, social, and political developments. They perceived their era no less as working stage artists than as former tradesmen. Thus, it is essential to gain a sense of the changes that the entertainment world underwent in the early twentieth century. For example, although Valentin's and Weiss Ferdl's understanding of industrialization had arisen out of their experiences in small business, it grew as the union movement spread to the stage industry. By about 1910, they were both too well established to be personally concerned, but they keenly remembered the hardships they had endured at the outset of their careers. The efforts of younger colleagues to find protection against similar hardships must have impressed them. Likewise, Valentin and Weiss Ferdl appeared under political conditions that affected their routines. Before 1918 they knew the authoritarianism of the Empire in the form of police censorship. Neither could have risked being seditious or indecent on stage. Weiss Ferdl was not particularly affected by the censor's limits, but Valentin was forced to state his occasional criticisms of the Imperial system in code. During the early years of the Republic, when censorship had been abolished, the National Socialists practically assumed its functions in Munich by holding demonstrations against entertainment that they found politically offensive or simply un-German. Again, this affected Weiss Ferdl less than it did Valentin. Generally, both folksingers faced the problem not only of how to say what they wanted to say but also of whether it was permissible to say it.

SINCE THE PUBLICATION of Rudolf Heberle's classic account of the peasants of Schleswig-Holstein during the Weimar Republic, historians have acknowledged that a local study of twentieth-century German political attitudes can serve two purposes.[29] First, it can provide a particular case for examining national economic, social, and political trends, for testing old assumptions, and for developing new hypotheses. Second, it can heighten scholars' awareness of the special role that one specific city or region played during these years of political turbulence. Munich is an apt subject for a local study in both ways. It offers an excellent local context for an investigation of the continuities of German middle-class social and political attitudes, ideas, and sentiments from the late nineteenth century to the Republic. Recently, several historians have dealt with the economic frustrations of tradesmen, shopkeepers, and employees in this era of industrialization.[30] They have tended, however, to neglect middle-class views toward politics and society. In the Bavarian capital, it is possible to see how sentiments from before 1914—longing for a preindustrial community, disdain for Jews, and unquestioning patriotism—fed opposition to Weimar. Further local studies could help determine the extent to which this was typical for Germany as a whole.

Munich also serves the second purpose of a local study of politics during the Republic. Historians have long recognized that Munich contributed to the early National Socialist movement by giving it a home after World War I and by being the scene of its ideological, organizational, tactical, and mass political development before the abortive Hitler putsch of 9 November 1923.[31] The opposition of the city's middle class to Weimar indicates yet another way in which Munich provided the early NSDAP with a friendly environment. Thousands of its citizens were at least potentially receptive to the Nazis' antirepublican politics.

I also hope to revise some common historical conceptions about early twentieth-century Munich. Preoccupied with Hitler and the rise of the National Socialist party in the early 1920s, historians of the postrevolutionary city have not delved into the pre-1914 social and political views of the middle class. As a result, they have not adequately uncovered the "insider" and "outsider" concerns that form the origins of resistance to the Weimar Republic in the Bavarian capital. Granted, these scholars recognize that the economic decline of many Munich shopkeepers, tradesmen, and white-collar workers had been fomenting hostility toward the Jews, the socialists, and the capitalists since well before the war. It is also clear from their studies that nationalism after 1918 represented the extension and intensification of sentiments common to the prewar period. Still, one misses a deeper interest in the history of this portion of society and a fuller appreciation that the years before 1914 were as important in creating attitudes as the years after 1914 were in hardening them.[32] Before World War I, the middle class's yearning for a preindustrial way of life, its resentment of Jews, and its loyalty to the Empire had all expressed the need of despairing people to feel that they belonged to a larger social entity. This need became steadily more insistent during the postwar era of crisis. By failing to meet it, the Republic disillusioned Munich's middle-class citizens and left them highly vulnerable to the appeals of the radical right during the economic turmoil of the early 1920s.

Prewar Munich has been the subject of insufficient study by historians of city politics in the Weimar era, but its history is far from unknown. Historians of Munich, above all Ludwig M. Schneider, have investigated the social ill effects of the city's rapid economic growth, depicting them as the origins not of opposition to the Republic but of the popular support that the Bavarian Revolution of 1918–19 attracted.[33] Others have concerned themselves with the dissolution of loyalty to the Empire during the war. Karl-Ludwig Ay and Georg Kalmer have shown that the middle class represented an integral part of the tens of thousands in Munich who were ready by 1918 to blame the Imperial government for their hardships and to join in the Revolution.[34] Linking the massive unrest at the end of World War I with wartime misery and prewar discontents, Schneider, Ay, Kalmer, and others have not completely ignored the middle-class swing to the right in the early 1920s. Nevertheless, they have marked it off as a separate historical issue. Only in a few suggestive but passing references do they acknowledge that resistance to Weimar did not constitute a wholly new phase of city history but rather arose out of those pre-1918 social trends that they themselves have taken such care to document.[35]

This study seeks to bridge the gap between the two groups of historians that have dealt with early twentieth-century Munich: the one that traces the development of long-term social problems up to 1919 but not on into the Republican years; and the other that overlooks these problems while focusing upon the dramatic rise of the early NSDAP. The historical picture of Munich that results is new in two regards. First, the prewar antecedents of middle-class disdain for Weimar receive proper emphasis. Second, the Revolution of 1918–19 looks less like the outcome of changes that had been going on for decades and more like an aberration. The Bavarian capital's tradesmen, shopkeepers, and white-collar workers may have welcomed the Revolution at first, but they quickly recognized their mistake and turned to the right.

2

The Middle-Class Origins of Munich Entertainers Karl Valentin and Weiss Ferdl

Belonging by his birth in 1882 to Munich's traditional middle class, Karl Valentin (born Valentin Ludwig Fey) spent his entire youth inhaling the musty air of middle-class ambitions and fears. His father, Johann Valentin Fey, had left his native city of Darmstadt in 1852, and found work with an upholstering company in the Au, a suburb of Munich. Twelve years later, the elder Fey had the company's license transferred to his name—apparently upon his employer's retirement. Under his ownership, the emphasis of the business shifted from upholstery to furniture transport; it seems that there were enough customers. In 1869 Johann Fey, then a widower, married Johanna Maria Schatte, a baker's daughter from the Saxon city of Zittau. The couple produced four children, of which the future folksinger was the last. Occupying the middle floors of the building that housed the transport firm, the Feys added to their income by renting out the upper floors. A backyard garden supplied them with vegetables and offered a pleasant spot to which they could withdraw from the city's noise and activity. If furniture transport brought the family years of lean to go with the years of plenty, the young Valentin knew nothing about it. He later recalled his boyhood as a time of comfort, if not of prosperity.[1]

Neither Johann Valentin Fey nor his wife left any historical trace of their personalities beyond the printed recollections of their son Valentin and their granddaughter Bertl. According to Valentin, the elder Fey was a very sociable man who drank heavily, a man with a good sense of humor to match an explosive temper. The folksinger's mother, by contrast, tended to be anxious and restrained. Her husband's drinking, for example, upset her enormously. Bertl portrayed her as "the typical good middle-class wife with a consciousness of social position" (*Standesbewusstsein*).[2] It was probably more from her than from his father that Valentin first gained an awareness of the "insider" and "outsider" issues that later pervaded his entertainment.

One of Johanna Fey's main fears centered upon her son's health, which is understandable, for he was the only survivor of her four children. The first, a daughter named Elisabeth, died of an unre-corded ailment three months after her birth in 1871; two sons, Karl and Max, born in 1873 and 1876, respectively, died of diphtheria within one month of each other in 1882, when their brother Valentin was less than half a year old; he himself contracted diphtheria as a baby and nearly died. It is an interesting reflection upon the scien-tific and technical accomplishments of the day that Valentin was saved not by a physician prescribing modern medicine, but by an old woman of the Au administering some kind of herbal juice. Grief had led Johanna to the edge of suicide, but seeing how precariously her infant held on to his life, she decided to hold on to hers. Throughout his youth, she treated him "like a raw egg . . . [and] ful-filled all his wishes even before he hinted what they were."[3]

Privately, the adult Valentin expressed many fears: of traveling, of performing, of lightning, of cemeteries, and so on, any one of which could practically immobilize him. As he once complained to a friend, "When I'm down, I'm afraid of falling up."[4] Fear was also a central theme of his entertainment. Whether he inherited his mother's anxieties or was suffering from the aftereffects of his own painful infancy cannot be ascertained; the available evidence does not nearly allow such probing into Valentin's deepest regions. Only a highly sketchy description of the surface is possible. Generally, it is clear that certain aspects of Valentin's personality emerged in the characters he portrayed on stage. Valentin found an outlet for his feelings of fear in many of the acts he delivered as a popular enter-tainer. In a hundred variations, he played the man who was afraid that the ceiling would fall in. The comic presentation of his own anxieties, moreover, formed part of his approach to the social fears of his audience. In the special world of a Valentin evening, a man who was afraid of the ceiling reassured people that their problems were small by comparison.

The primary source of information on Valentin's boyhood is a short autobiographical book he wrote as an adult, entitled *Der Knabe Karl* (The Boy Karl). Unfortunately, it offers few insights into the fears that later plagued him. According to *Der Knabe Karl*, between the ages of eight and fourteen the future folksinger was de-voted to causing trouble for virtually every grown-up with whom he came into contact. His life, as he recalls it, moved from prank to prank, each more elaborate and malicious than the last. When he was nine years old, for example, he accompanied his parents to visit relatives on his father's side at a farm near Darmstadt:

> In my childish ignorance, I threw cats into the manure pile, which was located in the farmyard, made the farm dogs rebellious with all conceivable means, mowed down the prettiest garden flowers and the rose patch with the scythe, knocked in windowpanes, tricked the cows by putting stickers up their noses, pinched the ears of the rabbits they were raising and of the goats with clothespins, and opened the doors to the pig stalls, in spite of being frequently warned that it was forbidden. And because there was nothing I liked better than riding, I set myself right away onto the best sow, and went off . . . For half a day, my uncle and his farmhands had to look for the sows in the surrounding area, and catch them.[5]

Apparently he was no less unruly at home—at the expense of his parents, his neighbors, his teachers, passersby, and even his father's customers.[6]

As an autobiographer, Valentin certainly exaggerated in places. Indeed, these descriptions of his boyhood read more like a continuation of his entertainment career than like an accurate depiction of situations and events. Undoubtedly, he wrote for his admirers, wanting to fit his youth into a legend that was as unique and bizarre as the routines he delivered on stage. Still, there is some additional evidence that tends to bear Valentin out, at least in general. His daughter's book, which was informed by hundreds of conversations with his mother, reports that angry neighbors frequently appeared at the Fey home to complain about Valentin's antics, and even at times to demand that he be turned over for revenge.[7]

Although it is impossible to tell the extent to which Valentin embellished these stories of his boyhood, they are useful for the picture of Valentin's early family life that emerges from them, a picture that his daughter later redrew in the same form, but less sharply. Often missing from this picture, in fact strikingly missing, is punishment. Valentin does not mention, for example, that either of his parents responded to the tricks on his uncle's farm at all. From other incidents, it is clear that he was able to offend his mother with impunity. Far from imposing discipline, she was the victim of some of his cruelest tricks. Once, in his teens, he stuck a piece of sponge into a reddish brown dye and held it up to his mother, screaming that it was his finger, cut off in the circular saw. Only after "my poor mother" had turned pale with fear did he reveal the joke; she was, in the words of her granddaughter, too "weak-willed" to control him. Nor did the future folksinger meet with much resistance from his father, who instead tended to view him, as Bertl put it, "with a real sense of humor." The elder Fey could even appreciate Valentin Ludwig's impish attacks on his own customers, as when the boy found the panama hat of one of them lying on a cart in the yard and nailed it down: "My poor father had to buy a new hat; but he laughed about it, like always, when I had done something. Of course, my mother cussed me out; but that didn't hold me back from thinking up my next trick." If Valentin's father was not strict with his son himself, he could fly into a rage with anyone else who was. Once, after a teacher had beaten the boy for not remembering the words of a prayer, it was all his mother could do to keep her husband from seeking out the pedagogue with the intent of assaulting him. Generally, the only father-son conflict that comes to light in Valentin's later stories had to do with his father's drinking: "With that, as the son I came for the most part pretty well into a fury, because our family chief was not exactly amiable in the third stage of intoxication."[8]

Young Valentin occasionally pulled a secret, anonymous prank, one that left its victims boiling in anger but uncertain as to who was responsible. Thus he described his days with the slingshot: "[They] hear the whistling of the stone, but no one knows where it comes from. I still bet today that I could shoot in all the windows of a four-story house within ten minutes at a distance of two hundred meters with such a slingshot, without anyone knowing who had done it."[9] But if Valentin wanted to stay hidden behind some of his most infuriating misdeeds, more often he wanted acknowledgment for his imagination and talents. This is evident not only in the things he did to make people mad but also in the things he did to make them laugh. Once, when he was eight years old, he and a friend dressed themselves like the clowns they had seen in the "Circus Bavaria" and entered a tavern where the elder Fey sat drinking with his friends: "For me, the criticism [of his friends] was a particular stimulus, because they were unanimously convinced never to have seen anyone look so dumb-assed [*saudumm*] as the Fey kid [*Fey-Buam*]." The "Fey kid" and his friends also gave little theatrical performances—including a twelve-minute version of *Faust!*—in the Fey's yard and even toured the Au with a puppet theatre: "The money we collected was divided among the players and went to buy sweets at the grocer's."[10]

The Au, Valentin's home suburb, presumably strengthened this impulse to amuse; by virtue of its popular theaters (*Volkstheater*), it had become "a kind of amusement center," as one historian has written, by the mid-nineteenth century. True, in Valentin's day the Munich folksingers had replaced this older tradition and were no more associated with the Au than with any other area. But the suburb retained a certain uniqueness of spirit as it grew within the city that surrounded it.[11] For example, its boundaries marked off the domain of dozens of "Munich characters" (*Münchner Originale*), those legendary figures of the city's taverns, street corners, and markets, of whom their friends and admirers said, "There is only one like that and there will never be another." Valentin later recalled them as "unique, humorous human beings." The "characters" of the late nineteenth-century Au included, for example, an innkeeper named Steyrer who was acclaimed for his strength as "the Bavarian Hercules," and a particularly entertaining drunkard who traveled the streets on a tricycle.[12] If the Au enjoyed these and other "characters" year-round, there was a special cause for gaiety each spring: the Paulaner Brewery's annual beer festival, a huge celebration of the new year's brew.[13] Local amusements such as these were basic elements of the "Fey kid's" environment; they stimulated him and, in later years, helped him to look back with fondness upon the Au. "I was not born in Munich itself, at least not in the old city . . . ," he once wrote, "but in the suburb of the Au."[14]

Attempts to visualize Valentin in the Munich of his boyhood must include the product that both turned the wheels of the city's economic growth and brightened the way its citizens spent their leisure time: beer. These were the years of the great rise of the Bavarian breweries, led by Löwenbräu in Munich, until in 1913—when Valentin was thirty-one—one glass of beer out of every ten in the world contained a Bavarian brew.[15] In Munich, beer was not only the usual beverage but a profound cultural phenomenon as well. When a man from Munich drinks a glass of it, observed the dramatist Max Halbe, "it is a cultic act."[16] Halbe, a man of letters, wrote with some detachment, but folksinger Andreas Welsch, a favorite of the 1880s and 1890s, performed nightly before audiences that emptied whole barrels of the drink: "Where would we Bavarians be with our culture, if not for our beer?" he asked, and one can imagine the roar that followed.[17] Beer's importance in the public life of the city was clear for all to see: during the festivals of the different breweries; at the Oktoberfest; in the Hofbräuhaus. It flowed no less through the daily routines of thousands of ordinary people, who drank it among friends at their neighborhood taverns, or ordered it from the taverns to drink at home. In the latter case, the head of the household sent a male servant or, if he had no male servants, one of his sons. For the Feys, this duty fell to Valentin; perhaps he resented having to provide his father with the intoxicant that made him so unpleasant. At any rate, as an observant boy, the "Fey kid" surely came to know the sights, odors, and sounds of Munich's beer culture.[18]

Valentin's recollections of his youth testify to the sheer excitement of growing up in a rapidly modernizing city. Late nineteenth-century Munich was undergoing changes of style, mood, and appearance at breakneck speed. For example, the new applications of technology that were seen in the city during the first fifteen years of Valentin's life included: electric streetlights; streetcars, first run on steam and then on electricity; automobiles; telephones; and moving pictures, which brought scenes of the battles of 1870 and of "Cairo and the Banks of the Nile" to an enthralled audience. Valentin found all of this fascinating. He later claimed to have conducted electrical experiments himself, and even to have attached some sort of shock to the knob of the house door, thereby providing the mailman with an unwelcome surprise. There were also new sports, full of action, to capture a child's imagination. Above all, Valentin loved bicycle racing. He and his friends idolized the best racers, he recalled, and practiced the sport on their own bikes.[19]

Munich's growth as a city led to the development and expansion of city services, some of which incidentally brought hours of pleasure to the city's children. Valentin's friends, for example, were enthusiastic about the volunteer fire brigades, which fought 117 fires in 1891, when Valentin was nine, as against 75 in 1882, when he was born. Perhaps the ceremonial, quasi-military aspect of the fire brigades helped to create a mystique; one can imagine the "Fey kid" in the crowd at the Nymphenburg Palace on German Fire-fighting Day in July 1893, watching the assembled brigades of Munich and surrounding towns march in formation. But most important was the fire itself. Valentin later remembered jumping onto moving fire wagons so as not to miss any of the thrills of a fire. More plausible are his recollections of playing fire brigade at home until the police made him stop because he was making too much noise.[20]

Valentin's interests in electricity, bicycle racing, and fire fighting serve as reminders that his early relationship to Munich's "popular entertainment" should not be considered too narrowly. With his active imagination, he found entertainment in the daily developments, pastimes, and activities of the growing city. But he did not, for all this, stay away from the entertainers proper: the singers, jugglers, and clowns who provided Munich's largely middle-class public with diversions and amusements. Certainly, he visited the circuses that set up their tents in Munich. He later remembered approaching the ticket stand at the Circus Bavaria on his knees, so that he could pass for a younger child and enter at a lower admission.[21] He also got to know the performers who were then practicing what would become his profession, the Munich folksingers. His exact reactions are not recorded, but he later remarked that "Papa Geis" was more popular in Munich than the Prince Regent, a sign that he was among those for whom this was true.[22]

The entertainer who most deeply impressed Valentin was certainly Karl Maxstadt (1853–1930), a native of Freiburg-im-Breisgau who sang original couplets and presented imitations before audiences throughout Europe. Indeed, the stage name "Karl Valentin" was chosen in honor of this traveling performer. Valentin was fourteen years old the first time he saw Maxstadt appear in Munich's Colosseum. He later wrote that this directly influenced him to become a folksinger.[23] But there was to be a delay; Johann Fey had reached a decision about his son's future, and in 1897, he sent Valentin to apprentice with a master cabinetmaker in the neighboring suburb of Haidhausen. "A trade," explained the father, "has a golden floor."[24] However well the furniture transport company was doing, the elder Fey would surely have realized that most trades had declined since his arrival in Munich half a century earlier. Entertainment, however, was too insubstantial an alternative for the son of a middle-class home.

Valentin stayed with cabinetmaking for five years, advancing in 1899 to the status of journeyman. Work certainly did not force him to give up his foolery. He and the other apprentices "used to ring doorbells across the street and were thievishly pleased when the people swore at us out of their windows."[25] There were laughs through the week, but real enjoyment came on Sundays, when Valentin and his friends wore their best suits to play billiards and drink in the beer gardens. If they swaggered more than usually on these occasions, there was a reason beyond the dictates of style: work-free Sundays were only then being introduced in Munich, as in the entire Empire; these apprentices and journeymen would have known that they were among the first to exercise the newly won rights of weekend leisure. In any event, Valentin relished these Sundays: "There was never any lack of things to talk about. We were so many-sided. That was just fun and foolery."[26]

It was also in this way—self-confident, entertaining, full of nerve—that the young tradesman made his first approaches to women. During his years in Haidhausen, around 1900, he met his future wife, Gisela Royes, a servant in his parents' home. She had recently come to Munich from a small town not far from Regensburg. At first, she found him shocking. Particularly offensive were his habits of sticking his hands in his pockets and of whistling rather than knocking at the door to her room. Moreover, as she later told her daughter, he was something of a "Don Juan." In time, she discovered that he also had an appealingly tender side. She kept a love poem he wrote in 1902, and later passed it on to her daughter. Entitled "Memory of the First Love," it began:

> As we sat lost in our dreams
> On a bench surrounded by leaves,
> And on your sweet lips,
> I found the way to love.[27]

That the poem was preserved is fortunate; it affords a rare glimpse of Valentin expressing himself seriously.

That same year, in 1902, Valentin Ludwig Fey reached the decision to quit his trade and become an entertainer—a comedian and singer. "I banged a nail into the wall," he later wrote, "and hung up the golden trade of cabinetmaking forever."[28] Certain aspects of his personality emerged in this decision. One was his need for amusement. Repeatedly, from his boyhood through his years as a young tradesman, this need is clearly visible in certain basic forms: passively, in his fascination for the spectacular, for example, for bicycle racing; actively, in games that stretched his imagination, such as fire brigade, and in his pranks. For Valentin, the middle-class working milieu—in spite of its occasional diversions—must have been dreary. Playing practical jokes and drinking beer with the other apprentices were not enough for a young man who had begun to imagine himself as a performer of the popular stage, as an inhabitant in a world of unfailing amusement. The lures of such a world would have been hard for him to resist.

Behind Valentin's decision to become an entertainer lay not only his need to find amusement for himself but also his impulse to create it for other people, that is, to entertain them. That this impulse had existed since his childhood is clear, for example, in the satisfaction he felt when his father's friends appreciated him in his clown costume. Much later, Valentin suggested that he became a comedian in order to help people live more easily with their troubles, in order to spread "the golden humor that helps us to get over so much."[29] This seems, however, more like the afterthought of an old performer who had lived through the upheavals of Germany and Europe that began in 1914 than the reasoning of a young cabinetmaker about to attempt a stage career in 1902. Generally, there is little to confirm that Valentin ever had any such sense of mission. Because of the lack of evidence, his deepest motives for becoming an entertainer lie in darkness. But there is clarity nearer to the surface, if one recognizes that in entertaining an audience Valentin was satisfying old urges: to provide himself and other people with amusement.

Although Valentin later wrote that starting as an entertainer and quitting his trade were parts of the same piece, he had begun to perform well before he banged his last nail into the wall in 1902. His daughter notes that in 1899 he was already appearing before local trade association groups.[30] He was, in short, an amateur; whether he sometimes retained a fee is not known. Actually, this does not single him out among Munich popular entertainers at the turn of the century. Many folksingers performed only occasionally, without giving up the trades at which they earned their livings.[31] Most of them were probably satisfied by the chance to sing and tell funny stories, and would never have considered trying to become professionals. Valentin may have been temporarily satisfied too, but he then decided to go further, to leave his first career and to proceed onto the hard terrain of his second.

Valentin probably had economic as well as personal reasons for becoming an entertainer. As a young tradesman in turn-of-the century Munich, he would have directly experienced the problems that faced the traditional middle class during Germany's age of industrialization. Cabinetmaking seems to have been one of the city's trades most hard-pressed by factory competition.[32] Unfortunately, neither Valentin nor his daughter later wrote about his years as a tradesman in any detail. However, the remark of a friend indicates that they had been difficult, and implies that they led Valentin to entertainment: "As a cabinetmaker who worked on caskets [Sargschreiner], Valentin was always out of work and therefore tried to earn his money as a musician on occasion."[33] Cabinetmaking did not offer him a very promising future. Perhaps the event that finally impressed this upon him was a strike that spread into cabinetmakers' shops throughout Munich in 1900, one year after he had become a journeyman.[34] Under such conditions, a stage career may have not only excited him; it may have appeared to be the surest avenue of escape from his distressed, declining trade.

Valentin's first step was to enroll in a "varieté school" directed by a Munich comedian named Hermann Strebel. After three months, Valentin left the school—having either graduated or withdrawn—for an engagement in a Nuremberg varieté. There he appeared as a comedian, twice each night, four times on Wednesdays, and six times on Sundays. Each appearance consisted, as he wrote home to inform his parents, of three numbers, one of which was a three- or four-minute song that he had written himself and entitled "Rezept zum russischen Salat" (Recipe for a Russian Salad).[35] Valentin's "Rezept" begins plausibly enough, calling for ground beef, then pepper and salt, then three lemons, but proceeds to name the most bizarre and even indigestible ingredients: sardines, spinach, and marzipan; turpentine, cement, and "two young white mice." So,

> If everything is in, just as I've dictated
> Stir it all with a spoon,
> Believe me, it really tastes wonderful
> You see, that way a funny salad gets made.

Certainly, there is the spirit of a prank, of passing something inedible off as good to eat, in this piece of nonsense. Imagining that the "Fey kid" wrote it is not difficult.

Regarding the success of Valentin's first venture as a professional entertainer, as regarding his early career in general, the evidence is conflicting and confusing. In *Der Knabe Karl,* he wrote: "Sure, instead of the star's pay of a [Karl] Maxstadt, I received only one mark and eighty pfennigs. And as for the princely hotel room of which I'd dreamed, that didn't turn out either. I got a little room in the attic, in which water dripped from the ceiling onto the bed, and where all the rats and mice of Nuremberg got together."[36] A letter he wrote at the time, preserved and later published by his daughter, tells a different, more detailed, and more convincing story. Appraising the situation in Nuremberg for his parents, Valentin complains that the audience of officers and students was more interested in the female performers than in him, and confesses that his "Rezept" was "not going over in the least." Overall, though, he was satisfied because he was winning not only applause from the public but praise from his director, who wanted to arrange appearances for him in Munich. The young comedian figured that he was in the position to earn three hundred marks a month—a comfortable sum for a bachelor, perhaps twice what he could have made as a cabinetmaker. Being an entertainer suited him; he stayed up late at night, got up late in the morning, enjoyed himself during the day, and ate well. Here, in Valentin's enthusiasm for his new life, one senses part of his frustration with his old life, with its heavy demands and unexciting routine. In a postscript to his letter, Valentin was frankly ecstatic. Apparently he had just returned to his room from the evening performance, and could report that he had stolen the show: "They screamed and stomped their feet. The applause lasted almost half a minute." Based on this letter, it seems that Valentin's 1902 debut as an entertainer was both successful and highly promising.[37]

Two days after Valentin wrote this letter, his father became quite ill and died. This not only saddened the young comedian but put his future as a stage entertainer in question. He appeared that evening in Nuremberg—"with a broken heart," he wrote Gisela Royes—and then returned to Munich, to his father's funeral, and past that, to the furniture transport company his father had left behind.[38] The next five years of his life are hard to reconstruct. Later, he rather vaguely portrayed them as years of failure and frustration in his performing career, and of poverty; he was a "poor, skinny devil." There is too little evidence to definitely rule this out, but it seems more likely that Valentin spent the four years after his father's death, until 1906, operating the family firm. Business was perhaps not good, but surely not bad enough to make him a "poor, skinny devil."[39] There is ample evidence that he did not give up entertainment. He appeared privately as a "song humorist" (*Gesangshumorist*) before several private Munich groups, although he may not have received anything in return other than profuse words of thanks and a general eagerness to have him back.[40] It is quite conceivable that he sang partly or mainly original material, like his "Russischer Salat." However, the door to life as an entertainer, which had opened briefly in Nuremberg in 1902, was all but closed.

In October 1906, Valentin's mother sold the transport firm. Either in the months preceding this sale or shortly after it, Valentin conceived and developed a plan to return to professional entertainment. He sank a great deal of his mother's and his money into building a musical contraption out of twenty-odd different instruments, the sounds of which he could then produce all at once. Before the end of 1906, he had taken his "living orchestra" to perform at the restaurant his uncle owned in Zittau. A local newspaper reported that its "exactness and uniqueness was admired on all sides."[41] This confirmed Valentin in his belief that a stage career lay ahead for him with his invention.

The year 1907 was to be crucial for Valentin, because it brought him first to the edge of ruin and then to the starting point of success. Incomplete and inconsistent evidence, again, permits only the most general description of his activities. At some point early in the new year, Valentin took his "living orchestra" on tour. Among his first engagements was a theater in the Bavarian town of Bernburg, and as a local newspaper reported, it went fairly well. Then, he headed north. On 16 March, he premiered in Halle at Süssmilch's Walhalla Theater. By one account, his act collapsed in Halle. Valentin's daughter, however, has written that he appeared for four months in Halle and ran into trouble only when he went on to Berlin, where no entertainment hall employed him. Whenever and wherever things fell apart, the evidence agrees that Valentin was forced to return to Munich and that his musical mechanism stayed where it was until a friend provided the money to have it shipped home. Valentin was thoroughly disillusioned with his "living orchestra." True, he went on tour with it to the Bavarian cities of Ingolstadt and Landshut late in 1907. But shortly thereafter—during a "big drunk from Löwen-bräu beer [*Löwenbräubierriesenrausch*]," as he later recalled—he hacked his once prized creation to splinters.[42]

Following his disastrous tour in the first half of 1907, it seems quite conceivable that Valentin was indeed a "poor, skinny devil" for a period of several months. His mother, her money gone, had returned to Zittau to live with relatives and was in no position to offer any assistance. During this time, Valentin slept in a hostel for trade apprentices for two marks a week. He remained an "entertainer" but was reduced to taking the lowest jobs in the smallest taverns: occasionally, he had a role in a "farmers' comedy" (*Bauernkomödie*); more regularly, he accompanied other singers on a zither for fifty pfennigs a night and supper.[43]

These experiences of 1907 amounted to the loss of status and income that Valentin would have learned to fear during his traditional middle-class boyhood and his years as a cabinetmaker; he had become a kind of proletarian. His later recollections indicate that he felt this very keenly. There is, for example, the small-business middle class's dread of having to work for wages in Valentin's reluctance to pass the hat after playing his zither. Above all, he feared the disgrace of being recognized by someone in the audience who had known him in his father's home. Once, the unbearable happened: "Miserable creature that I was, I'd gotten one of our neighbors from the Au." Twenty-five years old, Valentin was suffering from his bad luck and paying for his mistakes. Socially, he had fallen out of the class to which he had belonged as a youth. A friend of his later claimed to have talked him out of suicide during this darkest period of his life.[44] Toward the end of 1907, Valentin's fortunes improved, but not until after he had lived through this tradesman's nightmare.

Germany's industrialization had a direct and negative effect upon Karl Valentin's early working life. He remembered this as an entertainer, even at the height of success. Throughout his career, the folksinger dealt with the issue of middle-class social decline for Munich's small-stage audience; the fallen tradesman was one of his stock characters. Clearly, he was basing his acts upon his own decline. His brilliance as a performer lay in the ability to comically portray his own unpleasant experiences while standing as a symbol of the failure that the middle class dreaded. As a cabinetmaker, Valentin had become one of industrialization's victims. Economic frustration was to be a dominant theme of his folksinger routines and therefore of the message that he transmitted to a public of tradesmen, shopkeepers, white-collar workers, and their families.

Valentin later gave the impression that success came almost overnight, on the strength of some performances at the Baderwirt on Munich's Dachau Street; finally discovered, he moved up to the Frankfurter Hof, to recognition and good pay. However, the Baderwirt engagement may have been only one step of a more gradual improvement. Valentin's association at the same time with a group of traveling comedians on weekends—for ten or fifteen marks a day, according to his daughter—certainly helped him, both professionally and financially.[45] But the Baderwirt was important. There, Valentin delivered *Das Aquarium* (The Aquarium), an original comic monologue which delighted his audience and impressed the director of the Frankfurter Hof.[46]

Das Aquarium opens with the surprising explanation "because we were just talking about aquariums," and proceeds through three or four minutes of pointed nonsense. First, Valentin wants to explain where he lives: "on Sendling Street." Suddenly, he realizes that this would be ridiculous, because if he literally lived *on* Sendling Street, he would live directly in the path of a streetcar. He clarifies: "I live in the houses on Sendling Street." Such semantic bewilderment was to be characteristic of Valentin's humor; he would often bump his head on the literal meaning of an everyday expression. For a comic purpose, he would pretend that language had no conventions. A phrase would hang in the air, loosened from the meaning normally ascribed to it. It was as if anyone who uses language constantly begins anew, lacking the fundamental guidelines that develop over generations of usage and therefore personally having to come to terms with every ambiguity and imperfection.

After Valentin has explained that he lives in only one of the houses on Sendling Street, and there on only one of the floors, he moves on very artfully to establish that he comes from the milieu of his Munich audience. He has an aquarium, he declares, "in the living room where I sleep—I have an extra living room where I sleep and I live in the bedroom." On the face of it, this could mean that he actually has two living rooms, in one of which he sleeps, and a bedroom that he has converted into a living room. But the public would have understood something else: Valentin was referring to the considerable housing shortage in turn-of-the-century Munich. He did not have three rooms, but only one, which he was forced to use for different purposes. The generally middle-class men and women watching him surely caught this; if they were not living in cramped apartments themselves, at least they knew others who were. "I live in the bedroom": the sentence might have spoken for two or three hundred thousand people in Munich in 1907.

Valentin follows this vein of nonsense further. Just as he had turned the phrase "on Sendling Street" from something obvious into something new and barely conceivable, so he turns the aquarium itself into a wonder of parts functioning together to make a whole. "Underneath is the bottom," he explains, "which holds the water, so that the water doesn't run through when someone pours it in from the top. If it weren't for the bottom, you could pour ten, twenty, thirty liters in, and it would all run on through." But the bottom holds water, and this leads to the grotesque bit that finishes the monologue. One day, Valentin poured a bucket of water into his aquarium, and a fish spilled over the edge and down to the floor: "And that's where it lay, but only once it had stopped falling." The landlady saw the fish and convinced Valentin to kill it so as to end its misery. Valentin ruled out using a hammer because he was sure to bang himself on the finger. Then, he ruled out shooting the fish because "you don't hit it right and then it really has to suffer." Finally, he decided how to kill the fish and thereby gives the monologue a muted and ironic happy ending: he will drop the fish into Munich's Isar River to drown it.

Why Valentin's audience responded so favorably to *Das Aquarium* is at once obvious and hard to say; it is inventive and sharp-witted, but trying to relate its elements—sadism, absurdity, nonsense, and so on—to specifically middle-class attitudes in turn-of-the-century Munich would be pointless. Nor, besides the one shy reference to the housing shortage, is there any particular social or political message that might have given people a sense of belonging to a larger community. "Insider" and "outsider" themes, as Valentin was shortly to develop them, are also quite subdued in *Das Aquarium.* In this monologue, he proceeds no further than to identify himself as a man from the lower or middle layers of Munich's society who is especially confused by everyday situations and occurrences. Although the public could "say yes to themselves"—as Bergson would put it—by laughing at Valentin, it is not clear that they could feel socially superior to him, or that he had endured the status decline they feared. Nevertheless, *Das Aquarium* played a role in Valentin's mounting success. How great a role is open to question, but it helped bring—in Valentin's words—"my economic crisis to an end."[47]

In his recollections, Valentin first used the word "folksinger" to describe himself at the time of the Baderwirt appearance; up to that point he had been a "humorist." Of itself, this is not terribly significant. "Folksinger," in early twentieth-century Munich, was the general term for a variety of kinds of entertainers. Still, there is reason to consider whether Valentin had been a "Munich folksinger" in his earliest career. In some ways, he seems to have aspired to become something else. First, he was at least as interested in touring as in establishing himself with the Munich audience. The folksingers generally had a strong sense of rootedness in their city (or in Bavaria), and few would have undertaken Valentin's journey—with the "living orchestra"—into northern Germany, at least not so early in their careers. Moreover, the "living orchestra" itself distinguishes Valentin. With it, he defied most entertainment categories, even the broad one of "folksinger." On tour with his musical contraption: this is how Valentin thought his breakthrough would come. Perhaps he was surprised that it came locally instead, while he was appearing as a singer and comedian— as a "folksinger." Valentin had finally found people he could amuse for a living. Enabled by his private anxieties and even more by his personal experience of social decline to address their fears, he rapidly became one of their favorites. Consciously or unconsciously, he took the role of Munich's buffoon, a popular object of ridicule, an "outsider" whose hilarious misfortunes assured people that they were "insiders."

BETWEEN KARL VALENTIN's birth in 1882 and his engagement at the Baderwirt in 1907, the population of Munich more than doubled in size, from under 250,000 to over 500,000. Part of this was due to a sharp decline in the city's death rate during these twenty-five years. More decisive, however, was the influx of newcomers—tens of thousands of people who had left their homes in other places to try and find a foothold in Munich's expanding economy. They came from all over Germany and from foreign countries, but especially from elsewhere in Bavaria. This last group, Bavarians not born in Munich, amounted to nearly half of the city's inhabitants in 1907. Some of these had left peasant villages because of, as a contemporary observed, "less advantageous situations, the prospect of never being able to own their own land, and the rosy portrayals [of the city] by workers who go back home." There were also newcomers from Bavarian towns and smaller cities.[48] One of these was Ferdinand Weisheitinger, later known as Weiss Ferdl, a young printer who arrived around 1900 from Altötting, a city sixty kilometers to Munich's east, known for its beautiful Catholic churches.

Ferdinand Weisheitinger's childhood in Altötting remains more in darkness than Valentin Ludwig Fey's in the Au. This is because of a lack of basic evidence, which has several causes. First, in contrast to Valentin, as an adult Ferdinand wrote very little about his childhood. Perhaps he did not feel the attachment to his early years that Valentin felt to his, or perhaps he was less interested in turning them into a collection of funny stories for his admirers. Second, researchers have virtually ignored him, having neither conducted the interviews nor sought and preserved the documents that would shed light upon his time in Altötting. Third, there is no one in his family or circle of friends who has performed the biographical service in his memory that Bertl Böheim-Valentin has performed in her father's. The result is that very few episodes of his early years come into view.

The few pages that Ferdinand wrote about his childhood leave the strong impression that his maternal grandparents assumed the roles of parents in his life. His grandfather was an Altötting printer, and his grandmother—a woman of Swabian origins—operated a furniture business. Their daughter had given birth to Ferdinand in 1883, but lost her husband, a Frankian who had moved to Altötting, shortly thereafter. She remarried—this time to a local tradesman—but neither she nor her second husband appear in her son's recollections. Instead, he dismissed both of them in a comparison with his grandmother: "Anyway, my grandmother raised me and shaped my future destiny. She loved me above everything else." The family relationships that lay behind this statement are simply hard to imagine. Was Ferdinand so bitter toward his mother and stepfather that he later preferred not to write about them? Or was his grandmother such a strong figure that she simply took control of his upbringing, perhaps over her daughter's protests? Other hypotheses come to mind, but there is no evidence to support any of them. All that remains clear, on the basis of what Ferdinand later wrote, is that his relationship to his grandmother formed the emotional center of his early life.[49]

According to Ferdinand's later portrayal, this relationship was governed by a certain principle of fair emotional exchange: his good behavior in return for her unqualified, unquestioned love. Usually, he was an obedient, orderly, and good-natured boy. Even in the exceptional cases where his grandmother had to discipline him, her reasons were so clear and her sadness was so touching that it created no trouble between them. Once, a fire had broken out at a nearby farm, and Ferdinand had stayed to watch the attempt to put it out. As a result, he was late getting home, which made his grandmother worry that he had gotten lost. When he finally did appear, she hit him and "was so upset that she cried—I didn't cry." Nor did he become angry. Generally, for his good behavior, he received the feeling of being loved and accepted, of being another's favorite: "I was her sweetheart . . . I can still hear the sound of her voice in my ear, when she pressed me to her heart and said, 'You are my Nandy.' "[50] Of course, this is all open to doubt. Could such a mutually dependent relationship have operated so simply? Could it have been so completely loving? What Ferdinand later wrote may have been more a wish than a recollection. Even as a wish, however, it is historically important. Whether or not the child had actually been engaged in such emotional trading, the adult later believed so. Indeed, the theme of "being good" in return for security appears in the socially oriented entertainment he presented as a folksinger. In the early 1920s, for example, his acts voiced the outrage he felt that the middle class was not being justly repaid for its hard work and orderliness. As a Munich stage artist, one of his professional tasks was to transmit a message on the social crisis around him; popular attitudes informed his message, while private feelings lent it style and conviction.

Ferdinand's grandmother encouraged him to sing; he must have shown considerable ability, because it was here that her ambitions for him were to develop. She imagined him ultimately as a soloist in one of Altötting's old and beautiful churches, adding his melodious and clear voice to an inspirational mass. For this to happen, she knew, he would have to undergo a course of rigorous musical training. When he was about eleven years old, she sent him across the Austrian border seventy kilometers away, to the boys' choir of the cathedral in Salzburg. It must have been painful for her to let him go, but she understood that only an experience of this kind would set him on the road she was clearing for him.[51] His first several months in Salzburg were unhappy ones. Away from Altötting and from his grandmother for the first time, he was miserable. He later remembered quietly crying each night before he went to sleep. Far from comforting him, the other boys ridiculed his Bavarian dialect. After three months, relief came in the form of a visit by his grandmother and mother, but did not last long.[52]

Ferdinand learned something during his more than three years in Salzburg that was to be much more decisive in his later career as a popular entertainer than the basic vocal training he received: to love the trusted people and places of his Bavarian home above all else. He had become acquainted, as he later put it, with "the difference between being at home and being in a strange place." True, he overcame his moroseness during the course of his stay. He even established himself well enough among the other boys to lead a protest against the food they were given to eat, for which he was soundly punished. But the experience of being alone and feeling despised by everyone had left its mark. Above all, it had taught him an emotional yearning for home, for the family warmth he had enjoyed—or remembered enjoying—in Altötting.[53] Years later, as a Munich folksinger, he identified himself with the similar yearning of an urban middle-class public for its rural and small-town past. For anxious city dwellers, many of whom had been born in the Bavarian mountains and hills, an entertainer from Altötting offered a sense of home. Weiss Ferdl reflected their longing for the community feelings they had missed since leaving "old Bavaria." From his Salzburg years, he knew what it was like to be out of place in strange surroundings. It came naturally for him to express the "old Bavarian" nostalgia of Munich's out-of-place popular audience.

After Salzburg, when Ferdinand returned home to live in Altötting, he did not proceed the way his grandmother wanted—to become a church soloist, and work in her furniture business—because his grandfather stepped in to block it. In the view of this old Altötting printer, his grandson's future was not solid unless he learned a trade. He brought Ferdinand into the print shop as an apprentice, and there is no sign that the boy resisted. From the little that Ferdinand later wrote about this time in the printing trade, it seems that its effects upon him were discordant. One the one hand, through his grandfather's active chairmanship of a health insurance association, he was exposed to a modern trade-unionist attitude. On the other hand, by making the journeyman's tour to various printing houses in South Germany, his experience was guildlike and traditional. He did not stay long in this half-modern, half-medieval tradesman's world. Why he left is not clear. While he was in Altötting, he earned twenty-four marks per week: no fortune, but surely enough for a young man presumably living and eating at home. In Altötting he would also—through his grandfather's influence—have enjoyed some security at work. But, like thousands of Bavarian townspeople and peasants, he decided to move to Munich, where he arrived around the year 1901.[54]

Ferdinand's expectations of working at the printing trade in the Bavarian capital were not fulfilled. Instead, it was "impossible to find a position."[55] He did not, writing years later, attempt to explain why, but generally, printing presses in Munich had begun to rely upon machinery and unskilled labor in place of trained printers by 1900; he found himself in a declining trade.[56] Nor did he later dwell upon the disappointment he must have felt at being alone and out of work in a large, strange city. Nevertheless, he had grown up in the traditional middle class and had hoped—as a printer—to stay there. In Munich he fell out of his class and landed among the destitute and the jobless, the city's growing proletariat. He later glossed over this episode of his life, which lasted perhaps less than a year. However, for the son—or grandson—of a solid, middle-class Altötting home, the situation in Munich was surely cause for despair.

There was nothing in the course Ferdinand chose to get out of the impasse that would have soothed his traditional middle-class fears of losing income and status; answering an advertisement for a "beginning singer" and doing well in the audition, he became a member of a local troupe of folksingers, an entertainer. However successful he later became, he started his career, in late 1901 or 1902, at the bottom. Although his later claim of earning fifty pfennigs a day is perhaps too low, a "beginning singer" could not have expected very much. More disheartening than the pay was the behavior of the other performers, which constantly reminded him that he had descended to a lower level of society. He later wrote that printers were "much more refined." Upon joining the folksingers, he immediately felt abused as the low man in the troupe: "A beginner with the folksingers is one of the unhappiest creatures in the world . . . He has to drive the wardrobe chests from one temple of art to the next. He has to set up the stage, clean up, and fasten the dresses of the director's fat wife at the back—a very strenuous task—and so on. If anything goes wrong up on stage, of course it's the beginner's fault. He gave the wrong cue; he appeared too early or too late. It's always he—the others are infallible." Ferdinand's main consolation was that he gradually began to take a good share of the public's applause, which led to his advance within the troupe. Also, he appreciated staying up late nights and waking up late the next morning: his liberation from the working world.[57] But as long as he was among these coarse-mannered entertainers, he felt a sense of his own social decline. He no longer had a respectable middle-class career ahead of him, and his low pay and position conveyed to him that he had become a member of the working class.

Ferdinand Weisheitinger's young entertainment career was interrupted in 1903, when he entered the Imperial army and was sent to the garrison of Metz, in Lorraine, annexed by the Germans from France in 1871. His military tour was uneventful. He later complained about the work and the long periods of enforced separation from women. Once, he saw the Kaiser on a visit to the troops and found him strangely withdrawn and fearful. Regarding his development as a performer, he very quickly established himself in Metz as the regiment's singer and actor, and often appeared before his comrades in a local tavern. He even sang in the choir of some Wagnerian operas that were performed by—and presumably for—the soldiers.[58] This onstage activity kept him in form for his return to Munich, while the applause he won demonstrated that his decision to become an entertainer had been right.

As a civilian in Bavaria in September 1905, the young folksinger first went to Regensburg, where a local theater engaged him to perform during its winter season. Then, when the season was over, he returned to Munich and joined a traveling men's quartet, the "Munich Master Singers" (Münchner Meistersänger). During 1906 and part of 1907, he toured throughout the province with the "Master Singers." This was entertainment at a "higher" level: "No comedy and no makeup. Only a tuxedo with a white vest. Only four men and the director's son at the piano." He later remembered doing quite well financially at times, but also having to insist that the director arrange more performances.[59]

In 1907 Ferdinand appeared as a guest with "The Dachauers," the troupe of folksingers at Platzl, the well-known Munich music hall across from the Hofbräuhaus. He fully expected to return to the "Master Singers." Instead he stayed, in what was to be the setting of his rise to success as a popular entertainer. "The Dachauers," named for the Bavarian town twenty-five kilometers northwest of Munich, offered their audiences a good-humored and nostalgic view of "old Bavaria," of life in the villages and small towns from which so many in Munich had come. They sang songs and performed plays that brought the old customs and folkways affectionately to mind: courtship, rivalries between families, the priest in the community, and so on. At Platzl, Ferdinand found a home. Playing with the syllables of his name, he appeared as "Weiss Ferdl," "little white horse." With this stage name—as he later wrote—he became "well-known everywhere, not only in Bavaria."[60]

Ferdinand Weisheitinger of Altötting—who had learned to appreciate "home" during his Salzburg years—was truly at home as one of Platzl's "old Bavarian" entertainers. Although he was in Munich, not in Altötting, he was singing about the hundreds of Altöttings that a good part of his audience knew as home. Platzl was a monument to "old Bavaria," to "home," and this helps explain his satisfaction at performing there. Moreover, at Platzl Weiss Ferdl saw himself in the kind of relationship to his "old Bavarian" clientele that he believed he had been in with his grandmother: "being good," which in an undefined way meant roughly being obedient, in return for love and praise. Platzl entertainment, he later stressed, was "good" too: "If there were bad people [in our plays], it always went badly for them in the end. Love and goodness always triumphed."[61] The "good" characters in the Platzl plays—honest tradesmen, hard-working farmwives—were inevitably rewarded; for his part in making this happen, so was Weiss Ferdl. Later, he could devote pages to the acclaim he received: "Almost everyone in Munich knows me," he once wrote.[62] The principle of just exchange remained intact in his adult life. Just as the boy had obeyed his grandmother and thereby gained her complete acceptance, so the man made a career of obeying "old Bavaria," of upholding her values and demonstrating the innate strength of her customs. Thus, as he saw it, he gained his public's complete acceptance. One can complain that he was being naive and superficial. Nonetheless, this may have been what Weiss Ferdl liked most about his career as an entertainer; for "being good," or for presenting "goodness," he was able to feel loved in the way that he had felt loved as a child.

KARL VALENTIN'S and Weiss Ferdl's manifest differences of outlook and style relate to their equally manifest differences of personality and background. Valentin was a city boy, a unique mixture of brashness and anxiety who used his own fear-ridden idiosyncrasies as the basis of comic entertainment; Weiss Ferdl attempted to recreate the world of Altötting and of his grandmother by singing its praises and dramatizing its virtues every night at Platzl. Their economic situations, however, were similar. Both started their working lives in trades endangered by industrialization, and both fell from the traditional middle class into the lowest ranks of the performing business. This experience of social failure profoundly affected their routines. Whereas Valentin transformed his early setbacks into the object of a dark, self-degrading humor, Weiss Ferdl fled from his, seeking refuge in the dream of a traditional community where only success was possible, where no one's social status ever came into question.

Karl Valentin's and Weiss Ferdl's backgrounds sensitized them to the cares of Munich's middle class; they knew what kinds of messages their public found reassuring. On stage, Valentin was always an inept character who persuaded his viewers that their problems were, after all, relatively minor. Weiss Ferdl became a caretaker of the structure of political and social attitudes, sentiments, and ideas that the middle class had constructed to assuage its fears of social decline. Tradesmen, shopkeepers, and white-collar workers heard from him that they belonged to a traditional "old Bavarian" community, that they were right to be prejudiced against the Jews, and that they shared in the glory of the German Empire. After a night in a cabaret, *varieté*, or music hall with these entertainers, people felt like "insiders." Valentin and Weiss Ferdl appreciated the importance of this feeling. Having been "outsiders" themselves, having spent many degrading months at the proletariat's level, they were particularly aware of the endless worries of Munich's besieged lower middle class.

3

The Folksingers and Their Audiences Before World War I

At a time when Great Britain, France, and the United States were offering examples of representative government, when socialists were envisaging a takeover of power by the working class, and when anarchists were calling for the end of "the State," the Second German Empire (1870–1918) remained a fortress of authoritarian rule and of the large landed and industrial interests in German society.[1] It was determined not only to keep the gates of its power closed but to hinder those on the outside from voicing their anger and frustration. In this spirit, its police maintained a system of censorship over theaters, cabarets, music halls, and other public stages. The justification of the system was that it protected audiences from hearing opposition to the Empire's institutions and policies—and protected the Empire from the consequences. But the censor did not stop in public, political areas of German life; he entered private, moral areas as well. Thus, playwrights, directors, and performers were not supposed to express themselves in favor of sexual liberty or to dwell upon the scandals of "respectable" society any more than they were supposed to advocate socialism. Actually, this was just another aspect of censorship's function: to uphold the political, social, and economic order. Representatives of the Empire saw the habits of opposition and disobedience as the basic dangers, and sought to combat them however they appeared, whether in public or private behavior.

If the purpose of censorship was uniform throughout the Empire, its practice differed from province to province, and from city to city. In Munich censorship consisted first of the rule that theater directors submit printed copies of all songs, plays, monologues, and other material to the police censor fourteen days before they hoped to introduce them on their stages. Then, plainclothesmen would periodically check to see that only those acts that the censor had let through in fact appeared. Of course, the censor's decisions—and his existence—were subjects of endless controversy. This was unavoidable during an era in which artists all over Europe, and not less in Munich, were striving for original ways to express themselves and insisting upon their rights to do so. Otto Falckenberg, later director of

Munich's Chamber Theater (Kammerspiele), remembered taking part in a determined protest against censorship as a young drama student early in the century: "I joined the cause then with an active, almost political passion, as never again in my life."[2] In 1908, finally responding to the protest, the Munich police formed an advisory council (Zensurbeirat) of established writers and academicians to submit recommendations on the artistic merits of plays. For a time, members of the council included the dramatist Max Halbe, and even Thomas Mann. The council had a generally liberal influence in the years before the First World War, though its judgments were occasionally negative, and in any case nonbinding. It remained intact during the war, but fell in 1918, along with the censorship system of which it was a part and the Empire which that system had served.[3]

Despite censorship, in the official view Munich was still the friendly host of cultural activity that a series of benevolent Wittelsbach monarchs had made it to be during the nineteenth century. Thus, the chorus at the opening of the Prince Regent Theater on 20 August 1901 sang thanks to Prince Regent Luitpold for his tolerance:

> How many sounds, pictures, and shapes
> Thank your majesty for the air of life!
> So, let us celebrate your mildness,
> Oh first and noblest of Bavarians.[4]

Munich playwright Frank Wedekind would have known better about this "mildness"; trying to introduce themes like adolescent sexuality and middle-class decadence to the city's legitimate stages, he was involved with the Prince Regent's censor in several controversies. Indeed, with works like *Pandora's Box* banned from performance, he was reduced around 1901–1904 to showing excerpts in semiprivate cabarets. True, the situation improved over time. But Wedekind did not let the acceptance of some of his plays lighten his wrath over the rejection of others. In 1911, upset with the censor's advisory council for declining to endorse certain pieces, he published his bitterly ironic "Seven Questions to Munich's Advisory Council," in which he asked, "What essential difference exists between the secret proceedings of an Inquisition court and those of the Munich Advisory Council?"[5] Wedekind's case illustrates the problems that any theater artist with a critical view of German society would have encountered in prewar Munich.

The prominence of the "Wedekind case" should not suggest that the Munich censor was preoccupied with one playwright or with the theaters that had requested permission to stage his works. On the contrary, the censor's regulations affected all of the city's stage entertainment—everything open to the public, legitimate or popular. Thus, the management of the newly opened Kleines Theater (Little Theater), a literary cabaret, received a copy of the censorship code in October 1907, whereby it was required to submit its material to the censor and to accept responsibility for anything else its artists performed. Policemen seem to have been at theaters, cabarets, *varietés,* and music halls throughout Munich on a regular basis, making sure that nothing unapproved came on stage. For example, in the police file on the Circus-Varieté-Colosseum is the 3 April 1913 report of an inspector who concluded that the actresses' costumes "were appropriate to the requirements of decency"; two weeks later, the same inspector returned and again found nothing morally questionable.[6] The police were also at Platzl, and according to Weiss Ferdl, heard him tell the following uncensored joke in 1910:

> A traveling businessman met the daughter of one of his customers in the train. She was going to Paris [to live]. He didn't know what he should talk about with the young girl and so explained to her the meaning of colors. Red is love, blue is loyalty, yellow is jealousy, green is hope, and white is innocence. Two years later, visiting his customer at home, he met the good miss again and asked her whether she still remembered the conversation on the ride to Paris. "Yes," she said, and repeated the conversation, only she stopped at the color white and said: "You can't hold on to everything when you've been in Paris for two years."

Weiss Ferdl recalled that the police thereupon "confiscated my book of jokes," which is rather hard to picture.[7] Whatever really happened to him, this episode testifies to the inhibiting presence of the censor in the world of Munich's popular entertainment.

Throughout Germany, censorship was backed by "public decency leagues" (*Sittlichkeitsvereine*), all with a religious orientation and all strongly against a tolerant, secular position toward culture. Their campaigns against alleged perversities, of course, left them open to ridicule. For example, in one portrayal, *Simplicissimus* cartoonist Olaf Gulbransson had the leader of one of these leagues appearing at the Algeciras Conference of 1906 to convince the international delegates that their governments should abolish the belly dance.[8] Still, the leagues enjoyed considerable influence in society at large, and with the police. How they could make this influence felt becomes clear in the documents of a 1908 controversy involving Munich's Kleines Theater, where supporters of decency felt the police had been lax at enforcing the censor's standards. The controversy began with an editorial in Munich's *Allgemeine Rundschau* which, without naming the Kleines Theater, described a ballad that had been sung on its stage. According to the newspaper, the ballad placed the following line in the mouth of a priest counseling a duchess: "If I take off my spiritual clothing, I'm a person just like you." At this point, the duchess was supposed to have whispered, "Take it off!" To the writer, probably a teacher named Franz Weigl, the secretary of the Men's League for the Opposition to Public Indecency, this was outrageous. He wrote of a "flood of smut" in Munich, and—shifting metaphors—asked why the Bavarian Landtag did not "reach in with an energetic fist" to clean it up. The management of the Kleines Theater reacted by bringing suit against the newspaper for insulting their cabaret's reputation. In its defense, the *Allgemeine Rundschau* produced several "experts" to testify, including Franz Weigl. Weigl stated that he had seen the performance in question, but exercised his legal right not to name himself as the author of the editorial. He described for the court the costumes of a band of nymphs: "Of course they weren't stark naked, but I had the impression and I wrote it down in my program so as to mark it for later: 'flesh market.' I had the impression that they wanted to bring as much flesh—as they say—before the public as possible. How far the flesh was being shown and how far the tricot went is hard to distinguish." The court decided against the Kleines Theater, arguing that the paper had neither intended an offense nor erred in its remarks.[9] The forces for decency had scored a major publicity triumph and created an atmosphere in which the police could only try to be more vigilant.

CENSORSHIP WAS SIMPLY one of the difficulties of life in the entertainment profession in Imperial Germany. There were material difficulties as well, and none was more basic than the uncertainty of employment. For thousands of German stage performers, each theater season brought a challenge: to secure a place among the working, or take a place among the idle. Many failed. Estimating numbers in such a wide field is hard, but there was definitely a good chance that an artist would end up as Karl Valentin began: "a poor, skinny devil."

For those actors, actresses, singers, and other performers fortunate enough to have found employment, a whole new set of difficulties arose. First, most German theaters were open eight months of the year or less. This generally meant that each year theater personnel had to earn enough money during a period of work to subsist during a period of forced inactivity. On a typical salary, this was difficult.[10] Second, many came to their positions by way of theater agents, whose practices were notorious until set within some bounds by law in 1910. Prior to the law, an agent not only claimed a good percentage of his client's present earnings but of future earnings as well—whether he was to thank for them or not. Moreover, he would charge a fee for the "service." After 1910 the performers and the theaters that employed them split the payment of the fee, and agents could no longer take from future earnings. A historian sympathetic to the artists has named these features of the law "basic progress," but argued that the agent's percentage—even under the law—remained "not at all appropriate."[11]

Both the role of agents in bringing employers and employees together and the seasonality of work indicate the slow advance of labor rights in the German theater industry during the Empire, slow by the standards of German industry as a whole. The contracts under which most performers worked indicate it too. One clause, for example, might grant a theater the right to dismiss an artist during the month of rehearsal if it found him or her to be of low quality. Often, the theater would threaten to use the clause only to force the artist to sign a new contract for less pay. No corresponding clause, however, would give the actor or actress the right to leave at all; leaving anyway could bring a penalty, maybe as severe as a ban from the German stage for three to five years. Moreover, a theater frequently controlled its employees during the off-season too—by a paragraph in the contract that forbade them to appear on other stages in the same city.[12]

To promote and defend the interests of legitimate theater performers in the German Empire, a union was formed in 1872, the Brotherhood of German Stage Artists (Genossenschaft deutscher Bühnenangehöriger). Because it was not able to gain much influence over the way contracts were written, its success was limited. Still, in other regards, it was a quite effective organization. For its members, and after 1890 for nonmembers too, its greatest use lay in the area of old-age and disability insurance, where it compensated for the partial exclusion of theater employees from the state pension system created by Bismarck in the 1880s. The Brotherhood offered good coverage, and its insurance fund grew steadily up to World War I, even after the state policy was opened to most stage artists in 1911.[13] With accident insurance, however, the union had trouble. By law, a theater was responsible for paying the costs of a work accident only if its negligence was established. The stage artists' union tried to have the law changed to make the theater responsible in any case, but failed. This principle of employer liability, already law for some German industries, did not reach the stages until 1927.[14] Generally, the Brotherhood of German Stage Artists pushed for laws favorable to performers and was certainly a factor in the restriction of the agents in 1910. Local chapters of the union also supported their members in specific disputes. In Munich, for example, the union petitioned the police in 1912 to revoke the license of a theater director who had allegedly demanded sexual favors from his actresses. Apparently, the police chose not to do so.[15] All told, the union suffered most from the hesitancy of creative artists to act like proletarians and unionize; by 1900 it had recruited less than 40 percent of all German performers into membership.[16]

Clearly at the bottom of the entertainment profession, feeling its disadvantages most heavily, were the popular and small-stage performers: comedians, pantomimists, actors and actresses, folksingers, and others. The contracts that many of them had to sign were filled, according to one writer, "with arbitrary clauses, releases, and all kinds of possibilities for dissolution."[17] Those at the far edge of the profession did not even have contracts. Like Karl Valentin playing his zither in 1907, they could perform for fifty pfennigs a day and supper, in constant fear of being set out on the street. Hans Bötticher, who appeared under the name Joachim Ringelnatz at Munich's Simplicissimus Artists' Tavern in Schwabing, later remembered a pay raise—to one mark per evening with the privilege of no longer having to pay for his own drinks.[18] But if the present was hard, the future could be hopeless. Few popular and small-stage entertainers had pension plans like that offered to performers of the legitimate theater by the stage artists' union. In the words of an old man who had spent his working life in the cabarets: "Whoever did not save anything at the cabarets, or did not always think of the future, did not put his money into a piece of property or a house and save in addition, has nothing in his old age. He has to go begging or starve."[19] Anyone decided upon a career in popular entertainment had to be ready for a difficult and uncertain life.

Entertainers of the popular and smaller stages came much more slowly to the idea of professional unity than did their colleagues at the legitimate theaters. Thus, it was not until 1912 that the League for the Protection of German Entertainers (Schutzverband deutscher Vortragskünstler) announced its formation.[20] Locally, however, there were earlier efforts. The Munich folksingers, for instance, established a health insurance league in 1885 and met once a year to discuss its aims and operations. One researcher has written that "almost all of the known musical leaders, directors, players, singers, and humorists" belonged. In 1904 an organization with interests wider than health insurance was founded, the Local League of the Munich Folksingers (Lokalverband der Münchner Volkssänger). Five years later, the Local League gave way to the League for the Preservation of the Interests of the Munich Folksingers (Verband zur Wahrung der Interessen der Münchner Volkssänger). The membership in this second league was definitely no less than ten: a March 1914 letter to the police named ten officers.[21] Because they were all appearing in the same city, the Munich folksingers developed a quite exceptional sense of themselves as a group. Generally, popular entertainers in Imperial Germany led almost nomadic existences, on stage in one city after another; this hindered attempts to bring them together.[22]

BOTH UNIONIZATION AND CENSORSHIP, the two great conflicts in the entertainment field of early twentieth-century Munich, seem quite remote from the careers of Karl Valentin and Weiss Ferdl. With regard to censorship, there is no evidence that Valentin had any trouble at all, and Weiss Ferdl's reprimand for telling an "indecent" joke was probably not serious. Nor do the Munich folksinger leagues appear to have been very important for either performer.

No record exists to show that Valentin joined any of them. Perhaps he did, but either way, he was not active. Weiss Ferdl belonged to at least one of these unions, according to his widow, but his name does not appear on any list of officers or chairmen.[23] Both folksingers would have had little interest in a union, at least after 1907, because they were doing so well individually.[24] Neither had such a highly developed social conscience that he would have devoted a great deal of time and energy to pension plans and contract rights for less successful colleagues.

Nevertheless, unionization and censorship each occupy a place in the background of Karl Valentin's and Weiss Ferdl's lives in professional entertainment. Although the unions did not enlist either of them to be active in the laboring man's cause, neither was the type to be out of sympathy. Both remembered what it was like to be a struggling performer. Both reached near the top in their careers, but not without blocks along the way, and not without a fear of rolling backward. They may not have been dedicated unionists, but they would have had an interested awareness of the efforts of those who were. Censorship affected them too, even if there were no sensational disputes. Although neither fundamentally challenged the established order, each would have had to submit his routines two weeks in advance, and each would have known that he was being watched. Weighing a line of a monologue for its social or political connotations, looking for ways to make a point without arousing the censor's interest: these were aspects of their work. Karl Valentin and Weiss Ferdl were successful popular entertainers and the greatest of the Munich folksingers in the twentieth century; although they were highly regarded in their profession, they were not relieved of its everyday concerns.

APPEARING NIGHTLY at Munich's Platzl in the years before World War I, Weiss Ferdl and "The Dachauers" offered their audience of hard-pressed middle-class men and women a brief respite of light humor and song:

> Happy is he who laughs and sings
> And when worry is what life brings
> Don't take it bad, and let yourself be had.
> Ha ha ha ha ha![25]

Platzl customers sang along with this song, and with other songs, reading the words out of little booklets that they could buy for five pfennigs. Laughing, singing, and drinking were the activities of the evening. Another song reminds people about drinking, as though they could forget in the world's beer capital:

> Let the merry songs ring
> But song doesn't do it alone
> That's why we sing:
> Drink up, and fill it up again.[26]

To its song-singing, beer-swigging public, Platzl offered a sense of belonging; Weiss Ferdl recalled that "all Platzl was a happy singing family."[27]

This music-hall entertainment provided the audience with more, however, than an occasion to laugh and sing in half-drunken togetherness. In this age of economic growth and of widespread social uncertainty, these popular songs, plays, and comic routines reassured Munich tradesmen, shopkeepers, white-collar workers, and their families that they would overcome their problems and remain among society's "insiders." Filling the hall at Platzl was the structure of social and political attitudes, ideas, and sentiments in which the city's middle class sought refuge before 1914. Above all, the acts of Weiss Ferdl and "The Dachauers" reflected a yearning for the traditional "old Bavarian" community:

> It's back home I want to go
> To the precious place of our fathers
> Where you sing the happy songs
> Where you say the trusted words.[28]

This song, one of those with which the crowd sang along, rings with the nostalgia so deep in the Platzl spirit. It was a simplifying and idealizing nostalgia. Perhaps it found its clearest expression in the short "farmer comedies," or "farmer plays" (*Bauernkomödien* or *Bauernpossen*) that Weiss Ferdl and the others performed, of which there are apparently and unfortunately no remaining copies. Weiss Ferdl later recalled having a hand in writing these plays: "As literature, [they] were not particularly valuable, but there was a lot of hearty laughter."[29] One gets a general idea of what they were proba-

bly like from the songbooks, from songs with such titles as "The
Hunter's Farewell," "The Farmer Hymn," "Tegern Lake Song,"
and "Song of Our Bavarian Mountains."[30] These songs brim with
the Platzl longing for the past. In addition to evoking idyllic images
of Upper and Lower Bavarian scenery, they also refer again and
again to traditional, sturdy, folkloristic men and women who were
sure of their places in "old Bavarian" society in a way that few of
Munich's newcomers could be sure of theirs. Platzl took its audiences on an entertainment tour of the old villages and towns. It also
let them hear and speak their own language, German in the Bavarian dialect. Indeed, the dialect was an important element of Munich's "old Bavarian" attitude, as is clear from an 1890 controversy
involving Platzl itself, its name in particular. The management had
decided to change the Bavarian diminutive -*l* in Platzl to the high
German diminutive -*chen,* making Plätzchen, but then reversed itself under heavy public pressure.[31] One can imagine the vigor with
which a Munich audience would sing a dialect song like "Weibi
Weibi!" (Woman, Woman), also in the songbooks:

> Think, my little sugar bit
> Every woman needs a man
> O, woman, woman, don't be so hard!

> Denk, mein süsses Zuckerkanderl
> Jedes Weiberl braucht ein Manderl
> Weibi, Weibi, sei doch nicht so hart![32]

No less than membership in an "old Bavarian" community, the Bavarian dialect created a line between Platzl's "insiders" and "outsiders."

This song also expresses the "old Bavarian" view that men and
women behave toward each other by a fixed law of nature, that they
are engaged in a kind of mock conflict until in the end they admit
that they need to be together. Here one senses the reaction of country folk to the new sexual ways of the city, to prostitution, pornogra-
phy, and divorce. Exemplifying the concern that prostitution
aroused is an article in the 7 August 1912 issue of the *Münchner
Neuigkeits-Blatt* (Munich Novelty Sheet). According to the writer, a
man from Nuremberg was visiting Munich's famous art museum,
the Alte Pinakothek, and noticed a "fashionably dressed young
lady": "Then, suddenly, both of them are standing in front of a pic-

ture. No one is around. The lady opens her purse, and smiling, presses her card into the stranger's hand, whispering: 'Come on, fatty, I'll go first. You'll enjoy yourself.' On the card was: Frieda, Artist, Hohenzollern Street. So, prostitution is operating even in the royal buildings, looking for its victims there." The writer goes on to assert that sixty or seventy prostitutes greet a man walking along Müller Street at night.[33] News like this probably would have gotten a laugh from the least serious in the Platzl crowd. However, it may well have spread a certain disquiet among new city-dwellers, who in general did not feel very secure socially. Life in "old Bavaria," at least in Platzl's nostalgic depiction, was simpler: no traffic, no strikes, no housing shortage, and no prostitutes.

Bavarians of rural and small-town origins, new to Munich, found it difficult to adjust to urban ways in these years of economic and social change. This did not, however, preclude an attachment to the city, at least to symbols of its past. "Munich's good way of life [*Gemütlichkeit*]," so went the chorus of one Platzl song, "will never die out" as long as Saint Peter's Church, the Isar River, and the Hofbräuhaus exist.[34] The "old Bavarian" spirit also embraced the city for its role in preserving—or creating—the memory of the surrounding country. Thus, some Platzl songbooks mention that a "stranger" visiting the music hall will not only see "genuine Bavarian ways of performance" but will also get to know "the life and activities of the people of Munich."[35] For those on stage, and for the local people in the audience, there was no difference.

Resentment of Jews was also part of the message transmitted by the Platzl folksingers to their audience. As is obvious from the following song, the Jew appeared on the Platzl stage as a natural inhabitant of the new social world within which especially Munich's tradesmen and shopkeepers felt ill at ease:

> Cohen and Sarah
> Are driving their car
> Up front it stinks of garlic
> And at the back of gasoline.[36]

The symbolization is perfect: a product of the modern economic system being used by two beneficiaries of modern, liberal society. The foul-smelling automobile, which had been built in a factory and not in a traditional workshop, stands for the economic problems besetting the middle class. By riding in it, "Cohen and Sarah" show that they are unaffected by these problems. Distinguishing these Jews from Weiss Ferdl's public, no less than their car, are strange customs, in this case, the fact that they eat garlic. Fearing that industrial change was gradually opening their middle-class status to question, Platzl customers were looking for social groups to which they could feel superior. A song like this confirmed them in their belief that Jews were born for this "outsider" role. Contrasting themselves to the Jews, they were sure of being "insiders."

Loyalty to the German Empire occupied the place of honor in the structure of middle-class attitudes in Munich before World War I. Indeed, for all the Bavarian pride at Platzl, there was not the slightest hint of political separatism. The songs in the booklets sold by Weiss Ferdl and his colleagues express the most solemn patriotic feelings. Prussia may have had few friends at a Platzl evening, but judging from what was sung, there were hundreds of supporters of the military system that was enabling the nation to assert itself in the world. Men like Weiss Ferdl looked back upon their service in the Imperial army or navy as a time of participation in an urgent and magnificent national cause:

> Proud waves the flag of black, white, red
> On our ship's mast
> Woe to the enemy who threatens it
> Who hates these colors
> It is fluttering on the beach of home
> Back and forth in the wind
> Also far from our precious fatherland on stormy seas.

The German military was heroic, and German soldiers were heroes:

> No one knows the coward's shaking
> All are men of the deed
> And when the enemy crumbles—
> That's the work of the German soldier.[37]

While the men at Platzl identified with Imperial greatness, the women admired the men. Bravery, in Weiss Ferdl's view, had its inducements and rewards:

When the soldiers march through the city
The girls open windows and doors.[38]

"Old Bavaria" liked to think of sexuality in terms of a few basic, unquestioned, natural principles. That women found men in uniform irresistible was one of these principles.

During the Empire, Platzl was operating under the gaze of a police censor. Were these songbooks printed for the censor's consumption? Were the patriotic songs either not sung or sung in a broadly satirical way? Two considerations indicate that this was not the case. First, it would have been difficult for an establishment as well known as Platzl to perpetrate a hoax of this magnitude. The censor could hardly have remained unaware, with his plainclothesmen regularly in the audience. Second, Weiss Ferdl later had ample opportunity to present himself and his music hall as having been critical of German militarism before 1914. Naturally, after 1945 it would have been to his advantage to do so. Instead, he looked back on the songbooks with pleasure and did not suggest that anything in them was sung with less than full conviction. Weiss Ferdl was, in the words of his widow, "a follower of the fatherland";[39] it is difficult to imagine him as a member of a singing and acting troupe opposed to the Empire.

Unlike Karl Valentin, Weiss Ferdl of Platzl did not write his own material at the start of his entertainment career, at least not much of it. He began to do so later, during World War I. In these early years, he does not appear as the creator of messages to a receptive middle-class public, but only as the transmitter. One can wonder who did create the message, or to be more specific, who picked the songs for the Platzl booklets. Weiss Ferdl's influence may have been large or small. Either way, there was considerable understanding on stage—where there were enough former printers to open a press—for the problems of the people seated at the tables. This understanding informed Platzl's anti-industrial, anti-urban, anti-Jewish, and pro-Imperial message. Obviously, there were many who wanted to receive the message; filled night after night for years, the music hall became an institution of Munich's popular culture.

DURING HIS LONG and illustrious folksinger career, Karl Valentin repeatedly used one basic technique to address his public's fear of social decline. This technique is already in evidence in a three-minute monologue that Valentin wrote in 1908, dealing with the problem of hunger and entitled *Ich bin ein armer magerer Mann* (I Am a Poor, Skinny Man).[40] Its essential first point is Valentin's identification of himself with the audience's social milieu. He accomplishes this in part by language; his accent is strongly Bavarian, and his speech is filled with local words and expressions, like *Gaudi* (fun). Moreover, he demonstrates an "insider's" awareness of middle-class life. Wondering how he can weigh so little when his parents weigh so much, he adds, on an obscure line of thought: "And my sister got married to a freight man with the railroad." The public would have recognized one of their own: the son of an upstanding Munich family that has placed its daughter with a husband who works and earns solidly. Cleverly, Valentin proceeds to make it known that his skinniness is an effect of this Munich social world, of the hunger that makes itself felt in families that are struggling financially. Again, he conveys the idea implicitly. He repeats something his father has told him, that he can gain weight once his sister is married. Suddenly, for the audience, the relevance of the sister's marriage to Valentin's low weight is plain, as are the family circumstances. Valentin's father means that, with the sister gone to another household, there will be more for the brother to eat. The audience would have understood because—even if they might have preferred not to remember—such calculations were a factor in their daily lives too. Hunger was ever present in Munich not only for wage earners but also for the troubled middle class, if not as a reality, then as a fear.[41] Valentin, on stage, embodied this fear.

Having established that he comes from the middle class, Valentin proceeds to show that his situation is indeed much worse than an ordinary tradesman's or office worker's. It is particularly significant that he does not mention his work. Apparently, his time is free, and also unstructured, a sign not of upper-class leisure but of middle-class failure. His "insider" status recedes into the past; what remains is a series of laughable misfortunes and humiliations that mark him off as an "outsider." These all relate to his skinniness. Once, standing in a billiards parlor, he remarks, he was mistaken for a cue. Then, he continues, he was the butt of cruel jokes when he went to be examined for induction into the army. Of course, he was rejected. Later, he tried to sell himself to an anatomy professor for eighty

marks and ended up in a demeaning argument over the price.
"Then," he goes on, "I read something about a corpse-burning society, and I thought to myself, you go there and get burned when
you've died." He went to make the arrangements, only to hear that
they would have to rub him with ten pounds of lard for him to burn
at all, and that it would be more than normally expensive. When he
asked why, he was told that he would require a new oven plate because "you'd definitely slip through the one we've got now."
Repeatedly, the humor turns upon Valentin himself, upon the in-
dignities that his thin body has forced him to endure.

Like Zijderveld's "ceremonial clowns," Valentin confronts his
audience with an image of chaos, in his case, of the chaos that
awaits anyone who falls to society's lower depths. He is at once a
figure of warning and a reason to feel superior. This was not pleasant entertainment. Valentin had incited a certain meanness in his
audience, an aggressive urge to forget their own frustrations by
laughing at someone else's. Herein lay the reassurance of Valentin's
message; people felt that they would belong to a larger social whole
as long as there were buffoons like Valentin whom they could exclude.

Valentin's entertainment reflected not only middle-class fears but
also his own highly unique and legendary personality. The origins
of *Ich bin ein armer magerer Mann,* for example, are personal. Valentin's friend Ludwig Greiner, a Munich tavern owner, had persuaded him to use his slender form to comic effect, and the monologue followed.[42] "What must I have done," laments Valentin in the
act's opening line, "for Nature to have put me together so cruelly?"
Here, the folksinger gives vent to his deep-seated fear of being arbi-
trarily singled out as the victim of a disaster, or as the bearer of a
special pain. His daughter once encapsulated this feeling in the sentence: "That can only happen to me." Corresponding to Valentin's
fear, the figure he created in *Ich bin ein armer magerer Mann* sees his
skinniness as a personal affliction: "What must I have done?" he
asks. For the audience, the social context—middle-class impoverishment and hunger—would have been evident. Valentin's brilliance as
an entertainer lay in this unique ability to merge his private anxieties with society's concerns. In *Ich bin ein armer magerer Mann,*
he portrays his own vulnerable self while assuaging his public's
middle-class worries.

Karl Valentin's perspective upon social issues differed greatly from Weiss Ferdl's. The same is true of his perspective upon politics. "Der Schwere Reiter" (The Hard Rider), a song he wrote around 1911, for example, takes an openly satirical view of an important institution of the German Empire: the military.[43] Valentin, in battle dress, sang this song to the cadence of a military march, while he held a wooden horse between his legs:

> . . . The ornament of the German Empire,
>   that's the military
> We come up at attention—especially me
> And if a war breaks out, we take the field
> We hit them really hard—especially me.

> "Der Schmuck vom deutschen Reich, das ist das Militär,
> Wir kommen stramm daher—besonders i,
> Und wenn a Krieg bricht aus, ziehen wir ins Feld hinaus,
> Da hau'n wir g'hörig zua—besonders i."

Some of the humor is directed toward the folksinger himself. Spindly as he was and awkward as he seemed to be on stage, it was ludicrous for him to pretend to be a hero of the German cavalry. But he is not, as he broadly suggests, the only one pretending. Declaring that if it should come to war "we hit them really hard," Valentin was echoing—even mimicking—the fearsome threats then being issued, in these years of Balkan wars and Moroccan crises, by the Imperial German military. The point is clear. Valentin implies that the nation's saber rattling is as foolish and as empty as his own. His assertion in a 1913 letter that this number "made me popular in Munich" establishes that there were antimilitarist currents among the attitudes of the city's middle-class folksinger public. Loyalty to the Empire was Platzl's message; skepticism, at least in this song, was Valentin's.[44]

How did a politically critical number like Valentin's "Der Schwere Reiter" come through Munich's censorship offices? There is, unfortunately, no official "Valentin file" from which to draw an answer. It is possible that the song simply passed through unnoticed, but the greater likelihood is that the Munich censor would know of an openly political song that was helping to establish the career of a new local performer. Perhaps the official who read this number found it relatively harmless. Indeed, the Munich censor generally did not see it as his duty to ban all political complaints from the city's stages, only those that were especially sharp.[45] His focus does not seem to have been upon politics at all, but rather upon issues of private behavior, in particular sexuality. There was nothing directly political in the controversies over Wedekind or over actresses' costumes. It may be, therefore, that the censor—under the influence of the "decency leagues"—perceived moral perversion to be a greater threat to the Empire than everyday kinds of political dissatisfaction. Thus, he allowed light ridicule of the military or of the bureaucracy. However, it is conceivable that Valentin did indeed cross over the boundary of official tolerance with "Der Schwere Reiter" but could do so because he enjoyed a special status in Munich, a kind of fool's freedom. Perhaps he was able to speak behind the shield of his well-known peculiarity, not taken seriously by anyone with the power to silence him. In any case, Valentin's pre-1914 ridicule of militarism was permitted, and won him some public affection.

Throughout Karl Valentin's entertainment career, there was an antimilitary, anti-authority aspect of his humor which became pronounced in the course of World War I and in the uncertain years thereafter. Still, in "Der Schwere Reiter," the folksinger was uncharacteristically direct. For expressing such views, he generally employed a code that was simple but not necessarily understood by everyone. In evidence before the war, and in full form during and after it, the code's key was the use of small-town constables, militiamen, fire fighters, and others to stand for the German military, or for the principle of authority in militaristic German society. Making fun of yesterday's men in uniform at the local level, Valentin made fun of today's men in uniform at the national level. His code was the perfect language for satire; it enabled him to take critical positions at times when to do so openly could have damaged if not ended his career.

Dating from 1908, one of the first—if not the first—of Valentin's coded satires was a four- or five-minute monologue entitled *Der Schneidige Landgendarm* (The Sharp Country Constable).[46] From its first moment, it is a spoof upon the principle of authority. Valentin appears dressed as an old constable, carrying a large folder and holding a chain with a dog collar on the end of it. He introduces himself by singing four lines to the tune of a well-known German song, "Üb immer Treu und Redlichkeit" (Always Be True and Sincere), and thereby sets the theme:

I am a sharp constable from the country
And I have sharp eyes.
And just because I'm so thin
The bad kids have got to watch out.

As in "Der Schwere Reiter," Valentin presents a character intent upon exercising his authority yet ridiculous as he tries to do so. Both the folder and the dog collar, which Valentin has brought on stage, demonstrate this amply. The folder contains drawings of lawbreakers whom the constable has apprehended: because he cannot write, he cannot record the identities of those he catches except by drawing; often, to his dismay, they run off before he has finished. The dog collar is for his dog, but he notices while speaking that the animal is gone: "Now those wise, bad kids have stolen my dog. That's why I've been thinking how good he's been for the past week." Utterly entangled in his own basic confusion, the constable is anything but effective as an officer of the law. Valentin has succeeded at making the old system of local authority, which many in his audience would have recognized from their rural and small-town origins, appear laughable.

Very subtly, and especially at certain points, Valentin breaks through in this ridicule of authority from the quaint and provincial to the essential. Near the beginning of *Der Schneidige Landgendarm,* its character describes how sometimes the "bad kids" reverse roles on him: "There's only one thing I can't stand for the devil, when those lowly guys run after *me.* Then I go into a rage, because that isn't allowed at all." Then, a few minutes later, he complains that the school children force him to play with them, "or else they really hit me." In both situations, the constable is helpless to assert himself against people who simply do not recognize his authority. Here, Valentin has presented the most deep-seated fear of all governments, police forces, and armies: that the day will come when their uniforms suddenly mean nothing, when their places in their societies are open to question, when the "bad kids" turn around and chase the constables. The implications for Imperial Germany are clear—but only after some thought, perhaps more thought than the Munich censor would have given it.

Speaking in code, Valentin may not have made himself understood, which relates not only to the censor but to his audience as

well. How many of the common people who saw Valentin deliver
this monologue enjoyed the humor without sensing any particular
relevance for the politics of the day? Valentin, in making an old constable look foolish, aroused a certain popular impishness. It amused
people to see a uniform in so many predicaments.[47] There are signs
of an old aspect of Valentin's personality here; it is easy to imagine
the "Fey kid" as one of the "bad kids." As evidence of middle-class
attitudes, however, this monologue is not as reliable as "Der
Schwere Reiter."

Karl Valentin and Weiss Ferdl held and, more important, reflected different views on the authoritarianism and militarism of the
German Empire. They did not stand alone at their positions. Ludwig M. Schneider has shown that there was a Munich tradition of
popular resentment over the taxes paid to support the Imperial military. He tends, however, to draw his evidence from before 1900, that
is, before the "schools of the nation" could have a fuller effect and
before the propaganda about the navy's building program had
begun filling the middle class with dreams of glory and conquest.[48]
Nor were Weiss Ferdl's patriotic song booklets unique. For example, at the 1909 "Salvator Season," a May beer festival at the Paulaner brewery, the following was sung:

> Long live our Zeppelin
> The great German hero
> Who gave to his fatherland
> The greatest work of the world.[49]

There was room in middle-class Munich for diverging and even opposed attitudes. Loyalty to the Empire, like the yearning for "old
Bavarian" happiness, was not all pervasive. Although the acts of
these two folksingers reveal different popular views, a point of similarity should not be ignored. Making himself an object of ridicule,
as he did in all his entertainment, Valentin soothed the status anxieties of his public; in contrast to him, they felt like "insiders." Valentin's message was like Platzl's message in this one regard: it was
reassuring.

In 1911 Karl Valentin formed a lasting professional partnership
with a nineteen-year-old woman by the name of Elisabeth Wellano,
whom he rechristened "Liesl Karlstadt" in memory of his boyhood

hero, Karl Maxstadt. Liesl Karlstadt not only performed with Valentin in dozens of plays and dialogues over a thirty-year period but also took over secretarial duties in rehearsal, writing down what he improvised. Thanks to her efforts, most of his acts have been preserved. Valentin first saw her at the Frankfurter Hof, where he was the featured comedian; she sang soprano in a musical ensemble. To her surprise, he approached her one day to tell her that her bosom was too small for a good soprano, and besides, she looked too much like a communion girl. But, he said, she was funny. This took her aback. When he learned that she was appearing in a cabaret where the audience was ill behaved, he cautioned her: "That is not for you." Then, hearing that she was about to go on tour, he asked her if she knew that she would end up in the "white-slave trade." His offer followed. Their similar backgrounds worked to their advantage. The daughter of a Schwabing baker, she had completed an apprenticeship as a seamstress and had taken a job as a saleswoman before beginning her entertainment career.[50] She knew as well as he about the problems of Munich's middle class; on stage, as his partner, she portrayed them with great skill over decades.

Adding Liesl Karlstadt to his act enabled Valentin to branch out from writing monologues and couplets to dialogues and one-act plays. One of the first plays, *Alpensängerterzett* (Alpine Singers Trio),[51] given in heavy dialect, is a satire upon "old Bavarian" entertainment. This play centers upon a family of Alpine Singers: Valentin is the son, Liesl Karlstadt the daughter, and a third actor plays the father. Its humor arises largely out of the family's lack of musical ability. When the father sings a piece about a "sky-blue mountain lake," Valentin remarks that he has "too much pflegm in his throat." Then, Liesl Karlstadt tries "Edelweiss, Edelweiss," and cannot find her pitch. Moreover, if "old Bavaria's" ideal family had bonds of support and affection among its members, these three stand in open contrast to it. They not only bicker among themselves, but Valentin even pulls a knife when his father calls him a "damn kid" *(Hundsbua),* though he puts it back immediately. Neither of the men is at all patient with the daughter's singing difficulties. Valentin calls her a "dumb beast" *(Rindviech),* while the father hits her arm so hard that she begins to cry. Thus the show proceeds until the end, when Liesl's passing the hat in the audience brings an enraged manager onto the stage to evict these country no-talents from the house.

Valentin turns to the father near the end of *Alpensängerterzett* and complains: "There you have it with your fine *varieté* theater. If we'd gone to Mathäser [a Munich brewery and beer hall], we'd have done good business." The "fine *varieté* theater" was probably the Frankfurter Hof, the hotel with a restaurant where this play was first performed.[52] Valentin continues that "other establishments" have been more appreciative: "They are still happy to get folksingers like us!" ("Sie san no amal froh, wenn s' solchane Volkssänger kriagn, wia mir san!").

This raises questions about Valentin's place in a city where "old Bavarian" entertainment was so prevalent. Had Valentin left Munich's popular stages and popular audiences to entertain at "fine *varieté* theaters" like the Frankfurter Hof? Was the audience at the Frankfurter Hof at such a "level" that it could view the folksingers as objects of amusement but not accept them as performers? Was Valentin no longer a folksinger? Documents of his early career provide some answers. First, "fine" as the Frankfurter Hof may have been, it did not at all end Valentin's connection to Munich's popular cabaret and beer-hall audiences, to people "still happy to get the folksingers." Quite to the contrary, he often performed for them after his initial 1907 or 1908 engagement at the Frankfurter Hof: at Mathäser, and at other beer halls like the Kindl-Keller and the Augustiner-Keller.[53] Munich's popular stages were home base for Valentin. He ventured away from them occasionally, to Schwabing artists' haunts like Simplicissimus before the war, and even to literary cabarets in cities like Vienna, Berlin, and Zurich in the 1920s,[54] but he always returned.

Second, the Frankfurter Hof may have been "finer" than a Munich beer hall by only a few degrees. The entertainment was similar: a 1909 Frankfurter Hof program lists—besides Valentin—a "mountain comedy" *(Gebirgskomödie)*, some "farm songs," and a yodeler from Garmisch.[55] Perhaps "old Bavaria" was less in control there than, for example, at Platzl, but it was clearly present. Nor is it easy to imagine that the audience was at a different level of sophistication. Unfortunately, the Frankfurter Hof kept no guest books, but it is unlikely that many patrons of Munich's legitimate theaters would have gone there to see not only Valentin but also yodelers and "mountain comedies." Indeed, the one guest who made an impression upon Liesl Karlstadt was anything but "fine." She remembered a heavyset gentleman rising from his seat at the point in *Al-pensängerterzett* when the director appeared on stage to evict the family, and saying in a strong Bavarian accent: "Let them be—they sang fine!" (Lass steh—die ham schee gsungen!)[56] It may be that there were gradations among Munich's popular stages which time and the lack of documents have made indetectable. Frankfurter Hof audiences may have dressed a little better or earned a little more than audiences at Platzl or at the Mathäser brewery. Still, there is no evidence to suggest that they did not belong to the city's popular scene. Karl Valentin, appearing in front of them or at a beer hall, was a Munich folksinger—and never saw himself as anything else.[57]

Clearly, there were differences between Valentin and "The Dachauers." Valentin himself once remarked that the only stage on which he would not be accepted was Platzl's;[58] there was no place for the "poor, skinny man" with the "happy, singing family." Indeed, it would be better to see Munich's folksinger "audience" not as a block of people with common backgrounds and interests but rather as a group of "audiences," each finding its social and political views reflected in the entertainment. Here, the lack of documents is sorely regrettable. There are no lists of who went to see which performer. Moreover, the newspaper and memoir descriptions of the public, in general quite helpful, are not sociologically precise enough for concluding that clerks saw Valentin whereas tradesmen went to Platzl, or that Valentin's audience was born in Munich whereas Weiss Ferdl's was born in Bavaria outside Munich. It is reasonable to assume that Valentin had his crowd and that the "old Bavarians" at Platzl had theirs. Assuming, though, that there was an absolute dividing line would be wrong. On this, documents are available. At least once before World War I, Valentin and "The Dachauers" with Weiss Ferdl appeared on the same program, in 1909 at an annual brewery celebration. Both served frequently as after-dinner entertainment at public and private gatherings: at breweries, at church group or union banquets, and before veterans' clubs.[59] That there was at least some overlapping is not hard to imagine. These two entertainers generally appeared before different audiences with different attitudes, but there must have been a few thousand people who saw and appreciated both men. If Valentin and Weiss Ferdl represented the spectrum of middle-class attitudes in Munich, this spectrum existed not only between crowds but also within some individuals who enjoyed both folksingers.

GERMANY'S MAIN HISTORICAL trends of the prewar period form the context within which Munich folksingers Karl Valentin and Weiss Ferdl entertained. Industrialization, the rise of liberal society as typified by the advance of Jews, and military power were issues with which many of the small-stage acts dealt. Platzl's idealization of "old Bavaria" was a protest against urbanization, and Valentin's "hard rider" embodied a critical attitude toward militarism. The recurrence of such themes indicates the deep involvement of both performers with the major concerns of their time.

In 1913 the Munich folksingers and their middle-class audience were five turbulent years away from the founding of the Weimar Republic. If either Karl Valentin or Weiss Ferdl is to be seen as anticipating the opposition that the Republic aroused in the middle reaches of society, it is clearly Weiss Ferdl. The structure of middle-class political and social attitudes, ideas, and opinions, so firm at Platzl, became a center of disdain for the new state after World War I. Yearning for a preindustrial community, resentment of Jews, and patriotism all took on larger dimensions in the early 1920s, and all militated against a sympathetic view of Weimar. With few ties of loyalty to the Republic, the Platzl crowd entered that zone of political disillusionment where right-wing agitators like Munich's National Socialists sought supporters. Did Valentin's crowd do so too? In contrast to "The Dachauers," Valentin himself appears if not as a Weimar supporter, then as a critic of Weimar's enemies on the right. His antimilitarism was an implicit critique of the Empire before and during the war, and of the nationalistic spirit of revanche thereafter. It emerged, however, in coded form. That the tradesmen, shopkeepers, and white-collar workers of his public knew the code is open to serious doubt. Perhaps they did not understand that small-town constables and awkward militiamen stood for contemporary militarists. Valentin's own antirightist attitudes, then, may not have reflected the attitudes of those who paid for his entertainment. From another standpoint, however, Valentin's acts indicate the despair that underlay middle-class opposition to the Republic as much as Weiss Ferdl's. Repeatedly, in dozens of forms, Valentin appeared on stage as an "outsider," a man whose misfortunes reassured those watching that their problems were small by comparison. This was the basis of his success with the frightened middle class. In Karl Valentin, as in Weiss Ferdl, people of this milieu found the security that was lacking in their social lives; during the early 1920s, they found little security in the Weimar Republic.

4

The Wartime Munich Stage and Middle-Class Hardships

Munich entered World War I in a fury: with mass patriotic demonstrations throughout the city; with wild rumors that foreign spies were everywhere, including one that seventeen of them had been captured and shot in the suburb of Neufreimann; with a panic that the city's water supply was poisoned with cyanide; and with little boxes of Bavarian white and blue springing up on street corners and at streetcar stops, into which people could donate cigarettes and cigars for the front.[1] Not even old opponents of German militarism were immune to the war fever of late summer and autumn 1914. For example, playwright Frank Wedekind—who had written before the war of "the growing feeling of solidarity among the cultural nations against military rule"—spoke at a patriotic celebration held in Munich's Chamber of Plays (Kammerspiele) on 18 September 1914. "The unity of German Social Democracy with the Imperial High Command," he declared, is "the loyal brotherhood of arms...!" Not many months passed before Wedekind had lost enthusiasm, and was growing impatient with friends who were trying to call him to account for the speech: "They take everything literally, and simply cannot wait." But wherever Wedekind stood later, in September 1914 he was among the hundreds of thousands in Munich who stood with Germany.[2]

Swiftly, the war brought changes into the field of entertainment. Among these was a demand for singers, dancers, actors, actresses, and comedians to perform, often without pay, in support of the war cause in its various aspects. Some entertainers responded out of a genuine urge to do something for their fatherland in its time of need. As Robert Kothe, a singer of old Bavarian songs, expressed it in his memoirs: "I placed myself at the disposal of the army leadership. I often sang in Munich military hospitals . . . and in many elsewhere, with the satisfying feeling of being allowed to give at least something in the great struggle."[3] Without leaving a similar declaration of their motives, Karl Valentin and Liesl Karlstadt also performed at military hospitals—120 times over the course of the war, Valentin later wrote.[4] But the needs of the war-wounded were only the beginning. The actors and actresses of Munich's Theater at Gardener

Place performed in 1915, for example, for the benefit of the Bulgarian Red Cross; of the Welfare Establishment of the League of Former Members of the Thirteenth Company of the First Infantry Regiment; of Workers Harmed by the War; and of the War Support Fund of the League of Munich Districts.[5]

Even some of the stage entertainers who went off to war found, to their surprise, that the military needed them to perform for troops at the front. In France, Sergeant Weiss Ferdl—who had enlisted because he was "afraid the war would be over" without him—came to the attention of his superior officers when he informally began to sing songs he had written for the soldiers of his Bavarian infantry regiment. In 1915 he received the order "to locate himself with the other comedians of the battalion in the entertainment hall of the Seventh Company and to take care of the amusement there." Eventually, out of this command came a troupe of Bavarian field performers, including actors, singers, and musicians from Munich's establishments of popular entertainment.[6]

True to the Platzl tradition, there was patriotic group singing at the front. Included in one of the songbooks Weiss Ferdl used was "Heil Dir im Siegerkranz" (Hail to You in the Victor's Wreath), which recalls Emperor Wilhelm I as "the pride of mankind."[7] For the most part, however, Weiss Ferdl found that soldiers who had seen action in battle knew the war too well to enjoy this glib patriotism. He began, therefore, to deal very sensitively in his own songs with the daily problems of life at the front.[8] The best known of these songs was "Das Lercherl von Arras" (The Little Lark of Arras), inspired by a nest of larks between the German and French trenches from which there came, Weiss Ferdl later remembered, a sweet singing that pleased soldiers on both sides. The first verse of the song begins by recognizing the heroism of German soldiers who had died in battle. But the battlefield is also a "terrible" place, and the sight of a lark in flight fills those who are waiting for the next round of attack and counterattack with thoughts of home:

> The roar of the battle is rumbling heavily,
> Above us soars in the airy heights,
> A little lark which knows no fear
> And feels not the nearness of death.

It warbles without hesitation;
Little lark, we like you so much.
You are telling us something very dear
Of our homeland so far away.

"Grollt dumpf des Kampfes Brausen, oben schwebt in luft 'ger
Höh',
A Lercherl, kennt kein Grausen und fühlt nicht des Todes Näh',
Er trillert ohne Zagen; Lercherl wir haben dich so gern,
Du tust uns Liebes sagen, von der Heimat, die so fern."[9]

The song accepts the war and extends sympathy to German men
who have had to endure its horror. The experience of real battle
changed Weiss Ferdl from a music-hall patriot into a soldier who
sadly regretted the human sacrifices that the national honor was de-
manding. As a member of an entertainment troupe, he certainly had
firsthand knowledge of the suffering: he himself sustained a relatively minor back injury in May 1915; he barely missed being killed
when a French shell landed on an auditorium where an afternoon
rehearsal had just been held; and he often had to stay at the front to
entertain the troops when he should have been home on leave.[10]

One of Weiss Ferdl's songs, written in 1918, is frankly antiwar
and reflects the fear of soldiers that the lives they dreamed of having
after the war would not be possible. The song is the story of an ordinary Bavarian soldier named Sepp Huber who has received a letter
from home that accuses his wife of having been unfaithful to him. In
despair, he confronts her during his next leave home, but she assures
him that the news of her having a lover was not true. This relieves
Sepp enormously, and he resolves not to doubt her again. He has
also learned that returning to his wife is more important to him than
shooting any more enemy soldiers. Weiss Ferdl concludes:

The people of Europe are following the lesson
Of Sepp—it isn't dumb.
Sell the cannons and the rifles,
And kill each other no more.

Publishing the text of the song in 1933, at a time when Germany was
once again expressing its national will to power, Weiss Ferdl admit-

ted that the song was "a little pacifistic—one can understand that because I wrote it in the fourth year of the war."[11]

There is certainly nothing deceitful about this later apology. The song is more a sign of late-war disillusionment among the troops than it is typical of Weiss Ferdl's efforts at the front. As Frau Weiss Ferdl has indicated, the Munich folksinger was a "follower of the fatherland," and most of his wartime entertainment reflects his wish to inspire soldiers who were risking their lives for Germany. The army recognized this and decorated him with an Iron Cross; Wittelsbach Crown Prince Rupprecht personally thanked him several times for his patriotic service.[12]

THE MOST VISIBLE effect of the war upon entertainment in Munich was the removal of many of the city's favorite male performers—like Weiss Ferdl—to the battlegrounds. Almost immediately, dozens of actors, singers, dancers, and others left. Karl Valentin was with Papa Benz's troupe in Leopold Street when war was declared; eight days later "at least ten men" left the house, decorated with flowers and singing patriotic songs.[13] One gets an idea of how deeply induction into the army affected the body of Munich folksingers from a police document about the League for Support of the Interests of the Munich Folksingers. Established in 1909, the League disbanded in 1916–17 "because the largest part of the membership had been taken into the field."[14] Younger men almost vanished from the popular stages during the war. In 1917 at the Colosseum, for example, the management assured the audience that the few who were performing, "insofar as they were not citizens of neutral states, had in most cases been in the field repeatedly and released because of wounds or granted a leave of some months."[15]

The absence of young men from the stages was only the surface of change. How deeply the sudden national passion of 1914 touched the cultural life of Munich can first be appreciated by considering the new position of foreign artists in the city: foreigners living in the Bavarian capital before 1914 were accepted members of one of Europe's most cosmopolitan communities; suddenly they became objects of suspicion and scorn, not only for the general population but for the Bavarian government as well. Rolf von Hoerschelmann, for example, was a Baltic German who had moved to Munich with his mother in 1907 and established a name as a book and art collector.

When the mobilization for war was ordered, remembered a contemporary, "there was mistrust all around. The milk woman and the baker demanded immediate settling of their bills, and otherwise things were unpleasant too. When von Hoerschelmann wanted to convince the police that he came from the Baltic region, a sergeant explained to him brusquely that 'a Russian is always a Russian.' " He did stay in Munich and was free to move about, but only on the condition that he register regularly with the police.[16] What von Hoerschelmann endured was mild, however, compared to the experiences of some of Munich's "citizens of enemy states," for whom, according to a police document, "sharper measures" had been set in place. In extreme cases, this meant deportation of a suspected spy, or detainment in a jail, in a military prison, or in a special prison camp; at the least, it meant opening foreigners' mail, listening in on their telephone conversations, and requiring them to report regularly to the police and to obtain permission before traveling.[17]

The awakened nationalism of 1914 turned not only against foreign persons but against foreign culture as well. In the theater industry, one expression of this was the withdrawal of works by non-Germans or non-Austrians from theater schedules. For example, although Munich's Court and National Theater and its Residence Theater continued to perform plays by Shakespeare and to a lesser degree by Moliere during their wartime seasons, both dropped plays by modern playwright George Bernard Shaw.[18] There were, it is true, some artistic directors who returned as quickly as they thought possible to their prewar repertoires. But many felt the pressure of patriotic opinion in words like the following, which appeared in an Augsburg newspaper in 1916: "The main purpose is to liberate the German theater as much as possible from foreignism, and from the aping of that which is foreign."[19]

Munich's popular cabarets and music halls reflected the new nationalism as clearly as did the legitimate theaters. A critical contemporary described the change: "Now . . . the tinseled ladies, who earlier gladly passed out their coquettish adventures and alcove secrets in couplet form, are singing field-grey patriotic songs."[20] There was also resistance to "foreignism" on the popular stages. The famous Circus-Varieté-Colosseum, for example, besides running weekly films from the fronts, announced in its evening programs that its performing artists were "of German-Austrian nationality or were subjects of neutral states," and also ended the use of French terms in the programs. According to an October 1914 article in the daily *Münchner Zeitung:* "The splendid reopening performance on Saturday proved to a house that was sold out that a 'varieté' also runs without the Frenchman and the Englishman and particularly without the secretive names. Hoppkins, the mimic, shows as Hoppke that his act has not become worse for broadcasting his German name. No longer as a 'jongleur,' but as a 'catcher' does Franz Günther amaze us." At least for a time in late 1915, the Colosseum seems to have returned to the foreign words, as was noted with disapproval in the *Münchner Zeitung;* the practice of announcing that performing artists had been born in the German or Austrian empires, or in a neutral foreign country, lasted through the war.[21]

Neither the elimination of foreign elements from the entertainment nor the patriotic song-singing nor the benefit performances should, however, suggest that all support for the war was wholly voluntary. Many actors and actresses did what their directors told them, so as not to "go hungry";[22] the directors themselves were often responding to pressures from patriotic segments of the public, or from the government. Twenty years later, Karl Valentin recalled the position he was in as an entertainer for Papa Benz when the war broke out, and the position Papa Benz himself was in as director of the cabaret:

> Fourteen days after the outbreak of the war, we were allowed to reopen in order to give artists, actors, and so on the chance of an income, with the condition that our performances be attuned to the times. Every director of a theater ordered patriotic performances. I too had to do serious things, although no one was used to it from me as an interpreter of nonsense. Among other things, [I did] a war morality song which ended with the German anthem; it was a unique experience as everyone present rose up from their chairs and sang along. The success was great and for two months as a comedian I sang sad, serious songs. Then came the new order from the director to let humor reign in the difficult time of war, and that was good.[23]

Valentin's daughter reports that he once told her that he sang the war morality song "in order not to be without work," and that the sight of him and Liesl Karlstadt singing "in dead seriousness" brought some laughter from the audience.[24]

Valentin alluded to the closing of the theaters on 4 August 1914;

sharpened forms of police supervision accompanied their reopening a few weeks later. The most basic of these was preventive censorship, which required that texts of songs, monologues, plays, and so forth be submitted for approval to the police before they were performed.[25] German entertainment was expected to maintain a positive stance toward the war.

It was soon obvious that censorship would not stop at political dissidence, for the social and governmental forces that had favored controlling what theaters could offer the public before 1914 were determined to extend wartime supervision to matters of private morality and behavior. For them, the connection was clear: a play that dealt with sexual freedom, no less than a leaflet that called on the Kaiser to abdicate, detracted from the unity of the German people. An example of this thinking can be found in the national League for the Support of German Theater Culture, a group established in 1916 that listed "fighting against improprieties in the theater" among its purposes, and that had representatives in Munich. "In the area of art, the same danger is repeated," said a 1917 article of the League, "that we have hoped to overcome in the political area through the war: that individualistic and party-dogmatic exertions disturb and limit the higher purposes of the whole." With the system of censorship firmly in place, and with army officers attending their conferences, the League sensed final victory: "so shall this unanimity in the support of the highest cultural purposes exist after the war. We hope very deeply that the feeling of unity born in the war, the consciousness of belonging together within the whole of the people, will never be lost."[26] This vision was inaccurate, but that did not diminish its influence while the war lasted. Thus the Munich police instructed directors of the city's theaters and entertainment halls to hold back any item that offended "religion, morality, public decency, political institutions, [or] public order."[27]

Actually, wartime censorship was not as far-reaching as the League of Support wanted it to be. In Munich, Frank Wedekind's *Spring's Awakening,* a play about adolescent sexuality and generational conflict, was allowed onto the program of the Chamber of Plays in September 1915, where it stayed at least until 1917. To some, this was frankly unbelievable. In the words of one conservative journalist: "On our moral greatness rests the success that assured our national existence in this world war. We will always fight against the libertines. . . !"[28] The performance of some controversial works notwithstanding, however, the war was a major setback for Munich as a city of theater, and one reason for this was the intensification of censorship. More than before the war, the police tended to ban plays without first consulting the advisory council to the censor, which was left, according to a police document, with a "much narrower range of activity."[29] Munich author Kurt Martens found this when he tried to secure permission for a closed performance of another Wedekind play, *Schloss Wetterstein* (Wetterstein Castle), with proceeds to go to "suffering writers"; the police summarily denied his request.[30] Wedekind himself stayed at a distance from these issues, but he complained in a letter to a friend that "in spite of the twelve o'clock curfew, literary conflicts are again being handled in court. Thank God I do not have anything to do with that."[31]

Mention of the Wedekind controversies should not create the impression that censorship was more a problem for the "legitimate" than the "popular" stages. Both operated under the same police rules, and both had trouble. There was a policeman, probably plain-clothed, at the old Apollo Theater in December 1915 to make sure that no uncensored material was being presented there. He reported having seen "harmless entertainment . . . for [a] large, apparently lower middle-class public." His presence demonstrates police interest in the popular theaters and indicates how the police checked the effectiveness of their censor: by planting what were essentially police spies in the audience. It will be seen that the police actually banned Karl Valentin for six weeks in 1917 when he delivered an uncensored monologue critical of the war.[32]

Censorship was one expression of a widespread feeling within German government and society during the war that culture and entertainment were more or less dispensable. This feeling—that the war must come first—may have actually influenced some private citizens to cancel their magazine subscriptions; to not commission a certain painting; to take money they might have donated to a theater and donate it to a fund for wounded soldiers instead; or to stop visiting the cabarets as often. Probably a larger element in such decisions was wartime inflation, which forced people to cut spending for nonessentials. In any case, the war brought a depression to large sections of the cultural industries, and thousands of German writers, journalists, painters, actors, and actresses suffered without work. Six weeks after the war broke out, for example, the League for the Protection of German Writers, Local Group of Munich petitioned the Bavarian Ministry of Instruction and Culture on behalf of "many journalists and writers" who had been working for newspapers and magazines that had either stopped or cut back publication. "The war," began their letter, "has almost fully taken the possibility for existence from a large part of our colleagues who did not go along into the field or who were not able to dedicate their services to the fatherland in another way." Because their misery had become "unspeakable," the League of Protection requested the Ministry's help in placing as many as possible in new jobs where they could apply their typing skills or their mastery of foreign languages.[33] But the problem was not unique to the writers. Even Munich's street vendors of food and amusement felt the war's negative effects when Bavarian King Ludwig III banned the 1914 Oktoberfest because of the "present political situation."[34]

Stage entertainers who had neither established themselves before the outbreak of the war nor found work in patriotically inclined cabarets and theaters thereafter were in a difficult position. The temporary closing of the theaters during the first weeks of the war has been mentioned. The police had them closed again for a period of time in 1916.[35] But official restriction was not the only problem. The wartime shortage of coal, for example, forced theater managements to curtail their schedules during the cold months of the year.[36] In view of the effects of these conditions upon member actors and actresses, the Brotherhood of German Stage Artists printed the following in its magazine, Der Neue Weg (The New Way), in 1915: "We believe that we are not in error if we describe roughly half our members as unemployed during the winter 1914–15, and roughly two thirds to three quarters for the summer 1915 . . . Among the female members the misery created by unemployment is especially large, because a noticeable number of the male members are [with the military] in the field." Whether the percentages were quite that high is hard to say, but it is clear that the war brought layoffs: for example, of the 161 positions for performers at four Munich theaters during the 1913–14 season, 51 were lost one year later, nearly one third. Nor were performers who kept their contracts free from worry; a "war clause" allowed employers to release a performer with a notice of only eight days. This infuriated the Brotherhood of Ger-

man Stage Artists because members were left in uncertainty and because theaters used the clause to threaten actors and actresses into
accepting smaller salaries.[37]

Without a union to support them in the way that the Brotherhood
of German Stage Artists supported actors and actresses of the legitimate theater, popular entertainers had practically no defense
against the war's worst effects. In Munich police files, there is record
of a grievance at the Colosseum among musicians whose salaries
had been cut at the beginning of the war. Although the management
later restored the cut, it did so only on the condition that one of the
musicians be dismissed. This aroused the protest, but to no avail.[38]

UNEMPLOYMENT, low pay, censorship, the removal of foreign
influences and of young German male performers, patriotic enthusiasm: these were the conditions of popular entertainment in wartime
Munich. Performers were not alone, of course, in feeling the war's
impact. All of civilian society was affected, including the Munich
folksingers' middle-class public. Karl Valentin, with most of his
competition in military service, faced the task of dealing with his audience's increasing hardships. Successful enough before the war not
to have to worry about finding engagements during it, he remained
acutely sensitive to middle-class experiences. He understood that the
war had driven small-business and white-collar families beyond despair to desperation. This understanding paved his approach to entertaining them and formed the basis of his success.

Small businessmen, both shopkeepers and tradesmen, found that
the war was forcing them to take a few more steps down the stairway
toward losing their stores, their independence, and their pride. It
was an intensification of problems they had had before 1914: they
were not sure of having enough buyers for what they wanted to sell;
then, if they thought they had the buyers, they were not sure of
being able to purchase the necessary goods or materials because, following wartime centralization plans, they received their orders only
after the military and large companies received theirs. No less a figure than Bavarian Crown Prince Rupprecht pleaded with officials in
Berlin to consider the needs of his province's small businesses:
"Using the needs of the war in the most ruthless fashion, the Berlin
business people have managed, by the creation of all the central
agencies set up in Berlin, to bring the internal economic life of Ger-

many under their control and power, and the consequence will be that, after the war, the middle class, which already finds itself in dire distress, will disappear and a trustification worse than America's will set in. For Bavaria, where the middle class is rather numerous, this will be catastrophic."[39] Such advice, however, carried little weight in Berlin, and some small Munich businesses closed for want of supplies, especially coal.[40] Moreover, the middle class saw a leveling of its income with the working class's. Gerald D. Feldman has concluded that this "was due less to the improvement of wages than to the deterioration of the economic position of the middle class . . . The impression that the workers were being excessively paid . . . created resentment against them."[41]

Equally affected by the war was the new middle class of minor government officials, sales employees, and office workers. Having been too status-conscious to resort to working-class tactics and unionize before 1914, men and women from this part of society were powerless to force salary increases upon their employers during the war. As a result, they lost up to half of their purchasing power. Under these conditions, the movement to form unions gained strength, but nothing materialized until the last months of the war and the first months of peace.[42] In 1919 one of the newly established unions, the League of State Office Employees, reflected upon the wartime experience of its members: "Everyone still feels in his own belly what it means to feed a family with these hunger wages."[43] With this poverty came the humiliation of having slipped to the point where there was little to distinguish their living standard from that of manual workers.

Munich's middle and working class alike faced certain hardships during the war, one of which was that the housing shortage—bad before 1914—became acute. There were so many influences and counterinfluences upon the demand side of this problem that it is difficult to say which were most significant. Of course, the thousands of new soldiers left their apartments; often, their families either moved in with one set of parents or moved in together to cut the cost of living while the men were away. In either case, apartments became vacant. Also, hundreds of Munich's foreigners left, either having been forced out by the police or sensing that they were no longer welcome. However, hundreds of new families were formed as young couples chose to get married before the man went off to war, and although many of these postponed setting up homes until he returned, many did not. By the middle of the war, there was also increased migration of rural Bavarians into Munich, and these people needed places to live. The supply side of the problem is much clearer. With men and building materials like iron and cement going to the military and not to Munich's private construction industry, the building of family and apartment houses in the city virtually ended. Over four thousand new dwellings, built in 1910–1914, had not appreciably eased the housing shortage then; the less than three hundred put up during the war met neither the new needs nor the needs that had accumulated over several years.[44]

The lack of housing is the subject of a short song that Karl Valentin wrote in 1915, entitled "Auf der Wohnungssuche im Jahre 1915" (Looking for an Apartment in the Year 1915).[45] Probably sung by Liesl Karlstadt, the song is the lament of a Munich housewife who has walked all over the city, "up the stairs and down," to find an apartment. Finally exasperated, she decides not to look any longer. Her bitterest words, in her strong Bavarian accent, are reserved for the landlords:

> The landlords, the landlords
> The devil can take them
> They demand a lot
> But we sure didn't steal it,
> For two rooms in the building at the back,
> That's a bit too much—
> They are demanding, believe it or not,
> Forty marks these days.

> "de Hausherrn, de Hausherrn
> de soll der Teufi holn,
> de taten grad verlanga,
> ja, mir hams doch a net g'stohlen,
> fur zwei Zimmer hint im Rückgebäud,
> des is a bisserl stark,
> verlangens, sag und schreib,
> heutzutag schon 40 Mark."

There was no more humor in the song than there was in the situation. Valentin's personal background among people who were never far away from problems like those of this housewife enabled him to sense and express their frustration and anger, as well as their inborn skepticism about the motives of their social superiors. In 1915 the middle class had not yet reached the point of rebellion. "Auf der Wohnungssuche" indicates one of the dissatisfactions that would mount into the massive unrest of 1918.

The deepest worries of Munich's common people did not settle upon the quantity and cost of housing, however, but upon the quantity and cost of food. This was true since the very first days of the war, when, for example, a fifty-pound sack of potatoes, which had been sold at three marks, suddenly was sold at nine.[46] The official business explanation of the rise in prices was that the suddenly increased demand of the military for foodstuffs, together with the suddenly decreased supply from foreign countries, had created a genuine food scarcity.[47] Certainly there was less to buy in Munich's grocery stores; hunger spread to the point where many took to killing birds and animals whose meat, in less critical times, society found inedible. As folksinger Josef Benno Sailer described it in song:

> Squirrels, weasels, martens
> We did kill, and dog and cat,
> Fox and mole and jay and crow;
> Safe weren't even mice and rats.[48]

That this could go on testifies to the severity of the hunger. Indeed, the famous German "turnip winter" of 1916–17 was only one episode of a crisis which, for hundreds of thousands in Munich, lasted virtually throughout the war.

The Bavarian government stepped in to try to ease the worst effects of the food situation but succeeded only at angering the population by its ineptitude. A price control board, for example, established in 1915, set prices too high to satisfy the consumers, but too low to stop food producers from selling on the thriving black market. The next year, a system of government rationing was in place which included such staples as bread, sugar, meat, butter, and milk. But the government allowed too little to be given out and occasionally even failed to distribute enough ration cards. Generally, people in Munich felt that the government was lost in a maze of regulations concerning what could be bought and sold, and at what price, but was not seeing to it that there was actually enough food in the city to feed people.[49] The daily *Münchner Neueste Nachrichten* expressed this impatience with the government in a May 1916 article on the poor quality of potatoes in the city. There are better potatoes out in the Bavarian fields, the article argued, and therefore consumer complaints were "well justified." Responsibility lay, the article continued, with the Provincial Potato Board, "which apparently does not concern itself in the least with the quality of potatoes."[50] But this comment on the government's food policy was relatively mild: "a real disgrace," one of Josef Benno Sailer's songs called it.[51] All told, the Bavarian government's failure to deal adequately with the food crisis was the largest single reason for its becoming widely discredited in Munich by the end of the war.[52]

What made the hunger particularly unbearable was the belief, held by many, that there was not a real food shortage, that there would be enough to eat were it not for private hoarding. How could Munich's ordinary working- and middle-class people accept the official explanations when the rich were obviously getting food on the black market and when the farms around Munich were abundant with grains, vegetables, eggs, and milk? On the first point, a police document on civilian unrest is especially direct in reference to "the good life of many rich families for whom the war does not exist."[53] Nothing inflamed Munich's social antagonisms more than this: that the wealthy did not share the burden of wartime hunger.

The rich may have had special knowledge of the black market's operations, but others knew how they could get extra food. As Bavarian poet Oskar Maria Graf, who was then living in Munich, described the situation: "There were regular processions of pilgrims to the villages."[54] Once in the country, in what amounted to mass civil disobedience, people bought food from the farmers, or if they could not buy it, simply stole it. A song of the time, by folksinger Sailer, reflects this side of wartime Munich:

> We're going to the country all together,
>   there the things are everywhere
> Old and young, no one stays at home; they're
>   driven to go out to the country.

"Mir fahr's auf's Land all miteinand,
da gibts no Sachen allerhand,
Ob Alt, ob Jung, es bleibt koan's z'Haus,
mit G'walt treibts All auf's Land hinaus."

The song's chorus went: "To hoard, to hoard, they're going out to hoard."[55] In circumventing the official system of food distribution, Munich's citizens were showing that they no longer believed in their government. Even King Ludwig lost support in Munich because of food; people called him the "potato farmer," or the "dairy farmer," in reference to his large estates, which were supposedly not yielding their produce for sale in Munich either.[56]

Karl Valentin gave vent to several of Munich's wartime tensions in a ten-minute monologue entitled *Die Frau Funktionär* (The Official's Wife),[57] which Liesl Karlstadt first delivered during the last year of the war, 1918, probably at a small Schwabing cabaret named Serenissimus.[58] It is ironic that the cabaret was located near Munich's Victory Gate in Schwabing, for this monologue reflects the utter defeat of the city's civilian population. It refers to problems that plagued virtually everyone in wartime Munich who was not extremely wealthy, although there are places where the official's wife expresses specifically middle-class views. An opening couplet sets the monologue's helpless, pessimistic tone:

Well, the world is a theater
In the world, everything's speeding up
Wherever you look, it makes you mad
You never have your peace and quiet
In the marriage, with the children
With the apartment, with the husband
In the morning when you open your eyes
The cross is pinning you down.

"Na, die Welt ist ein Theater,
Auf der Welt, da geht's jetzt zu,
Wo 'st nur hinschaugst, muasst di ärgern,
Nirgends hast a Rast und Ruah.
In der Ehe mit de Kinder,
Mit der Wohnung, mit 'm Mann,
Machst du in der Fruah die Augen auf,
Geht das Kreuz scho wieder an."

This woman is especially interesting in that she senses disorder in "the world" around her by way of its effects in her private, domestic life. Thus, she asserts that "everything's speeding up," and points not to the war or to Berlin or to the national economy as examples, but to her own home and family. This is one of Valentin's sharpest observations about how common people experience political, social, and economic crises: as added strains in their family relationships; as the growth of worry and conflict in their homes. Valentin had not idealized the institution of the family before the war. The "poor, skinny man," for example, had evidently been given too little to eat by his gluttonous parents. In *Die Frau Funktionär,* the folksinger developed the theme that economic pressure worsens the quality of family life.

Because the official's wife tends to wander from thought to thought in her monologue, it is often hard to follow her meaning. With regard to the family, for example, she mentions that her husband "can't do anything with the children at all" and has even "recently" given their three-year-old boy, Pepperl, a razor to play with: when she screamed "For God's sake! Take that razor out of the boy's hand," the husband replied, "Leave him alone. He can't shave himself yet." The woman exclaims to the audience, "You see, that's how stupid the men are talking!" but then immediately leaves this frightful incident to talk about something else. Does the father do this often? Is there not as much sadism as ignorance in what he did? The woman has said too little to provide a context that would help explain what happened. But this is one of the monologue's points: that the woman does not see contexts and explanations herself. Valentin has her simply react to whatever happens, and in the vagueness and confusion of her words, he conveys her despair. In this case, where her husband has placed the child in danger, all that is clear is that she cannot rely on him to help her raise the children and that this is an added burden upon her.

One family problem with which she deals at greater length is sickness. First, she mentions a son, presumably her eldest, who has undergone an operation to drain his sinuses. Unfortunately, she goes on, the doctor performing the operation stepped on a lemon peel, slipped, and accidentally rammed the lancet he was holding into the boy's head. All she can say is "Thank God" that the child has recovered, before her mind jumps ahead to her second son, soon to turn sixteen years old and "not really healthy" either. He also has suffered from a doctor's mistake. In his case, the family doctor failed to diagnose an infection of his gums and treated him for rheumatism of the joints. But neither of these bizarre cases of maltreatment excites the woman to anger; she seems to accept them as two more misfortunes that she and her family simply have to endure.

The official's wife adds that the general health of her second son is like that of his father, who "suffers . . . from a kind of sleeping sickness." Apparently, she means that her husband sleeps a lot, because she describes his ailment as "not painful, but very time consuming." A father and his son in wartime Munich, both with a problem of exhaustion: though the woman never directly says it, they are hungry. One wonders whether the hardships of her life have bewildered and demoralized her to the point where she cannot see that malnutrition lies behind her family's illnesses; or whether she herself is so hungry that she has blocked the need for food out of her conscious thoughts. In any case, the hungry people of Munich in *Die Frau Funktionär*'s audience would have known what was wrong from their own situations, from having watched their own children slowly starve.

In describing her life, often the woman cannot help but come to the point where she would have to discuss the shortage of food, but invariably, she backs off. For example, when she considers the difficulties of shopping and keeping a family budget "these days," she declares: "You just think that you can start cooking, and you're missing this and that." Obviously, she would be missing food because it was either not available in the stores or too expensive on the black market. But suddenly she is complaining about something else: that she has too little coal to heat her stove, and that coal is scarce. If the coal dealer has coal, she has certainly forgotten to bring her coal-rationing coupons; and if she goes home for the coupons, the dealer is certainly out of coal when she returns.

In this story of one thing going wrong after the next, the official's wife pauses occasionally to consider the larger disorder around her, even if she looks for its marks only in the events of her own life. What she finds is a rise of cruelty and mistrust among people. At the monologue's beginning, for example, she blurts out in her heavy Bavarian accent:

The whole world is a big lie, a swindle. Everybody swindles everybody. You can't trust anyone anymore. No, no, it's a mess, but you have to go along with it 'till you die, and when you're dead you still don't have any peace, because they're still swearing about you.

"de ganze Welt ist eine Falschheit, ein Schwindel, oana schwindelt den andern o, koan Mensch derfst mehr traun, naa, naa, is des a Jammer, aber mitmacha musst, bis d' stirbst, und als Toter hast na aa no koa Ruah, da schimpfa s' na aa no über di."

Moving on to a concrete example of what she means, she describes a funeral she has recently attended, for the husband of one of her friends. The deceased had been, she says, "such a good, decent, hard-working man," a Munich streetcar conductor. It had therefore irked her when, at his funeral, she heard someone behind her murmur that he did not deserve the praise of his eulogy because all he had ever done was ride around in a streetcar and say, "Show your tickets please. Thank you." For her, this is the clearest possible confirmation of the decline of human compassion. "You see," she demands, "people are so mean." A man can devote himself to "a profession so worthy of sacrifice" and no longer expect that people will honor his memory after his death.

While the war has brought out meanness and pettiness in people in her own circle of acquaintances, it has also heightened her consciousness of her social position in relation to people who are richer or poorer than she is. She is extremely bitter when she looks either up or down the social hierarchy. She resents the rich, very simply, because "some people still have everything their hearts desire." Here again, what they have, although she does not name it, is obviously food. "The injustice is too great in the world," she continues. "For that reason our Lord God should let a [flood] come again and let everything be swept away." This is not the language of a woman who would raise her arm to defend the well-to-do bourgeoisie when the Bavarian Revolution set its wealth in jeopardy several months later.

Her attitude toward social inferiors, in the person of her servant, the thirty-five-year-old woman who cooks for her family, is less clear but more filled with anxiety. Fear that the family will not be able to afford a cook is a small part of this attitude; more important, she senses a new insolence in the woman, named Fanny, and in this insolence, a warning that society is on the verge of going through convulsions that will leave her own status and position uncertain.

Fanny has had her own bed, and a noon meal out of what the family did not care to eat, but wants to leave because the family does not pay her health insurance bills. How this catches the official's wife by surprise—"I mean, when you meet a person halfway"—is one of the monologue's subtlest points. Like a person who is finding her way blindfolded on a piece of ground she has never seen, the official's wife tries to cope with a servant whose behavior reflects none of the discipline and loyalty that she expects from a servant, and to understand that, on the terms of employment she is offering, she can find no replacement.

Her fear of the social change that Fanny represents is nowhere more implicit than in her remarks about the cook's ambition to become a film actress. She is haunted by the thought of her servant going to work in the theater, and generally, by the specter of an entire class of domestic servants leaving their employers to take new jobs, twentieth-century jobs of the kind she could barely imagine in 1918. She has confronted Fanny once: "You had better think about your cooking . . . so that you learn which side to butter the bread on. Do you really think with the warts and worry wrinkles on your face and with your chopped wood complexion that you'll be an actress?" ("Denka S' liaber an Eahna Kocherei . . . dass S' amal lerna, auf was fur a Seite man Butterbrot schmiert, moana denn Sie mit Eahnan gwarzerten Verdrussfaltengsicht und mit Eahnan Baumhacklteint wern Sie a Schauspielerin?") This is the rage of a woman who no longer has any say; the cook has gone out of her control.

There is a reason why this middle-class woman insults her cook regarding the beauty of her face, in other words, regarding her sexual attractiveness: of all Fanny's qualities, she finds her sexual freedom most deeply distressing. Twice she mentions that Fanny is too preoccupied with men to be a good cook; and she angrily disapproves of Fanny's abusing the privilege of a free afternoon every fourteen days to spend the night elsewhere and return the next morning "with a twinkle in her eye" (*mit grasgreane Froschaugn*). The official's wife would like to bring an end to the promiscuity, to supervise her servant's moral conduct in a traditional way. But worst of all is that she not only would get no support from her husband but would be opposed—because he and Fanny have been more or less openly carrying on an affair! She hints at this when she mentions how Fanny serves her spouse at the dinner table, and how her husband presented the servant with a gift of earrings one

Christmas when money was especially scarce. She proceeds to admit that she must bear the humiliation that her husband is in love with the unruly cook: "It is unbelievable, so conceited is the person. She makes herself believe that my husband is crazy about her. She doesn't have to make herself believe that, for it's the bitter truth." This is not the place to psychoanalyze the official's wife; what is important here is that, through her cook, she senses a coming sexual liberty that will threaten values—like propriety and restraint—at the base of her middle-class life.

Her anger with the cook is of no use; generally, powerlessness has resigned her to the inevitable. She herself expresses this near the beginning of the monologue, when thinking about the streetcar conductor's funeral leads her to think about another streetcar conductor whom she does not personally know, the sister-in-law of a woman who lives on her floor in the apartment building.[59] She is supposed to be a "dear, nice woman," but the official's wife wonders about someone who would work on Line Thirteen: "You, holy Joseph, I'm not superstitious, but how can someone not have second thoughts? Imagine it, if the woman right on the thirteenth takes in thirteen marks on Line Thirteen, then a misfortune will surely happen." But Valentin's character stops to correct herself: if numbers indeed rule events, then a person who knew the numbers could foretell the events; in her opinion, the world is too mysterious for that. "It's just fate," she continues. "The way it's determined for a person is the way it goes." This was certainly true for her husband, she says, who had always believed that he would receive an official decoration. Without mentioning whether he did or did not receive it, she insists that "something like that comes up suddenly, and often we don't have the slightest idea from where." This is one of the woman's basic life attitudes: that people do not control their own lives but are bound to await the inexplicable effects of distant happenings. It is important to remember that she has lived through four years of war, away from the battlefields, and outside of the centers of political power. During this time, her life—as a member of the white-collar middle class—has become steadily more difficult. One may wonder whether this woman's belief in "just fate" can be counted as an effect of the war, or whether she had had it since before 1914. But however the belief originated, the war—visible behind the woman's complaints—strengthened it.

The war is everywhere in *Die Frau Funktionär,* but the woman herself does not see it. There is no record of why Valentin created this amazingly myopic character. He may have simply passed the limits of his own vision on to her, or he may have wanted to avoid a fight with the censor. Or perhaps Valentin recognized the dramatic irony of a woman struggling to surmount obstacles in her path without knowing why they are there. In any case, the monologue conveys a sense of her mental and emotional exhaustion. Her vagueness, her inability to concentrate, her submissiveness, and her sense of decline are the subjective effects of having lived and suffered for four years in wartime Munich. Although she is too tired to deal intellectually with the history of her time, she is one of its victims, and one of its witnesses.

Actually, the official's wife does allude to the war once, when she expresses her hope that her second son will not be conscripted into military service. Here the line of antiwar satire that runs through the monologue comes clearly into view. According to the ideal of the German wife and mother, this woman should accept the possibility of her son's induction stoically, and should even be prepared to accept his death if the nation requires it. But Valentin's housewife is far from the ideal. She talks on in her dull-minded way about a funeral, about her cook, about needing more coal—about the worries of her daily life—but never once expresses interest in the outcome of the war. Nor do her two frail sons and her sleepy husband approach the ideal of brave and hearty German fighting men. Delivering this monologue in war-ravaged Munich, Liesl Karlstadt was in effect holding up a mirror in which the middle-class men and women of her audience saw themselves.

Die Frau Funktionär confirms what "Auf der Wohnungssuche im Jahre 1915" had strongly indicated: that World War I moved Valentin to present characters who, by comparison with his prewar and postwar entertainment, were extremely realistic. Perhaps it is no accident that he put Liesl Karlstadt into these two roles; his reputation as the city buffoon would have made him an ineffective man-on-the-street. *Die Frau Funktionär* continues the technique that Valentin had used so brilliantly in pre-1914 routines, like *Ich bin ein armer magerer Mann*. The character identifies herself with the social milieu of her middle-class Munich audience by revealing an "insider's" knowledge of its basic conditions: of having to fetch coal, of trying to cook with too little food, and so on. The official's wife differs from the "poor, skinny man," however, in remaining a member of this milieu. She has not lost her middle-class status, but like thousands in Munich, has watched it shrink; she is dazed and confused, but not absurd. Her misfortunes are not so bizarre that no one from the public could identify with them; she does not provide a reason for people to "say yes to themselves." Much less than the standard Valentin figures is she an "outsider."

Karl-Ludwig Ay and other historians have established that by 1918, when Liesl Karlstadt first delivered this monologue, the hardships of the war had brought Munich's civilian population, including its middle class, to the verge of revolution.[60] As a Munich folksinger, Karl Valentin reflected these developments. First, it was his task as an entertainer to adjust to the changes that his audience underwent. Prewar economic problems had turned into hardships; people went to Valentin less for the old reassurance than for his articulation of their deepened fears and misgivings.

Second, Valentin was himself the son of a traditional middle-class home, and a failed tradesman who never forgot the bitter and frightful if only temporary loss of his own middle-class position. During the war, as before it, he understood the social and political attitudes of his audience implicitly. *Die Frau Funktionär* stops far short of calling for revolution, but it reveals the grievances that led the middle class to answer the call when it was made. It should not be overlooked, however, that this monologue also indicates why the Revolution ultimately disillusioned its middle-class followers. The official's wife is not only angry at the upper class because of its selfishness but also afraid of the lower class because of its demands for equality. It is not surprising that the people for whom she spoke later opposed a revolution that pledged to raise the working class, and in effect to dismantle the barrier between "insiders" and "outsiders." Indeed, it was the fear of working-class upheaval that turned large sections of the middle class against the Weimar Republic.

ONCE, in 1917, Karl Valentin went so far as to openly express the popular resentment of Bavarian King Ludwig that fueled the rebellion of November 1918. A short, untitled monologue makes the angry point that the monarch was living a life of ostentatious ease while ordinary soldiers suffered. Of course, the folksinger had not submitted this act for the censor's approval:

The day before yesterday I was at the main train station as they were
laying the ones with brain injuries from the front into Red Cross
cars to take them to Schwabing hospital. The Red Cross cars didn't
have rubber tires because of the rationing. They were bumping and
bouncing, these cars for the sick. But it was the purest miracle: the
wounded didn't lose their brains riding in them. They arrived in
these cars! And yesterday the king visited them: with his car, which
of course had fine rubber tires. But he wouldn't have needed rubber
tires, because in any case he wouldn't have lost his brain.[61]

Valentin's monologue serves as a reminder that the war was, above
all, a time of death and enormous suffering. Of this, he had firsthand
knowledge from his 120 performances at military hospitals. Seeing
the terrible, almost inconceivable wounds of thousands of young
men deepened the basic despair and melancholy of his nature; this
pointedly gruesome monologue is the result. Unfortunately for Valentin, someone reported his remarks about King Ludwig to the Munich police; or perhaps a police spy in the audience heard them
directly. In either case, the police forbade the folksinger to appear
on any stage for six weeks. Munich's discontents were rising in 1917,
and Valentin had helped to give them expression.

Generally, Valentin was too careful to suggest in performance
that Bavarian soldiers were fighting for a monarch whose personal
luxury mocked their sacrifices. But, by the middle of the war, he was
often taking aim at the German war effort, specifically, at Bavaria's
contribution to it. In his short play *Der Herzog kommt* (The Duke Is
Coming),[62] Valentin ridiculed Bavarian fighting men—these "brave
militiamen of the upper country," as one Munich patriot called
them[63]—while staying out of the censor's reach. His method was to
work his satire not upon Bavarian soldiers then under arms at the
fronts of World War I, but upon their ancestors, the men of Munich's old citizens' militia *(Bürgerwehr)*. This represented a continuation and a refinement of the code he had developed before the
war in *Der schneidige Landgendarm.*

In the prologue of *Der Herzog kommt,* the Child of Munich
(Münchner Kindl) requests the audience to think back on the "good,
old times" one hundred years past, when happy militiamen protected happy citizens. True, there was a "darker side" of life then,
but no one remembers it:

> ... and only the good and comfortable,
> the cosy and the pleasant
> appear to us in our nervous haste
> as a near ideal of life.

> ". . . und nur das Biedre und Bequeme,
> das Mollige und Angenehme
> dunkt uns in unsrer Zappelhast
> als Ideal des Lebens fast."

Of course the people in the audience knew that they were living in a "nervous haste"—worried about sons, brothers, and husbands away at war, or about whether they would have enough to eat. They also knew that the war was largely to blame. But the general message of the prologue is that they should relax, forget their troubles, and let a story from an earlier time entertain them.

It is therefore ironic, and must have been quite jolting for the audience, when the play returns a few moments later to a sensitive present-day issue. The militia has marched on stage, led by Valentin, who sings an introduction of his character, a soldier named Josef Stuckmeister. He is not far into his song when he asserts that he is the best-looking of the militiamen, and that although his wife forbade him to go on maneuvers with the soldiers, he went anyway. The implication that a handsome soldier can always find a girlfriend when he is on duty away from home cannot have been lost upon the soldiers' wives in the audience. Not even the obvious joke—considering spindly Karl Valentin to be the best-looking of any group of soldiers—could have taken the sting away from a young woman who was upset by doubts of her husband's loyalty. Valentin only seemed to beckon people into the past; in fact he led them to where they would have to face the present.

In a short monologue that follows his song, Stuckmeister describes his life as a soldier and again confronts the audience with the contemporary meaning of his words. He declares that he has been "nearly three years with the citizens' guard"; the audience would have realized that three years was also the duration of the present war up to 1917. "The time goes quickly," he continues. "For me it's just as though I'd been with it for twenty years." As is obvious from his verbal mistake, Stuckmeister's time was not going quickly at all. Between his attempt to make his life as a soldier seem exciting and his blundering admission that it was indeed very tedious, the audience must have seen a comic reflection of what they were experiencing in wartime Germany: the rhetoric of enthusiasm and the reality of hardship. Poet Oskar Maria Graf later recalled how the people of Munich had come to view official patriotism by 1917: "Meanwhile the great mass of the lower classes dragged on their lives in sullen apathy. The daily queues before the food shops grew longer . . . Nobody read the yellow telegraphic announcements from the front any longer . . . Victory or defeat, heroic deeds and battles, the Emperor's messages, Hindenburg and forty-two centimeter mortars—overnight they had lost their importance."[64] Valentin understood how the war had fostered the cynicism of Munich's common people. Stuckmeister's slip of the tongue was meant for those who no longer wanted to hear optimistic reports about a war they knew to be a disaster.

Stuckmeister and the drummer boy Alisi, probably played by Liesl Karlstadt, had been discussing an upcoming visit to Munich by a duke, when Alisi remembers that he has a letter from the militia captain for Stuckmeister. Here the critique of the military begins in earnest. The captain wants Stuckmeister to lead the men in an exercise of the cannon; he himself cannot do so because he is playing skittles. This absent officer lets his men do the work: in wartime Germany, the work of soldiers was not exercising a cannon, but risking their lives in battle; the thought of an absent officer would not have amused people, but enraged them. Then, the attention turns from the irresponsibility of the officer to that of the men themselves. Where is the cannon? Stuckmeister, in charge of this band of legendary Bavarian fighters, suddenly remembers that he has left it out in the rain. In exposing the old militia's inefficiency, Valentin implies that inefficiency also plagued the militia of his day: the German army and, specifically, its Bavarian units.

After the cannon is retrieved, Valentin uses its exercise to continue his satire upon the military. First, the anal implications of cleaning the cannon barrel excite the fantasies of Stuckmeister and Alisi to the point where they can hardly perform their duties. The barrel is "stopped up," Alisi remarks as he tries to swab it out, using the German word *verstopft,* which also means "constipated." "You have to have your nose in every hole," Stuckmeister replies. When Stuckmeister wants Alisi to work faster, the drummer boy snaps at him: "If it's not going fast enough for you, you can wipe your own hole." Then, when the cannon will not fire, Stuckmeister reveals his physical cowardice by refusing to look down the barrel to find out what is wrong. "He's shitting in his pants," Alisi calls out; this is hardly what Munich's twentieth-century patriots would want to have said about the old Bavarian heroes, or by implication, about the great-grandsons of these heroes fighting in France and Russia.

The cannon finally does fire, but the image of its not firing has already insulted the legend of the militiamen by raising doubts both about their battle effectiveness and about their sexual potency. Stuckmeister had acknowledged the relationship of the two, military and sexual achievement, in the line of his introductory song that alluded to the soldiers' love affairs. Helplessly, these militiamen stand by while their cannon does not function. Perhaps they themselves do not always function sexually. Valentin's soldiers—possibly impotent, certainly incompetent, afraid, and indecent—are the opposite of what their legend presented them to be. In their failure, they ridicule success; in their pettiness, they ridicule grandeur. For anyone who could not see that he was calling the war into question, Valentin threw a phrase of French, the enemy language, into his orders for cleaning the cannon: "Is everything vis-à-vis? Oh—now I've gone into French!" With that the soldiers march off the stage, and the play ends.

Clearly, if there is a point in Valentin's entertainment career when his antimilitaristic code became transparent to his middle-class Munich audience, it is with the performance of *Der Herzog kommt.* That this play was actually permitted on stage in wartime Munich raises doubts about the censor's vigilance.[65] Its critical references to the war are unmistakable: Stuckmeister's "three years" in service; the irresponsible absence of an officer while the enlisted men carry out their duties; and the French phrase at the end. Valentin was transmitting the message that his public wanted to receive. From his position at the home front, he fully realized that the middle class's war enthusiasm of 1914 had passed into sullen resistance. Beyond *Der Herzog kommt,* it passed on into revolt.

PRESUMABLY, World War I affected the size of Munich's folksinger audience, but it is not clear in what way. Did many people stop coming to the tavern cabarets because they did not like being entertained while their brothers, sons, or husbands were being terrified, maimed, or killed? Did others seek the release of laughter more often than they had before the war? There is insufficient evidence to answer either question. Throughout the war years, Karl Valentin drew enough of an audience to be able to perform regularly at various small stages in the city.[66] Perhaps this was even a time of special popularity for him, with rivals like Weiss Ferdl off at war. But this is speculation; the only indications of how his entertainment was received are press reviews, which were quite favorable.[67]

It is possible to be more definite about Valentin's message than about the numbers of people who received it: opposition to the war. Although neither *Der Herzog kommt* nor *Die Frau Funktionär* comments openly upon the war, both point at it with the finger of ridicule. This the people of wartime Munich—hungry, tired, distressed, and grieving—would have seen. Indeed, in both the play and the monologue, Valentin depended upon his audience to recognize the unnamed nationalistic myths against which he hurled his satire. Stuckmeister was no more the brave and high-principled German soldier of whom the propagandists spoke than this pitiable official's wife with her sickly sons and her undisciplined cook was the indestructible German mother. Valentin's point was that people could not live up to their myths, could not attain the level of greatness, heroism, and dedication that their leaders expected of them. It is a common man's view of large events, and his hope that he will not become their victim. What sacrifices would he really choose to make in order to satisfy the national honor? How long can he overlook the fact that he has too little fuel to heat his home, or that the beer he drinks has had to be thinned until it tastes like water? *Der Herzog kommt* and *Die Frau Funktionär*, performed before Munich's popular audience in the last years of the war, are signs of widespread exhaustion; in November 1918, a fairly small revolutionary band relied upon this exhaustion to take political power from King Ludwig, the "potato farmer."

5

The Middle Class Against Weimar

The Bavarian Revolution of 1918–19 offers a picture of contrast. Although its leadership consisted of a small, disparate group of intellectuals and agitators, mostly Jews, the Revolution enjoyed wide support among the middle and working classes. On 7 November 1918, a war-weary crowd assembled upon Munich's Theresa Field (Theresienwiese). Quickly, it came under the sway of radical socialist Kurt Eisner, who proclaimed a Bavarian People's Republic. Eisner himself was to become the new state's minister president, though his past experiences did not fully qualify him for a political office of such importance. Before 1914 he had been a journalist in the Social Democratic press and had been associated with a group within Social Democracy that foresaw the triumph of socialism on the basis of universally recognized moral principles. After the war broke out, he belonged to the minority of socialists that opposed it on grounds of conscience and that separated from the SPD in 1917 to form the Independent Socialist Party (USPD). For his role in a January 1918 workers' antiwar strike in Munich, Eisner had been in jail until a few days before the Revolution.

As a Jew who was not Bavarian by birth, Eisner was not able to inspire the lasting popular loyalties that would have certified his leadership. In January 1919 his party, the USPD, won only a small fraction of votes in the Landtag elections, and he was forced to resign. Walking to the Landtag building to do so on 21 February, however, he was assassinated by a young right-wing aristocrat. Bavaria entered a ten-week period of utter political confusion, governed by one left-wing faction after another. Ernst Toller and Erich Mühsam, both Jewish intellectuals from northern Germany, led a short-lived Bavarian Soviet Republic in early April 1919. A playwright and a poet, respectively, their ties to the local population were no closer than Eisner's had been. Eisner, Toller, and Mühsam were, however, at least living in Munich at the end of the war, and as a result knew the city better than did Eugen Leviné, also Jewish, the professional revolutionary whom the KPD in Berlin sent to represent it in Bavaria. Leviné became the main figure of a Second Soviet Republic which lasted for nearly three weeks in April and May 1919, until counterrevolutionary Free Corps (Freikorps) troops entered Munich and fiercely suppressed it.[1]

By 7 November 1918, much of Bavarian society was disillusioned with the war, unwilling to endure any longer the food and coal shortages it had brought, furious with the government—Bavarian and German alike—for being aloof through four such difficult years, and open to socialist radicalism. This was especially true for Munich. Otherwise, Eisner, Toller, and the others would not have emerged into such prominence in the Revolution. Support for the radicals was greatest among workers in the Krupp munitions factories, which had been established in Munich-Freimann in 1916. It extended through the working class and for a time into the middle class: to tradesmen, who had seen raw materials that they sorely needed go to the military; to sales and office employees, whose incomes had not kept pace with inflation; and to overworked, underpaid lower-level officials. Not everyone who had cheered the Revolution at the start, however, was there to defend it at the end. This was due partly to growing apathy and partly to the feeling that the new "state" could not withstand the attacks that its enemies were openly preparing. Concerning the middle class, the Revolution did little to foster loyalties and much to arouse fears. First, it did not succeed at lessening the basic hardships of life: food, coal, and housing scarcities; inflation; and unemployment. Second, after Eisner's death, its radical leaders made the mistake of opening some banks for plunder, and thereby horrified thousands of middle-class people who naturally opposed any violation of the principles of legality and property. In many cases, the Free Corps soldiers who arrived in Munich on 2 May 1919 enjoyed a hero's welcome; the middle class saw them as liberators from the Communist threat.[2]

It might be expected that the entertainment of the Munich folksingers would reflect the highly volatile political attitudes of their public. Karl Valentin, in this regard, proves disappointing. Throughout the Revolution, he performed in a small cabaret in Schwabing named Serenissimus, in front of a middle-class audience mixed with some students from Munich's nearby university. There is no indication that he expressed any political views or that he developed any new stage material whatsoever. He performed privately at least twice for soldiers home from the front—in January 1919, both times at welcoming ceremonies given by the city's voluntary fire brigade. Which acts he chose to give, whether he referred to political events, and what the general political tone of these gatherings might have been are, for lack of evidence, unanswered questions. It is probably correct to assume that he did not take a public stand on the Revolution.[3]

Weiss Ferdl, by contrast, disapproved of the Bavarian Revolution from the first and expressed this to the audience at Platzl. On 7 November, on his way home from the war in France through Belgium, he heard of the events in Munich. Although he and his comrades were tired of the war, they "did not want to believe" that the monarchy was gone, as he wrote in his diary. As early as 16 November he was back on his familiar stage with an antirevolutionary song he had written, "Das Revoluzerlied" (The Revoluter Song):

> Lord, do we bring freedom when we
>   whistle through our fingers.
> Pull a king right off his throne—
>   he packs his things and goes.
> Revolutilatilutilati! Holaridium!
> Turn everything around
> Bring everything around
> And shoot everything up. Boom! Boom!

This was the first verse, a satire on the revolutionary whose deeds arise out of uncontrollable impulses. In the sixth and last verse, however, a more piercing criticism emerges:

> Freedom and justice rule over the country,
>   Take whatever you like from the
>   stuffed-up bunch [geschwoll'na Bande]
> Whatever's not nailed down belongs to us—
>   that's for sure.

Weiss Ferdl was voicing the middle class's misgivings about the new socialist state. Was the revolutionary—despite his high-sounding pronouncements—no more than a common thief? For all its bluntness, this song does not call for opposition to the Revolution. In November 1918, amid the surprise, hope, and excitement that followed the armistice and the formation of a new government, such a call would have had little response. Still, this song—presented by one of Munich's "old Bavarian" favorites, by an entertainer whom the city's popular audience had surely missed during the four long years of the war—evinces a reserve and skepticism toward what Kurt Eisner and his supporters were undertaking. One could object that Weiss Ferdl had not been in Munich for very long, that he had not yet fallen back into step with his public. He later asserted, however, that "Das Revoluzerlied" was "one of the biggest successes." The Revolution, then, does not seem to have broken his contact with the Platzl audience or to have made his "message" outmoded. Weiss Ferdl did not like what he saw in the first weeks of November 1918; many in his middle-class audience must not have liked what they saw either, or else "Das Revoluzerlied" would not have been so well received.[4]

Weiss Ferdl's song indicates that Munich's middle class stood at a greater distance from the young Revolution than has recently been argued.[5] Munich had not ceased to be a city with deep roots in its surrounding countryside, in "Old Bavaria." The thousands of people who yearned for the "old Bavarian" community had, of course, gone through the social and political convulsions of 1914–1918 like everyone and everything else. Nevertheless, they had not lost the reactionary nostalgia of prewar times. Evidently, the men and women who had gone to Platzl for years, who had consumed pitchersful of its beer and amusements, did not genuinely accept "outsiders" like Kurt Eisner and Eugen Leviné as leaders. This is not surprising. Both the traditional and the white-collar middle class had greeted the Revolution in November 1918 because it offered peace and seemed to open the way to social and economic recovery. By May 1919, there were no signs that a recovery was under way, but there was every indication that the Revolution would lead to the very assaults upon status and property that the middle class most feared. This awakened old "insider" and "outsider" worries; tradesmen, shopkeepers, and white-collar workers quickly rebuilt the structure of attitudes, sentiments, and ideas that had made them feel safe before the war. After their frightening experiences of 1918–19, they also doubled their watch against socialism. Naturally, in the early 1920s they would turn to Weiss Ferdl, whose "old Bavarian" acts had always made them feel like "insiders," like members of a large, protected social group.

* * *

FOR ALL THOSE who earned their livings in the fields of art and culture, the Revolution held great promise. None was better at articulating this promise than Minister President Kurt Eisner. Declaring that "the conduct of politics is just as much an art as painting a picture or composing a string quartet," he went on in his 3 January 1919 address before the Bavarian National Council to proclaim that "the Revolution should not have a stronger inner relationship to anyone than to the artists." Moreover, the Revolution needed artists to "uplift and spiritualize the masses." Thus, Eisner mused, it was "completely possible" that painters, writers, and actors might soon come to receive their subsistence from the government. Such words, coming from the top of the new regime, brought hope to many artists who had felt hemmed in during the Empire and whom the war had driven to near desperation. It appeared that the new era would be one of state support for the arts and of vastly expanded opportunities.[6]

Hundreds of Munich artists expressed their support for the Revolution's planned initiatives by joining the many artists' organizations that had formed in the city after 7 November 1918. Generally, the purpose of these organizations was to represent artists' interests in the new state. One example is the Council of the Plastic Arts (Der Rat der bildenden Künstler). It "expected," as worded in a 21 December 1918 letter to the Bavarian People's State, "to be heard in all artistic questions." Recognition by the governmental ministries followed shortly. Specifically, what the Council hoped to achieve included rights of consultation in the design of stamps, coins, and paper currency, and in the purchase of art works by state museums and galleries.[7]

A second, more broadly based organization, which dated from 27 November 1918 and also enjoyed official recognition, was the Artists' Union of Bavaria (Künstlergewerkschaft Bayerns). It encompassed four subgroups: artists from the theater; from the creative and graphic arts, and architecture; from music; and from creative literature. According to its opening manifesto, it "strived for an improvement of the economic situation of artists," and it proposed insurance plans and desks for employment information, for example, as steps to attain this improvement. Prominent Munich artists belonged to the Union, including Thomas and Heinrich Mann, the dramatist Max Halbe, and the writer Kurt Martens.[8] These were the well-known names of a much wider movement. On 7 February 1919, the Artists' Union wrote to the government that the Council of Plastic Artists should be seen as a union subsidiary—and claimed that a joint assembly had brought together fifteen hundred artists![9]

Because it concentrated upon advocating the economic interests of its members and left politics alone, the Artists' Union survived the fall of the Peoples' State and went on to represent artists in the 1920s: one last mark of the cultural politics of a Revolution "whose fine and useful suggestions have not been realized," as Kurt Martens put it later.[10] Even while the Revolution lasted, it was at best a mixed blessing for artists. True, there were some state outlays for special performances. They were not large enough, however, to cause the Artists' Union to describe the employment situation for performing artists as any better than "endlessly difficult—not to say hopeless."[11] Part of the reason for this lay in the Revolution itself, in its ongoing crises and disruptions. Between 7 November 1918 and 2 May 1919, rather than expand their programs, Munich theaters tended to cut them back. During the six months of the new state, for example, the National and Residence theaters not only shut their doors for three days of "revolutionary celebration"; they also closed for a solid week in April because of "unrest." Likewise, the Theater at Gardener Place (Theater am Gärtnerplatz) closed for a week after Kurt Eisner's assassination. None of this helped unemployed actors, actresses, and other performers who had hoped that the Revolution would bring them greater opportunities. Indeed, theaters were releasing personnel, not taking new people on.[12] The Revolution had meant well by the artists and had even viewed them as special citizens of the new state. But ultimately lacking the power to defend itself, it had also lacked the power to give these special citizens the rights and advantages that it felt they deserved.

Just as the Revolution did not live up to its promise in artistic policy in general, so it fell short in the specific area of small-stage entertainment. However, the entertainers could not feel ignored. No less a figure than Ernst Toller followed Kurt Eisner to the speaker's place on 3 January 1919 to represent the "circus, varieté, and cabaret performers." He made it clear that they would enjoy the new state's beneficence. He proposed that they be guaranteed an income of 200 marks per month to end their "economic need," and that they be further protected by the creation of a union with compulsory membership. In addition, he felt that the government should intervene between small-stage artists and their employers to make sure that the artists no longer had to sign contracts that restricted them from later seeking work in the same city or province. Ambitious and helpful, these proposals were mere pieces of paper on 2 May 1919 when Toller and the other revolutionaries went to defeat.[13]

Looking beyond the disappointments of Munich in 1918–19, the general effect of the new German Republic upon the work conditions of stage artists was quite positive, both in the legitimate theater and at the small stages. First, because the system of Imperial censorship had been abolished, the artists were much freer to express themselves on political and social questions. In this regard, however, Munich was an exception. After the war, the city became the national center of extreme right-wing opposition to the Republic, of violently nationalistic, anti-Semitic groups like Hitler's NSDAP. Frequently, these groups took away what the Republic had given. Without hesitation they would disrupt the performances of a director or entertainer whose political ideas aroused their disapproval, and in this way they exercised a kind of practical censorship over the city's stages.

Second, the German Republic improved the stage artists' basic financial and legal situation in Munich as elsewhere. Already in November 1918, the Brotherhood of German Stage Artists won government recognition to act as the sole negotiator for theater personnel in contract bargaining with the employers' organization. This meant that every German actor and actress had to become a member, and led in 1919 to a contract that forbade some of the least progressive conditions of theater work during the Empire, such as unpaid rehearsals, and that was valid at every theater in the country. Such gains were not restricted to the legitimate theatre. In 1924 cabaret and *varieté* artists, affiliated with the General Employees' League (Allgemeiner freier Angestelltenbund), also moved ahead, to a contract that eliminated the most abusive clauses of their previous agreements.[14]

Neither the lifting of state censorship by the German Republic nor the improvement of the stage artists' legal and economic position greatly affected Munich's two best-known popular entertainers, Karl Valentin and Weiss Ferdl. Even when the censor was gone, Valentin still had to be careful about how he expressed himself on stage. With the Nazis in Munich, it would have been a risk for him to unambiguously voice his old disapproval of German militarism. As during the Empire, he resorted to secrecy, to his code of satire, to making post-1918 advocates of national might look foolish by poking fun at past defenders of local order. Regarding Weiss Ferdl of Platzl, the removal of the censor indeed had a visible effect, but only within the larger context of Germany's changeover from an empire to a republic. For the first time, he was able to criticize the government. But this was not something he had wanted to do before November 1918: the Republic had given him the right to be a critic, and he took full advantage of it; had the Empire given him such a right, it would have gone mostly unused. The new system of government invited all Germans, and not only performers, to speak their minds freely, and in so doing to take part in the shaping of a national purpose. Weiss Ferdl was one of those Germans who accepted the invitation only to undermine those who had issued it. His opposition to the Republic showed that he was yearning for, and even still serving, the Empire it had replaced.

Having less of an impact upon Valentin and Weiss Ferdl than the end of censorship was the advance made by the entertainers' unions in the first years of the Republic. The two folksingers were too successful to be affected. Still, this advance was made within the environment in which they worked, and should not be forgotten. It would certainly have sharpened their awareness of the historical changes that their era had brought. Karl Valentin and Weiss Ferdl saw the world as entertainers. In the roughly two decades between the start of their entertainment careers and the early 1920s, Germany underwent an enormous transformation: from Empire to Republic; from an aggressive national pride to defeat; and steadily if less dramatically, from an economy of small shopkeepers and tradesmen to one of large-scale business and industry. Few were able to comprehend all of these developments. Most had a sense of change, but only as mediated by their own particular surroundings. Valentin's and Weiss Ferdl's surroundings were the beer halls, cabarets, *varietés,* and music halls at which they appeared. They would have seen that even the least successful of their fellow performers enjoyed rights and benefits that they could have desperately used twenty years earlier. This cannot have failed to make an impression. They may not have had clear ideas about how swiftly German political, social, and economic history was moving, but a look at the people with whom they were working would have reminded them that they were living through times of great consequence.

LARGE SECTIONS of Munich's middle class opposed the Weimar Republic. Different features of their opposition are reflected in the routines that popular entertainers Weiss Ferdl and Karl Valentin delivered in the years 1919–1923. Weiss Ferdl returned to transmitting the messages that had characterized Platzl before the war, and the music hall became a center of anti-Weimar sentiment. The audience's disdain for the Republic had emerged during the Revolution, when it seemed that the new state was on a course toward socialism. There was more to the middle class's rejection of Weimar, however, than lingering anger over the radical deeds before 2 May 1919. Weiss Ferdl sounded a retreat to the prewar social and political standpoint; from there the new state looked very dismal. By the standards of old music-hall patriotism, the leaders of the Weimar Republic had virtually committed treason by assenting to the terms of the Versailles *Diktat*. Moreover, the prominence of several Jewish politicians during the Revolution and in the first years of the Republic enflamed anti-Jewish prejudices like those to which Weiss Ferdl gave vent. The "old Bavarian" faithful also resented the new state's obvious lack of interest in fulfilling their dream of a traditional, rural community. Valentin's relationship to the Weimar Republic, by contrast, had two opposing aspects. First, he used his on-stage code to express his disapproval of the revived militarism of the early 1920s; although this was not directly favorable toward Weimar, it was at least unfavorable toward Weimar's most relentless enemies. Second, he resumed his position as Munich's buffoon, making his audience laugh at his misfortunes until theirs seemed inconsequential. Consciously or unconsciously, he became an "outsider," and reassured people that they were "insiders." Through Valentin's comedy, it is possible to observe the middle class's need for security. The persistence and intensification of this need during the economic crisis of the 1920s enlarged the new state's difficulties at winning middle-class loyalty and support.

There are many anecdotes to tell about Munich during the inflation of the early 1920s: for example, in August 1923 the image of the new city hall, a symbol of late nineteenth century prosperity, appeared on a newly issued banknote for one million marks; three months later, a ride from one streetcar stop to the next cost 250 billion marks.[15] Life in Bavaria's capital also had a grim side. In 1923 a Munich city councilman named Michael Gasteiger published a short account of the inflation as it ravaged the city.[16] Assessing his subject as a whole, Gasteiger declared that "Munich behind her glittering displays and intoxicating parties ... struggles and suffers." Each day in 1923, the city's inhabitants went looking to buy essential goods and found them, if at all, unbelievably more expensive than on the previous day. One kilogram of rye bread, at 34 pfennigs just before the war, and at 3.80 marks at the end of the summer of 1921, cost 16.40 marks one year later, and 6,200 marks in July 1923: a price rise of 18,200 times over nine years, 1,600 times over less than two years, and 400 times over less than one. The inflation affected other grocery staples too, like flour, potatoes, pork, butter, and milk, and also clothing. Incomes rose, even millions of times over pre-1914 levels, but not as quickly as living costs.[17]

Some of the inflation can be attributed to genuine scarcity. While the Versailles Treaty of 1919 stripped Germany of rich agricultural areas, refugees from the annexed territories crowded into what remained, 50,000 of them into Munich alone. Taking milk as an example, on a day in 1923 Munich had slightly more than half of what it had had on a day in 1914, with 5 percent more people.[18] Apartments were also scarce. This long-term problem became acute after the war, when veterans started families, and when refugees and new arrivals from the countryside added to the need for housing. Rents climbed, to the point where there were street protests in June 1921, and then went even higher. The building industry was not nearly able to satisfy the demand. The war had slowed private construction by drawing men and materials away to the army and to more vital industries; the early 1920s did not afford the economic stability that was necessary for a dramatic recovery. Before the war ended, the municipal apartment office was attempting to cope with the shortage, and both revolutionary and postrevolutionary governments continued its work. This included converting barracks, offices, and even part of the Nymphenburg Palace into living quarters. An official report issued in April 1920 claimed, however, that the situation was worsening. By the height of the inflation in 1923, 26,000 persons or families were looking for apartments. While they looked, they presumably lived in temporary city-built "cabins," or were crowded into private apartments.[19]

Shortages of both coal and kindling wood made Munich's scant living space cold during the long winters of the inflation.[20] With people undernourished, inadequately clothed and housed, and often freezing, it is not surprising that birth and death rates in Munich approached each other in 1923, until nearly as many people were dying as being born. City and private welfare agencies served people according to their means but could not reverse the basic trends. Gasteiger's investigation cited reports from Munich's schools to emphasize how serious the situation had become: 13.5 percent of all schoolchildren were considered "undernourished" in 1923, as against 6 percent a decade earlier—and in some quarters of the city, the proportion was nearly half; on the average, during the school year 1922–23 a schoolchild missed half again as many days because of sickness as a child before the war; there were more skin and tooth problems, more tuberculosis, more stunted growth; and children lacked proper clothing and shoes. Gasteiger remarked that "it is getting frightfully close to the circumstances of 1918 and 1919, when the war and the blockade heavily restricted the possibilities for life."[21]

If the inflation made nearly everyone more or less desperate, class and occupation shaped the way its effects were felt. For the traditional middle class of tradesmen and shopkeepers, as well as for clerks, salespersons, and low-level state officials, the economic upheaval intensified pressures that were simply part of the rise of industrial Germany. The December 1919 issue of a short-lived publication called *Der Bayerische Mittelstand* (The Bavarian Middle Class), an organ representing the "entire small-business middle class," expressed the fear of social decline:[22]

> To the empty mouth comes the empty hand
> Talking and praying do not help
> Yes, we—we of the middle class
> Are the true proletarians today.[23]

Falling into the working class was a terrifying prospect for people at this level of society. In 1921 or 1922, the Munich Chamber of Commerce, which tried to represent both large and small enterprises, discussed tax relief for small businessmen in order to prevent "the complete disappearance of the middle class and increasing proletarianization."[24] Small businesses found themselves less able than ever to withstand big competitors. Not only did they lose customers to cut-rate department stores, but suppliers of finished goods and raw materials tended to sell first to large operations, leaving orders from the shopkeepers and tradesmen unfilled. The occasional protective measures of the Empire,"holding actions," as one historian has called them,[25] were gone and many owners of small businesses felt left to their fates during the crisis of the early 1920s. Michael Gasteiger concluded in 1923 that "the destruction of their existence is only a question of time."[26] Actually, the prophesies of doom were wrong. In general, small firms cut the size of operations and "proved able to resist" the upheaval around them.[27] As long as businessmen kept their shops and tradesmen kept their tools, they survived into the calmer mid-1920s. They may have lost their savings because of inflation, but they also lost their debts.[28] Still at a disadvantage to big companies, they lived on. That the storm would pass was not clear while it raged, however, and the sense of danger spread through these middle-class groups.

The economic breakdown made it impossible for the new middle class to recuperate from the war. As a group, its purchasing power declined in the early 1920s, more steeply than that of manual workers.[29] One gains a sense of its plight from reading the journals and annual reports of its occupational associations. In 1920 the League of Support for Women Teachers in Munich, for example, confronted the problem of hospitalization insurance at a time when the cost of staying one day in a hospital had climbed from 5 to 17 marks, or 240 percent, in a span of eight months. The teachers finally decided to raise each member's "hospital fee" from 2 to 15 marks.[30] But inflation began in earnest shortly after that, and the teachers' insurance fund lost all value. What could a League of Support do when staying one day in a hospital cost nearly 11,000 marks, as it did in June 1923?[31]

The economic climate also affected the cultural and entertainment industries.[32] People bought fewer books and paintings, and went out less often to be entertained. Already in January 1921, representatives of the provincial ministries of culture met in Munich to discuss "the emergency of the German arts." The Prussian representative portrayed the literature, music, and theater industries as extremely depressed: regarding the first, he proposed subsidizing the publishers; and regarding music and theater, he favored support for publishing new works, for performances, and for instruction.[33] The "Munich People's Stage" (Münchner Volksbühne), formed in 1914 to sponsor performances for its members, encountered "serious difficulties" in the early 1920s; inflation forced up membership fees and in winter the coal shortage made heating a problem.[34]

Among the artists themselves, there was great hardship. The Brotherhood of German Stage Artists had built up pension, sickness, disability, and life insurance funds, but saw them dwindle into nothing because of inflation. As a historian of the stage artists described it: "In this way the entire insurance operation came to rest, as many old artists, who had nothing more, were counting on help. Left by everyone, they were sent to their fate, and often reports of this time tell of misery driving many among the artists to voluntary death or, half-starved, to become burdens of the state."[35] With regard to the Munich folksingers in particular, there was less work. A colleague of Valentin's from the Hotel Wagner, Karl Flemisch (1878–1938), moved north to Nuremberg, hoping that an authentic Munich folksinger could draw crowds there.[36] Valentin and Weiss Ferdl had established reputations by the 1920s and were not desperate. Still, Weiss Ferdl later recalled losing both the shares he owned in a bank that collapsed and his savings;[37] his widow remembers running to buy groceries with their money before it devalued.[38] Nor was Valentin immune to the inflation: "Millions, billions, trillions rained in Germany. You couldn't bear it! Money earned in the morning was nothing by afternoon."[39] Both folksingers were familiar with the hardships that encircled their middle-class public.

KARL VALENTIN dealt with the effects of the economic crisis upon middle-class family life in two one-act plays, *Der Firmling* (The Confirmation Candidate) and *Das Christbaumbrettl* (A Board for the Christmas Tree),[40] both first performed in 1922. In order to connect with his audience, he returned to the technique he had successfully used before the war, for example, in *Ich bin ein armer magerer Mann*. The crucial first point of this technique was to identify the character he portrayed with his public's social milieu. He accomplished this by speaking the local dialect and by revealing an "insider's" knowledge of middle-class affairs, values, and habits. Then, he proceeded to take on the role of a buffoon, of a man whose life consisted of a string of outrageous misfortunes. Naturally, this created distance between himself and his audience; they were at least still struggling with their hardships, whereas he had been utterly overcome by his. He presented them with an occasion "to say yes to themselves," to exclude someone, to regain the feeling that their place in society was secure. Gratefully, they received the Valentin message that they belonged.

Der Firmling is set on the wine terrace of a fine Munich restaurant, where a father (Karl Valentin) has invited his son, Pepperl (Liesl Karlstadt), to celebrate the boy's church confirmation. This plain middle-class man (*Mittelständler*), as he identifies himself, has brought his son to a place of quality, where they clearly do not belong. Valentin injects considerable humor into this situation. After the two have entered, the dialogue begins when the father shouts in his Bavarian tongue for two half-liters of beer, only to hear in the waiter's polite high German that the establishment serves only wine and liqueurs. Valentin had signaled the beer-drinking men and women in the audience that he was one of theirs, a common man with ordinary tastes. Proceeding to further identify himself with the clientele, he slaps the waiter's rear end. Horrified, the waiter swings around: "What are you allowing yourself to do?" "Oh—I just thought I was with Marie in the Hofbräuhaus" is the impish reply, which must have evoked howls of laughter from people who frequented Munich's famous beer hall themselves and who perhaps knew "Marie."

Next, as the father attempts to place his order for macaroni with ham, he, Pepperl, and the waiter become entangled in a confusion of words—an echo of Valentin's earlier semantic clowning, and a first indication of the mental disarray that marks the father as an "outsider." Pepperl, the father says, wants a portion of the macaroni with ham, and the waiter assumes that the father does too. He repeats the order: "So, two macaronis with ham." The father corrects him; there should be only one, presumably Pepperl's. Then Pepperl interjects that they want one portion—"for each," and the waiter feels confirmed that they both want macaroni, therefore two portions. The father looks for a clarifying formula: "No, no—one—but for two." He thinks, perhaps, that he has told the waiter that they want one plate of food at the table. The waiter is uncertain; he still wonders whether the father also wants macaroni. Then, Pepperl states *his* wish, which is "only one" portion. Having assumed again that the father also would like a portion, the waiter asks: "Then you do want two?" The father returns to his formula: "No, one for us two." His frustrations mounting, the waiter concludes that a double portion is being ordered, which would be "one—for two." The father seems to accept the new concept but then renders it meaningless when he replies, "Yes, a small [*einfache*] double portion." "Blast it all [*Zum Donnerwetter*]," explodes the waiter, "shall I bring one or two portions?" The father, himself angry and evidently not seeing the source of confusion, fires back: "Bring one and then get lost. . . !" The waiter exits. Smarting from the exchange, and probably also from Valentin's failure to address him with the polite language form, the waiter curses under his breath that the two belong in a "farmers' tavern," in other words, in a place like the one where this play was being performed.

As he had in *Das Aquarium* at the outset of his career, Valentin presents a fantasy world in which language's inherent ambiguities and imperfections form barriers to communication. It is as if society had no conventions to avoid such misunderstanding. The father chooses words—"one—for two of us"—that are ambiguous: does he want one or two portions? There is potential confusion in what is often said in the same situation: "We'd like one." Is the person placing the order summarizing the desires at the table, or saying that each person would like one? It is the convention of usage that points to the former. Valentin's character, however, has used a phrase that has no such generally ascribed meaning and has baffled the unfortunate waiter.

Although the father's inability to place the order makes him appear ridiculous, his difference from the middle-class men and women of the audience is not yet firmly established. In two respects, the situation on stage corresponded to the situation of the people watching. First, the character was not only trying to place an order but also trying to avoid placing a large order. Why does he not want macaroni for himself? Surely it would have occurred to the public that he did not have enough money for two portions. *Der Firmling* was first performed in Munich as the inflation entered its harshest phase. Thousands of middle-class people had seen their savings disappear and had been forced into a day-to-day struggle for existence. This restaurant scene must have reminded many men and women in the audience that they themselves had not ordered the sausages or fried potatoes they wanted because they could not afford them.

Second, in spite of Valentin's comic exaggerations, the father is at the social level of ordinary tavern customers. One of his problems is that he has not been accustomed by ordering beer from Marie at the Hofbräuhaus to handling waiters in an upper-class establishment. He is out of place, as common people invariably are when they venture into the world of their superiors.

Valentin also uses this opening scene to demonstrate the lack of affection and understanding between the father and his son. Pepperl interrupts twice—without effect—to end the confusion, thus attempting to show that he is more clever than his father. Their relationship is poor. Although the father does try to find out what the boy would like to eat, he also strikes him for laughing over the trouble with the waiter: "Now quit your stupid-ass [saudummes] laughing." Pepperl begins to cry, but starts to laugh again immediately, mocking his father. Later, when the father tries to sniff tobacco, the son jars it out of his hand twice. He stops only when he is threatened. That Pepperl is not interested in celebrating his confirmation is obvious; beyond the irreverence lies a basic malice toward his father.

After his failure with the waiter, the Valentin character tries to regain his poise by resuming the fatherly role. It is his responsibility, he maintains, to see that Pepperl's youth is happily and meaningfully spent. He sings: "Wonderful is youth, the happy times, wonderful is youth, it comes only once." Then, however, a typical Valentin misfortune befalls him and ruins his attempt to play this role. For no apparent reason, he bends over the table, and jabs his nose into the toothpick container. Hurt and suddenly panic-stricken, he wonders: "What if I get blood poisoning and my nose gets cut off?"Pepperl shows no sympathy: "I can't do anything about it. Why do you have to put your nose into everything?" The father, still afraid, rubs schnapps into the wound. As Pepperl starts to sing, his father pushes him to the floor, saying: "He's beginning again about his stupid-ass youth." In pain, the father gives up his attempt to act like a father is supposed to. Clearly, this episode arises out of Valentin's personal anxieties; the folksinger's fear of being struck by unexpected disasters is legendary. Valentin made a career out of drawing laughter onto himself and, frequently, onto his own fearful nature.

When the pain has subsided, the father expresses his pride at providing his son with a confirmation. This is his way of asserting himself against the poverty around him, of distinguishing himself from those who have become demoralized by the economic upheaval: "No one in the world would have been your *pate* at confirmation. Everyone promised it. Everyone said 'I'll be your boy's *pate* at confirmation.' And the way it all happened, everyone pulled out . . . Why wasn't [your uncle] your *pate? . . .* Because he didn't have the dough . . . couldn't have bought you a watch. I was your *pate.* I kept my word." The father sips his drink and begins a rambling monologue about how he acquired Pepperl's communion suit. He went all over Munich looking, but the store price was sixty-five marks: "As a plain middle-class man, I can't allow myself that, that I should put sixty-five marks on the table for the kid—I'm not from the burschoisie [*sic*]. I must earn my money with the hard work of my hands." He went to all his taverns, but no one had a communion suit for sale. Then he meets "a war comrade of mine in '70. We stood together . . . man by man, shoulder to shoulder, right on the banks of the Isar, where it was so damp. He heard that I wanted to buy a communion suit." This friend did not want to accept payment, but the father insists "because you yourself are a poor devil, and if you give me the suit, we want to regulate the thing financially. In these matters, I'm a man of honor." It is this traditional middle-class concept of honor that moves Valentin's character: he functions as a father, he works for what he earns, and he accepts no charity.

Despite the comedy, the father has become a solidly middle-class and almost inspirational figure at this point. In other words, he appears to be an "insider." The hilarity that ensues, however, makes it clear that he has failed miserably to provide his son with a respectable confirmation. He is indeed an "outsider," whose place in society has become marginal. What the father finds most "terribly interesting" about the suit is that, although it had been tailored for another boy, it fit—poorly, but well enough. The father returns with astonishment to the thought again and again, slamming the table each time: "It fit!" With the last slam, he falls to the floor, drunk and unable to get up. Pathetically, he assumes that his legs have given out and wonders aloud if he will have to ride a tricycle in his old age, again a characteristically bizarre Valentin fear that made him seem inferior to the audience.

Quickly the situation degenerates into chaos. Pepperl, openly disgusted as he helps his father back to the chair, becomes cross when his father starts to sing, and declares: "Shut your mouth."

Father: I have fought for king and fatherland.
Pepperl: That's baloney [*Wurscht*] now ... (Father falls down.) It's getting too dumb for me. Next time you go alone to the confirmation ... (Father falls down.) I'm going to go insane pretty soon.

As this point, when the son has insulted the father's patriotic and religious feelings, *Der Firmling* simply erupts. The play ends with macaroni spilling onto the floor, which the father picks up and stuffs into his pockets. Pepperl suggests that they "get out of here," and his father instantly consents: "Then we don't have to pay." They exit, the father riding Pepperl piggyback, as the waiter chases, calling "Stop and pay! Pay!"

Valentin's character has placed much value upon functioning as a father and as an honorable middle-class man, but in the end he functions as neither. Pepperl's "special day" was transformed into a wild scene, and finally into a family act of thievery. The father did not, after all, have much money, and the bill at an upper-class restaurant would have been high. Drunk and bewildered in a place where he does not belong, his facade of middle-class honor slips until he can agree to rush off without paying.

Considering how Valentin came to create *Der Firmling* is instructive for understanding both his work method and his artistic relationship to the middle-class people he entertained. Liesl Karlstadt has recorded that she passed near a Munich cigar stand during the inflation and overheard its owner loudly telling customers that he had nearly given up looking for his son's communion suit when a friend offered him a used one. The suit fit. To the cigar dealer, this was a positive miracle: "It fit!" he roared, again and again: "By the end tears ran down all our cheeks, the storyteller from being so touched by his tale, and the rest of us from laughing."[41] Valentin literally took an episode off the streets of Munich and fashioned it into a piece of popular entertainment. Fifteen years had elapsed since he had actually belonged to the small-business society of this cigar dealer. His attachment, however, remained strong. He understood middle-class fears and worries because he had had them himself and had never fully lost them. During the hardships of the early 1920s, he was well suited to transmit reassuring messages to a frightened and extremely receptive middle-class public.

Two young Munich playwrights, Bertolt Brecht and Arnolt Bronnen, wrote of *Das Christbaumbrettl* that "it caught the era and the people of the era in the mirror of comedy."[42] From the stage setting alone, it is clear that the play deals with the declining middle class. The action takes place in a family living room where disorder reigns. According to stage directions, the room is in "colorful confusion"; signs that the family's life is hard include the broken plates and cups in the cabinet. Inexplicably, Christmas music is playing on the gramophone, but a spring scene is visible through the window. Alone on stage for the opening monologue, the mother, played by Liesl Karlstadt, adds to this chaos: she lights a cigar; nonsensically, she concludes in late afternoon that "the sun will rise soon." She is a type very dear to the Munich small-stage audience: a wife complaining about her husband. She has sent him to get a Christmas tree "for the small children, and now he's late coming home. I think he can't find his way home anymore, the old fool [*der alte Depp*]."

The father, with Valentin in the role, arrives with the Christmas tree. Confusion and discomfort are the first impressions he makes. He wears a heavy overcoat, appropriate for the Christmas season and for the obviously fake snow on his shoulder and hat, but he is overdressed for the spring weather out of which he has come. Explaining the time it took to buy the tree, he says he had to go to "two Christmas tree factories." The absurd suggestion that Christmas trees come from factories surely found resonance in the audience, at least among the tradesmen who felt that too much had been taken over from the traditional workshop by mass production.

When the mother discovers that the father has not brought a board with which to stand the Christmas tree upright, she complains, "I expressly said, bring a tree with a board."

The Father: This one has nothing.
The Mother: I see that it has nothing.
The Father: How can you see it, if nothing's there?

Valentin is playing with language as he had with the macaroni and ham order in *Der Firmling*. The mother has used an expression that most people simply recognize; she does not mean that she sees "nothing" in the way that she sees the tree or sees her husband. Nevertheless, the figure of speech confuses the father, as though he has never heard it before and needs to ponder its meaning. Again, Valentin has constructed a short piece of dialogue in which his character evidently forgets the most basic information about the society in which he lives. In this way, he is an "outsider."

Several lines later, the father signals the audience that he lives in the same Munich as they and that he shares their hardships. He offers to hold the tree for the children's celebration, to which his wife sarcastically replies, "Go on, you can't stand there and hold the tree until Twelfth Night!" His answer fits the era perfectly: "Why not? I have nothing to do—I'm out of work." With time on his hands, he leaves to get a piece of board to cut to size for the Christmas tree.

As in *Der Firmling,* Valentin focuses in this play upon the effects of impoverishment upon the quality of middle-class family life. There is little tenderness between husband and wife. When he has left, she comments that "he is a good man, but an awful jackass [*furchtbares Rindvieh*]." There are also problems with the children, who draw her attention to the next room (offstage), where they are waiting for the Christmas tree to be set up. What they are doing certainly detracts from the sentimentality that normally surrounds the theme "children at Christmas": "Hey, who hung the baby upside down? All the blood'll run into his head," the mother calls.

The father, who had left confident that he could make a Christmas tree board, returns, following the stage directions, "with two long boards, gets tangled up in the lamp, and strikes everything around him with the boards. The table breaks apart, and the fly paper sticks to his face." He proceeds to reveal his utterly hilarious incompetence as a tradesman. When he finally manages to saw off a piece of wood and holds it in his hand, he forgets himself and his purpose for having it; for him, it becomes a sexual instrument and he reaches it under his wife's skirt. As inadequate as it is impulsive, the gesture only irritates her: "What are you doing? Today on Christmas Eve he does such stupid-ass things." Still thinking of sex, he suggests that they have the time: "It's still afternoon." But the mother concentrates instead upon the board he has cut. She finds it too short, criticizing his workmanship and rejecting his sexuality. The wife honors her husband in neither of two domains that the traditional marriage places under male control: sex and work with tools. His failure at both, and her criticisms, emphasize that their married life has completely broken down.

As *Das Christbaumbrettl* proceeds, it becomes more and more apparent that the emotional bonds in this middle-class family have loosened considerably. The father and mother are not loving parents. Although they are trying to give their children a Christmas celebration, hearing the children scream in the next room has unnerved them until they cannot hide their contempt: "Be still, you miserable sons of bitches [*Hundsbankerten*]," shrieks the mother. "You don't need to say sons of bitches to those pig cripples [*Saukrüppel*]," returns the father. Indifference and hostility characterize the mother's attitude toward her husband. When he suddenly begins to weep, she assumes that "he has gone insane." Seeing the cause, that a clasp on one of the candles with which he is decorating the tree has pinched a finger, she offers no comfort but exclaims, "For God's sake! Another misfortune!" This is a device Valentin used in *Der Firmling*, when the father in that play pricked his nose on a toothpick. He conveys the depths of emotional misery in the family through this extremely pitiful image: the father, vulnerable and inept, suffering alone without the least bit of sympathy to console him.

With the tree finally in place and the children ushered in, *Das Christbaumbrettl*, like *Der Firmling*, closes with the parents encouraging their children to steal. The mother receives a bonnet as a gift from one of her children, and thanks her: "It's beautiful, and I can use it. Yes, did you knit it yourself?"

Child: No, Mother, I didn't knit it myself. I stole it.
(The father and mother are noticeably moved . . . and begin to
    cry.)
Mother: A good child! Everything's so expensive now—you can't
    still buy things.
Father: Of course, you have to do it.
Mother: I hope no one saw you.
Child: No, mother, no one saw me.

Mother: Then go back next week and bring me another.
Father: And if you go by Henne's, bring me a Mercedes.
Mother: You are a good child, already ripe for prison.

The satire of the Christmas exchange of gifts is complete. It is a genuinely joyful occasion, not because the children have been "good"
but because the parents realize that they can exploit their children's
thievery to get what they want at a time when buying is impossible.
Carried away, the father puts a cap on the absurdity by asking for
an expensive car.

A chimney sweep, tall and wearing a top hat, interrupts them in
their mood when he appears to clean the oven. Like *Der Firmling,
Das Christbaumbrettl* turns to pandemonium before the end: the father rides around the stage on a tricycle given to him by his wife; the
chimney sweep sits in the Christmas cake; the children scream; and
from their visitor the family learns that the day is the twenty-fourth
of June, not December. Still not able to comprehend the mistake,
the father asks for his calendar and turns to his wife: "You see, old
lady, that's why I got the Christmas tree so cheap today!"

By dramatizing incidents of family stealing, *Das Christbaumbrettl*
and *Der Firmling* touch upon an important contemporary issue. For
nearly ten years, people in Munich had lived in a perpetual state of
emergency. As Munich folksinger and poet Josef Benno Sailer wrote
of the wartime food shortages:

> Everything that was forbidden
> suddenly was quite all right.[43]

Das Christbaumbrettl goes further than *Der Firmling* to suggest that,
in a family, such times are thrilling for parents and children alike.
Children find themselves actually encouraged in a hitherto forbid-
den adventure, and the adults can finally express their resentment,
sharpened by worry, of wealth and property. Emotional bonds form
in *Das Christbaumbrettl* only as the family transforms into a band of
criminals.

These twin plays of 1922 reflect the need of frightened middle-
class people in Munich to find someone or some group whose inferi-
ority appeared to guarantee the security of their own places in society. Valentin and Liesl Karlstadt took this role. Their entertain-

ment derived its humor from their ability to pose as laughingstocks, in effect as miserable but funny proletarians. There are, it is true, numerous points of similarity between them and their middle-class audiences: the language; their attachment to middle-class traditions, like family Christmas parties and confirmations; their concepts of honor; and even their willingness to steal during these years of economic crisis. These indicate their class origins, however, not their current status. Their bewilderment and inadequacies reveal that they have fallen below the level of the middle class, that they no longer belong to their former group, that they have become inhabitants of a marginal, classless realm of society. They are not declining; they have declined. It reassured the shopkeepers, tradesmen, and clerks of Valentin's public to see these two convincing reminders of their own superiority. During the economic and political turmoil of the early 1920s, however, they needed more reassurance than a folksinger could provide. The inability of the Weimar Republic to satisfy this persistent middle-class need hampered the new state's efforts to gain that class's loyalty and support.

ALTHOUGH POLICE censorship had officially fallen with the German Empire, in effect the National Socialists took over the censor's functions in Munich's cultural life. They waged a bitter campaign against Munich's "decadent" artists—in other words, against those who reflected none of the national quest for power and glory, those who criticized or ridiculed this quest, and those who were Jewish. To all their enemies in the arts, they applied the label "cultural Bolshevik." Demonstrating against the performance of certain plays or harassing artists at their homes, the Nazis succeeded at transforming Munich from a center of artistic freedom into a cultural danger zone. "It is no longer a secret," wrote a contemporary, "how seriously Munich has suffered in its reputation as a city of the arts and as a generally beloved cultural middle point of the German South through the unhealthy amalgamation of artistic-moral and supposedly political points of view. Actually [it is] street agitation."[44]

Particularly high on the Nazi list for removal from Munach stages were plays by Wedekind and by an important young dramatist, Bertolt Brecht. The Nazis' tactic was to take places in the audience and wait until a prearranged point when they would begin to shout and to stomp their feet. This made continuing the performance impossible. Sometimes the Nazis also threw rotten eggs or stink bombs. Brecht's *In the Jungle,* performed at the Residence Theater in May 1923, made it through the last scene, but only because Brecht's followers outnumbered the agitators and shouted them down.[45] According to Brecht's friend and fellow writer, Arnolt Bronnen, these experiences embittered Brecht, who came to see the Nazi Sturmabteilung (SA) as "the excrement of Adolf Hitler, which began to pollute the Isar city." The Nazis focused considerable hatred upon another Brecht friend, Jewish author Lion Feuchtwanger, who told how, according to Bronnen, "in the past weeks, each evening groups of boys had pulled up before his house, heaving out anti-Semitic screams and then throwing stones . . . 'We cannot wait here for long,' said Feuchtwanger . . . Brecht saw similar dangers."[46] Brecht and Feuchtwanger left Munich for Berlin in 1924–25, in part because of Munich's new, stifling atmosphere.

The NSDAP made its opposition to "cultural Bolshevism" a rallying point for party supporters and sympathizers. As early as October 1921, a Nazi official spoke at the Landtag about the "Jewish influence" in Munich's cultural affairs.[47] Then, after their success in the 1924 Landtag elections, Nazi deputies denounced "the seduction of the people by the Jewish operetta, with one hundred women turning their legs up in the air, and by the Jewish movie house." This attitude found friends among prominent conservative politicians.[48]

Munich's police supported the NSDAP on cultural matters, for example, by banning "dangerous" plays from theater schedules; rather than arrest the Nazi demonstrators, police often used them as a pretext for closing the plays. The Nazis needed only to threaten to create an incident, and in spite of constitutional guarantees of free expression, the police would force a performance's cancellation, explaining that they could not keep order. Munich's daily newspaper, the *Münchner Neueste Nachrichten,* echoed the frequent complaint that because the police cooperated in this way, the theater disturbances "have stepped in to replace the censor, who has been abolished." A police document of February 1921, concerning the performance of an Arthur Schnitzler play, reflects basic police sympathy for the right-wing extremists. Forbidding further performance of the play because of incidents at a previous showing, the document concludes: "The police are not in the position, without neglecting more important tasks, to place such a large contingent at the constant disposal of the business directors [of the theater], in order to insure the quiet performance of a play that mocks all healthy sensitivities of the people, and that therefore has rightly awakened heavy protests in wide circles."[49] It is not surprising that artists like Brecht were leaving.

In conservative, Nazi-influenced Munich, on occasion theatergoers actually had to walk past armed men to see a play. The Einwohnerwehr (citizens' militia), which had been formed in 1919 to fight the Revolution, struck a blow at decadence during the March 1920 Kapp putsch by occupying Munich's Theater of the Prince Regent. This did not matter during the three-day general strike, which theater personnel joined, to bring Kapp down.[50] But the Einwohnerwehr stayed after the Berlin crisis had passed and the theater had resumed its schedule; some performances were given while militiamen with machine guns stood at the theater doors.[51]

These were the political conditions under which the Munich folksingers appeared in the early 1920s. Weiss Ferdl was unaffected; "old Bavarian" entertainment stood in no danger of being labeled "cultural Bolshevism." Valentin, however, continued his old opposition to German militarism and was forced to use his code. He kept his personal opinions to himself. The Kapp putsch prompted one of his few recorded responses to a political situation. At the time, Valentin was appearing regularly at a tavern cabaret named Charivari, a few blocks south of the main train station.[52] There was some debate among the personnel there as to whether the general strike involved them, but they decided that it did and that they would not perform while it lasted. Theo Prosel, later manager of Schwabing's Simplicissimus, recalls walking with the folksinger and Liesl Karlstadt during the strike, when they saw a line of Einwohnerwehr men blocking their way: "Valentin took Liesl Karlstadt's umbrella away, and held it like a bayonet. Armed this way, he moved against the Einwohnerwehr. But when these defenders of Munich noticed that the attacker was Valentin, they gave us free passage."[53] Valentin, it seems, enjoyed a kind of village fool's status in Munich. He could afford to make this gesture of protest without having to fear demonstrators at his performances or outside his home: it was just Valentin! However, he and Liesl Karlstadt had performed for the Einwohnerwehr of Munich's twenty-sixth district in the Löwenbräu beer hall three months earlier. Inasmuch as Nazi theoretician and writer Dietrich Eckart authored that gathering's opening remarks, its mood was no doubt passionately nationalistic and anti-Semitic. Nor was this Valentin's only appearance before a right-wing audience: on 12 September 1919, he entertained the "Bavarian Rifle Brigade 12" at the Hotel Wagner, near the Sendlinger Gate.[54] Although there is no record of a performance for the NSDAP, the evidence remains: Valentin was willing to perform before Munich's right-wing, paramilitary groups. This does not prove, however, that he shared their attitudes. Valentin, it must be remembered, was a stage artist, not a politician; entertaining was his business, not his way of demonstrating support for the politics of the audience.

After World War II, Karl Valentin affirmed in a questionnaire that he neither belonged to a political party during the Weimar Republic nor saw politics along party lines.[55] He occasionally made fun of republican institutions on stage. For example, an autobiographical sketch whimsically dated 8 February 1935, although written in the early 1920s, stated: "He lives from the fabrication of nonsense, like most other people. By changing positions he expects sooner or later to be able to become a Reichstag deputy." He also held local political officials up for sharp satire. A comical depiction of a session of the Munich City Council found one of the councilmen proposing the "replastering of our mayor's restaurant." When the proposals were not self-serving, they were nonsensical: raising the tax on dogs from thirty to twenty marks; setting more distance between streetcar tracks in the busiest streets; and founding a rest home for a singing men's club in the center of the city.[56] If Valentin occasionally gave vent to the common man's doubt that people in government really cared about him, his references to politics were too few and too vague to convey much sense of a viewpoint. Perhaps his disclaimer of interest in politics should settle the matter.

Why have leftist intellectuals embraced Valentin as an entertainer who spoke out against right-wing extremism? Brecht and his friends were sure that the folksinger had no sympathy for the fanatic nationalism and intolerance with which Hitler had overrun Munich.[57] Thomas and Heinrich Mann's younger brother Viktor even called him the "direct opposite" of the "opportunist" folksingers who became Hitler's "propagandists," probably a reference to Weiss Ferdl: "With the most grotesque nonsense, he holds a fool's mirror up before the people."[58] Eugen Gürfter of the Berlin magazine *Die Weltbühne* (The World Stage) polished this assessment of Valentin when he wrote: "Yes, behind the Munich whose clouded picture is being given to us by the panic-stricken and sleepy-headed lower middle class, there is another, brighter, humanly wiser Munich."[59] Perhaps Karl Valentin, who rarely mentioned politics on stage, did not deserve this praise.

Valentin's admirers among the intellectuals may have assumed that his portrayals of thievery in *Das Christbaumbrettl* and in *Der Firmling* implied a wider rejection of capitalist private property. Rejecting capitalism, however, does not qualify him as a left-wing opponent of Hitler's, any more than it makes him a Nazi supporter. That is part of the confusion between the radical right and the radical left in the early 1920s: both claimed that they were anticapitalist, as the name "National Socialist" indicates.

Whatever it was about Valentin that made essayists see a "brighter, humanly wiser Munich" in him, some of his entertainment does indeed point critically at the paramilitary groups that had virtually taken over the Bavarian capital in the early 1920s. He never had to face an unruly crowd because he had woven his attitudes into a satire so thick that they were partly concealed. Without naming names or referring to contemporary politics at all, Valentin aimed at the Bavarian tradition of citizens' militias. He did not invent the relationship between the militarism of his day and that of the past. He understood that groups like the Einwohnerwehr and like Munich's assorted marching and shooting clubs found widespread approval because people saw them as the heirs of this local military tradition: Bavaria's fighting men, spirited and courageous, stepping hard as they marched through Munich's streets. Although the Nazi leaders were not Bavarian, the party had in effect merged with this tradition. Valentin thought these superpatriots were fools. He exposed them from the stage, but only for those who realized that in making fun of the past he was holding up a mirror to the present.

One way to resist militarism was to doubt that the enemies of old had been genuinely dangerous. Thus, Valentin announced on stage during the early 1920s: "At around six o'clock this morning, an army of war, consisting of four men and seven hundred horses, armed to the teeth, advanced on Ringelberg."[60] How ridiculous to think of the local defenders standing at their cannons while this army approached! The parody turns upon Hitler and his followers. By implication, they looked ridiculous too, holding their beer-hall rallies about Germany's peril when there were no enemy soldiers anywhere near them.

Valentin's most developed piece of pacifist satire from these years, a two-act play entitled *Die Raubritter vor München* (The Robber Barons before Munich), does accept the existence of a dangerous enemy.[61] It premiered on 1 April 1924, when Germany's memory of French troops in the Ruhr Valley was still fresh. Although the play took only thirty minutes to perform, Valentin had worked at it on and off since 1914, ten years during which military imperatives were constantly before the German people in one form or another: the need to fight, the need to rearm, the need to resist, and so on. Valentin vented his opposition to this into *Die Raubritter,* which Munich writer and journalist Hermann Sinsheimer has called "the most biting satire on militarism, even if that went unnoticed in Munich."[62]

Valentin's parody takes military alertness as its first object. It is six o'clock in the morning at the city wall, one hour before the changing of the guard. A drummer boy named Michl, played by Liesl Karlstadt, knocks at the sentry box to awaken Bene, played by Valentin, who has been sleeping cramped up inside. Not fully awake, Bene stumbles out to start his watch, but turns to go back for more sleep when he learns the time. Michl tells him to stay up; he should be glad to be wakened so early. Bene protests that he was in the middle of a "completely exotic dream," obviously a play on the words "exotic" and "erotic."

Bene wakes up as he recounts this remarkable dream, in which he was a duck, swimming in a pond, when he spied a long, yellow worm on the bank. He had been about to seize the worm in his beak when Michl woke him. Michl replies that being awakened from such a dream should not matter; Bene insists that in the dream he was a duck, so it was a perfectly good dream. This goes on until the following exchange:

Michl: You can be thankful to me that I woke you up, because if
    I'd let you eat the worm, you'd be feeling real poor just now.
Bene: But a duck doesn't feel poor from a worm—don't you understand that?

Unable to resolve the disagreement, they leave it.

A man dreaming he is a duck about to eat a worm: this bizarre and pitiful image conveys a sharp idea of Bene's life as a soldier to the audience. The laugh-getting nonsense of the dialogue does not ease the awareness that he is hungry, so deeply hungry that he can even imagine swallowing a worm, and wants to go back to sleep, to reenter his dream, in order to do so. Bene stands in satirical contrast to an idealized city defender: he is sleepy rather than alert, his thoughts on food rather than on duty.

Whatever code of honor Bene has learned in the militia, it does not hold him back in the next scene from stealing food, any more than middle-class respect for law held back the hungry civilians in *Der Firmling*. The butcher's helper enters, carrying a tray of sausages on his shoulder. Unaware of Bene, he walks straight to a lilac bush growing at the wall, with the idea of breaking off a branch for himself. Muttering to himself that "you shouldn't be stealing so early," but probably thinking that a sausage would more than adequately replace the worm he had missed, Bene sneaks up behind the butcher's helper, grabs a sausage, and to his surprise pulls all the sausages off the tray, for they are linked end to end. Only after he has stuffed them into the back of his shirt does he let the would-be lilac thief know of his presence: "Leave it be!" Startled and angry, the butcher's helper exits without noticing that his sausages are gone. Michl returns, and after Bene has confided in him about the stealing, demands that they share the plunder, which they are about to do when they hear approaching hoofbeats and the cracking of a whip. Frantic to find a hiding place for the sausages, Michl shoves them down the barrel of a cannon, symbolically completing Valentin's statement about the real relationship between the call of duty and the need to eat.

Bene and Michl have just assumed innocent poses when an excited traveling merchant rushes up to tell them that robber barons have attacked Berg am Laim, a nearby village, and have already hung the mayor. He demands that Bene lock the city gates, but Bene refuses:

Bene: Yes, that's all perfectly right, but in this matter I am not allowed to undertake anything.
Merchant: Why?

Michl: Bene means that without the captain's order he is not al-
lowed to undertake anything.
Merchant: That's garbage [*Schmarrn*]! Who else is supposed to
close them up? As the sentry, you've got the key.
Michl: Yes, he does close up, but not until nine o'clock in the eve-
ning.
Merchant: But that's too late! The robber barons will already be
here!
Michl: So, they should go slower.
Merchant: Are you fools?
Bene: That we don't know.

Exasperated, the merchant cries: "What do you do as sentries?" The
question sends Bene and Michl into a detailed explanation of their
official duties, according to which Bene may call out the guard—
which he does four times to impress upon the merchant that he
really has this power—but not issue any further orders. This is finally too much for the merchant, who goes off swearing, and for the
soldiers of the guard, who have marched out four times without reason. The corporal tells Bene to stop. When Bene replies that he can
ring the bell as often as he wants and that the guard has to come
each time, the corporal threatens to report it to the captain. "All this
running around on an empty stomach," he complains. "It's so unhealthy too."

Nothing can shake Bene out of this structure of military rules and
regulations: neither the merchant's alarm, nor consideration for the
guards, toward whom he shows the same insensitivity that Michl
had shown in waking him. It is worth noting that when Bene and
Michl list their duties, they drop the Bavarian dialect, which they
had used between themselves, and speak official high German. This
emphasizes that they are conducting themselves by the book, following explicit orders, as does the fact that it is often Michl who explains Bene's unwillingness to "undertake anything."

Valentin has carried his parody into the area of military efficiency. No longer tired and hungry, Bene has become a functioning,
efficient soldier within an utterly useless and ineffective system of
giving and obeying orders. These are the proud defenders of yesterday, and extending the satire, of today. Bene and Michl had no
more effect on the robber barons west of Munich than the Nazis and
the shooting clubs were having on the French west of the Rhine. But

Valentin does not stop with a laugh at military efficiency. Bene conceives of his function so narrowly because he is *unable* to conceive of it broadly. What does it mean that robber barons are threatening the city from Berg am Laim, or that they have hung a mayor he has never seen? Is his interest in the city of Munich so strong that he should jump to its defense? What is he supposed to do? Bene is not a war resister; he is refusing to look for meaning in a situation that, to him, is essentially meaningless. Valentin has let Bene, his universal soldier, ask the universal question: Why should I fight?

Left alone on stage, Bene and Michl discuss the merchant's story. Could there really be robber barons at Berg am Laim? Bene is doubtful, but not sure. If there were robber barons, Michl asks, would he be afraid? At first missing the point of the question, but then coming to it in his answer, Bene replies, "Me? Be afraid? Not me—out of the question." Then: "Except if they did come, then I'd be afraid." Michl would also be afraid, but says he would run away so they could not catch him: a natural conversation for two soldiers, about battle and their fears. They drop the subject immediately and amuse themselves as Bene calls out the guard for a fifth time; then, Michl tells how the corporal's mouth had gotten stuck yesterday when he bit into a piece of bread on which the drummer boy had spread shoemaker's glue, an unmistakable reminder of the "Fey kid." Valentin has briefly introduced the issue of fear, which has only been implicit up to this point. In his satire of militarism, he is presenting soldiers for whom fear is more natural than courage, the need to turn and run more urgent than the will to stand and fight.

Still laughing about the corporal, Bene and Michl do not notice that the city actuary has come to speak with them. When Bene sees him, he suddenly draws his sword and begins to march back and forth, as though on patrol. Why all the noise so early in the morning? the actuary wants to know. Needing an answer fast, Michl seizes upon the story they had just heard from the merchant: "The traveling merchant was just here and told us that the robber barons want to invade the city." Bene, to make his repeated ringing for the guard seem reasonable, embellishes this, recounting how "the storm wind howled in pain, the fire raged, the heavens were bloodgreen." Michl, however, cannot concentrate well enough to sustain the story and quickly confuses it with the one other remarkable story he had heard that day, Bene's dream. The robber barons were set to kill the merchant, Michl says, "but then he hid himself behind a tree and fell asleep, and all of a sudden he dreamed that he was a duck and that he had eaten a worm this long!" This bewilders the actuary for a moment, but Bene steps in and says, "That's a completely different department," implying with his matter-of-fact explanation that such mental mix-ups are common.

Although Bene and Michl have gone along with the story about the robber barons to get out of trouble, the actuary is no more successful at getting Bene to close the city gates than the traveling merchant had been. He makes one last appeal, to Bene's manhood, warning that the robber barons take women and children, but this means nothing to Bene: "Ah, if that's all!" As indifferent to the fates of women and children as he is to the fate of the city, Bene is a spoof on the "old Bavarian" legends about the valor of Munich's fighting men.

The actuary has evidently taken the report of robber barons to the police, because a police officer appears at the city wall to read a state-of-emergency proclamation. This finally impresses upon Bene and Michl that their lives are endangered. For a minute, Valentin stops the clowning, as the two militiamen consider the situation. "So it's been quiet since the Thirty Years' War," moans Bene, "and now they have to start up again, now that I'm young and married, and have opened up a grocery store." He does not even try to tighten his courage for battle, the way soldiers are supposed to, but is overcome by a kind of grief, sure that he will be one of the unfortunate victims. When he notices that the eastern sky has gradually turned red before sunrise, he cries "Ow! Ow!" because of a folk adage, "today dead, morning red." Despairing, he reaches into the sentry box for his accordion and joins Michl in song:

> Morning red, morning red.
> Lighting my way to an early death.
> Soon the trumpets will blow
> Then I must leave my life—
> Along with my comrade.

> "Morgenrot, morgenrot,
> Leuchtest mir zum frühen Tod.
> Bald wird die Trompete blasen,
> Dann muss ich mein Leben lassen,
> Ich und mancher Kamerad."

These sad and thoughtful moments are mentioned time and again by those who saw *Die Raubritter vor München* performed: "reflections on war and death," Hermann Hesse called them.[63]

Humor returns as the entire militia assembles to receive battle instructions from the captain, a hearty officer who knows his soldiers and speaks their language. "Grüss dich Gott!" (God be with you), declare the captain and the corporal, exchanging the Bavarian greeting. "Bravo, bravo, they're a tough bunch," says the captain of his troops. "So, how's it going, people?" "Fine, Captain!" comes the reply in unison. The captain pays special attention to one of the men, who has just fathered his ninth son: "Meier doesn't let anything get away." But this picture of masculine self-assurance starts to fade when the captain notices Bene, who has been in a private conversation with Michl the whole time. The corporal has to call his name three times before Bene realizes that the captain is watching him; he then rushes into an exaggerated patrol, back and forth near the empty sentry box. "Stop it!" orders the captain. "Do you run back and forth like that the whole day?" "Only when you come," Bene answers. The captain patiently tries to involve Bene in this Bavarian military ritual: "Grüss dich Gott," he says, stretching his hand out to Bene. But Bene cannot even competently return the gesture. "Grüss Gott, Captain," he says, but extends his sword rather than his hand for the captain to grab. The captain almost cuts himself, but he gives Bene one more chance to show that he can behave like a soldier, and asks: "Do you have something to say to me?" Having evidently forgotten about the robber barons, Bene seizes the moment to request a little oven for his sentry box. The captain even seems to agree to this, but grows impatient when Bene persists: "He's forever talking about his oven with the robber barons in the area." Bene is an utter misfit among these Bavarian fighting men.

As is apparent in their preparations for battle, however, this militia is much sharper as a parade unit than as a fighting unit. It turns out, for example, that the corporal has loaned the cannon swab to the chimney sweep. But there is a second swab, the captain remembers, where is it? "It's in the cannon," Bene answers, but since the cannon is pointed out through a hole in the city wall, "you won't find anybody to climb over" for it.

Captain: Surely there's someone who'll climb over!? Corporal, show the people you've got the nerve. Climb over.

Corporal: . . . Go on, Captain, send someone else over. I think
   that's better.
Bene: He's lost his nerve.
Michl: He doesn't have it to climb over. He's shitting in his pants.
   Now he's afraid.

Hardly soldiers any longer, Bene and Michl have stepped into new
roles as commentators on the fear—which they have felt all along—
now spreading through the militia.

Finally, the captain orders the corporal to climb over the wall.
But Valentin had already established this hard-luck militiaman as
the butt of jokes. As the corporal sticks his body over the wall, a shot
is heard, and he falls back, dropping a cannonball to the ground and
screaming, "Ow! Ow!" This incredible spectacle—a man catching a
cannonball, then falling in pain to the stage—is also quite useful: it
is a stylization of death in battle and conveys the stinging hurt a soldier feels when hit, yet at the same time it enables Valentin to go on
with his humor without dead and dying men on stage. The reactions
to the wounded man are also important. Michl walks over to him
and, with sadistic curiosity, exclaims, "Right on the head—you must
be completely dumb!" "I already was," replies the corporal. Nor is
the captain's response more human; he sends this unfortunate soldier back to the wall where, predictably, he is hit again. This was the
spirit of comradeship in the old militia under fire at the city wall, or
despite what the Nazis and their allies said, among German soldiers
in the trenches of World War I!

Of all these uniformed Bavarian heroes, it is unbelievably Bene
who arrives at the right idea for getting the cannon swab out of the
cannon: "We simply pull the cannon back out of the hole. Then we
have the swab." Bene and Michl actually do this, but setting the
cannon back into action is unexpectedly interrupted when the
butcher's helper appears with the police officer to claim the sausages
Bene had stolen. The battle preparations come to a halt while Bene
and the butcher's helper argue. Bene denies taking the sausages, but
accidentally knocks them out of the cannon barrel with the swab.
The policeman is about to arrest him, when the sentry shouts that
the robber barons are coming closer to the city wall. At this, the officer turns and runs, and Bene and Michl push the cannon back up to
the wall.

Singing a broad parody of a Bavarian fighting song, such as could never be sung at Platzl, the militiamen begin firing. According to the third verse, they have neither affection for the king, whose honor they are supposed to defend, nor confidence in themselves as soldiers:

> When the king gets a child,
> We quickly fire a salute.
> And at every procession,
> We fire with the cannon.
> In short, at every dumb-ass thing
> Our cannon is in view.
> The cannon is famous,
> But in war it doesn't work.

> "Wenn der König kriegt ein Kind,
> Schiessen wir Salut geschwind.
> Auch bei jeder Prozession
> Schiessen wir mit der Kanon.
> Kurz bei jeder Viecherei
> Ist d'Kanone auch dabei.
> Die Kanone ist famos,
> Bloss im Krieg, da geht's net los."

As in *Der Herzog kommt,* the image of a cannon that will not fire suggests sexual impotence. Here, Valentin is at the heart of "old Bavaria's" myth about its men: the equation of strength and courage in battle with masculine vitality. Soldiering tests sexual prowess at the same time that it tests military capability, and the militiamen of *Die Raubritter vor München* fail at both.

The battle scene itself is complete pandemonium, with cannons on both sides booming loudly. Bene has become the first-aid man, and the way he performs his duties is hilarious: he sees a soldier with a head wound leaning on a lantern post, and wraps not only his head but also his helmet, rifle, and the lantern post in a large bandage; then, he and Michl roll a soldier onto a stretcher but leave him on the ground when they pick up the poles, because the stretcher has no bottom. Finally, defeat comes. The theater lights are turned on and balloons meant to be enemy cannonballs float from behind the city wall into the audience. The robber barons appear at the top of the wall, and one of them sticks his pike through the unfortunate corporal. Bene runs to his sentry box and pulls out a white flag, which he waves madly. Michl tosses cannonballs into the audience.

Die Raubritter vor München contains both exaggerations and inconsistencies. No one would really refuse to lock the city gates before an attack, or set a wounded man onto a stretcher with no bottom. Nor does it make sense that Bene, who follows military regulations to the letter when dealing with the merchant, would be in a private conversation with Michl as the captain is reviewing the troops. This is the license of satire. Seen as a whole, Bene is not a person but a cluster of qualities: tired and hungry, thieving, malicious, blindly efficient, then not efficient at all, frightened of battle, yet unable to imagine it. What does Valentin mean with this unsoldierly soldier?

A few moments after recounting his dream to Michl, Bene sends the drummer boy for coffee and gives him "fifteen crosses" (*Kreuzer*), explaining—whether to Michl or in an aside to the audience is unclear—that there were no pfennigs back then. It was as though Valentin wanted to jolt his audience out of the past, to remind them that they were not actually at the old city wall, but seated in a theater in the 1920s, and to suggest that the significance of this story about an earlier citizens' militia lay in the present. Bertolt Brecht, then Valentin's young admirer, would later call such intentional breaking of the audience's concentration the "estrangement effect" (*Verfremdungseffekt*), a technique that keeps the viewers at an emotional distance from the stage, so that they will objectively consider the social and historical context of the action before them.

For those in the audience who understood Valentin, the context of *Die Raubritter vor München* was contemporary Munich, where thousands had made a cult of military life and were at a fever pitch celebrating the virtues of a soldier ideal: courage, self-sacrifice, sense of duty, and so on. Valentin dissented from this, suggesting that there was a Bene in all the soldiers, marchers, and shouters who claimed to follow high principles. According to Munich's Hitlers and half-Hitlers, the most crucial event of the past decade was Germany's signing away of her honor at Versailles; for Valentin, the battle dead were more important, as was the fact that soldiers and civilians in Germany had experienced gnawing hunger with few interruptions from the first months of the war through the inflation.

Was national honor really more important than individual survival? Valentin was a pacifist in an armed camp.

Valentin's *Die Raubritter vor München* represents a sharp if well-coded attack upon contemporary German militarism, of which Munich's National Socialists were the most prominent exponents. Premiering on 1 April 1924, less than five months after the putsch and a few weeks after the Nazis polled more than one third of the city's vote in Landtag elections, this play raised an isolated voice in protest against the tumult of impassioned nationalism. In this regard, it did not reflect but rather opposed widespread middle-class attitudes. Indeed, even if the men and women of Munich's usual folksinger public would have recognized current problems in the guise of the past, they did not have the chance to do so, because Valentin did not perform *Die Raubritter* for them. Instead, he took it to a more refined audience, to people who would be more likely to appreciate its nuances and to share its anti-Hitler views. He first presented it at Munich's Chamber of Plays (Kammerspiele), in other words, on the legitimate stage.[64]

Die Raubritter vor München's premier at the Chamber of Plays is the main event of a phase of Valentin's career that had begun in March 1923 and that lasted until 1926 or 1927. During this phase, Valentin not only became a cult figure for Munich's upper-class public but also performed frequently as a guest artist in other cities. In 1923, for example, he spent no less than two-and-one-half months in Vienna, fifteen days in Zurich, and ten days in Nuremberg. Evidently, the younger man's ambition to be a famous touring entertainer had subdued the older man's legendary fear of traveling. In Munich, he appeared most often at the Chamber of Plays or at a small stage that the Chamber was operating in Schwabing. These engagements grew out of an idea of the Chamber's young assistant directors—among them Brecht—who knew Valentin from his tavern cabarets, found him outrageously funny, and hoped that he would attract customers. Since October 1922, he had been appearing at the Chamber's Schwabing stage occasionally. What changed in March 1923 is that Valentin began performing less and less frequently at the cabarets where he had risen to local prominence.[65] Many of his cultivated admirers felt that he had become theirs. As Gerhard Gutherz, an assistant director of the Bavarian state theater, wrote: "The admirers of Valentin can only be pleased to have pulled him out of an atmosphere of beer and tobacco, to see him in a circle that brings his discreet and penetrating art to the fore." Fritz Strich, professor of literary history at the University of Munich, agreed that "his plays do not belong at all to the genre of the music halls, but rather are comedies that belong on the stage of a literary theater." Taking note of this attitude among such observers, Liesl Karlstadt once wrote that "even the sharpest critics had recognized that he was no cheap beer comedian."[66]

Valentin returned to Munich's popular middle-class audience a few years after his engagements at the Chamber of Plays; his main stage during 1927–28, for example, was Munich's old *varieté*, the Colosseum.[67] Why had he left? Valentin himself never answered this question, but two hypotheses seem convincing. First, he had reached the point in his career when some of the finest entertainment houses not only in Munich but throughout German-speaking Europe were beckoning him to come. He cannot have failed to recognize that this constituted a major opportunity. Although it entailed more traveling than he wanted, it offered both fame and material rewards. Declining it would have been hard.

Second, the politicization of Munich's middle class by the National Socialists may have alienated Valentin from his old public. As long as tradesmen, shopkeepers, and white-collar workers were coming under Hitler's sway, they did not need a buffoon to make them "say yes to themselves"; they had been promised "insider" status in a magnificent, glorious "national community." It is probably not a coincidence that Valentin withdrew at this time. True, *Die Raubritter*'s anti-Nazi protest was too well-coded to have aroused a rude, Nazi-inspired counterprotest at a tavern cabaret. Valentin chose, however, not to show it to people who would have appreciated it only to the extent that they did not understand it. Instead, he sought a more discerning and less right-wing audience at the Chamber of Plays. Generally, in the politically charged months leading up to and following the putsch, Valentin ceased transmitting messages to Munich's middle class; Weiss Ferdl, by contrast, transmitted hundreds. While Valentin was performing at the Chamber of Plays, or in Zurich, Vienna, or Nuremberg, Munich's "old Bavarian" favorite was drawing large crowds every night at Platzl. He, not Valentin, expressed the mood of the times. Since before World War I, Valentin's acts, with their "insider" and "outsider" themes, had reflected the middle-class social attitudes that formed the basis of popular disdain for Weimar; as rightist opposition to the Republic began to intensify, Valentin dissented. It is in Weiss Ferdl's entertainment of the years 1919–1923 that the political responses of Munich's middle class clearly appear.

WEISS FERDL'S post-1918 stage acts reflect the middle-class economic fears to which industrialization had given rise, which the war had intensified, and which the Weimar Republic was powerless to relieve. A short monologue of the early 1920s, for example, articulates a master tradesman's grievances against factory capitalism. Delivered by Weiss Ferdl himself or by one of Platzl's other artists in the role of a locksmith named "Wamslinger," the monologue takes the form of an answer to two questions: "Who is responsible for the war?" and "Who is responsible for losing the war?" "I'll say this—we wouldn't have needed the war at all. It just came to ruin the middle class [Mittelstand]. How can a small master like me pay the wages people are asking today? How? I'd like to know!—You have the work, you don't have the materials; have the materials, you don't have the work . . . Who's responsible that the middle class is folding? Who pushed for war? Who?—Big capitalism, the factories." Wamslinger was surely played to the hilt: a red-cheeked, beer-loving, finger-wagging, outspoken Munich Original of the kind that a music-hall public would instantly take to heart. Wamslinger's message, however, was quite serious. This tradesman, called "typical of our popular life" when he is introduced to the audience, voices the traditional middle class's despair at being caught between the pincers of big capitalism and big labor. Weiss Ferdl attempted to overcome this routine's gloom by adding a short song at the end:

> People, we're all people
> Get along with one another, wise up
> Then you'll enjoy life again
> Then the good times will come back.

> "Menschen, Menschen san mir alle,
> Vertragt's euch wieder, geh seid's gescheidt,
> Dann wird das Leben euch wieder freuen
> Dann kommt wieder a gute Zeit."[68]

Entertaining people was Weiss Ferdl's business, not depressing them. This closing song may have provided a light transition to the next act, but it did not erase what Wamslinger had said. "Getting along with one another" was hardly a solution to the problems that the locksmith had described. The middle class realized that it was not the people of the economic system but the economic system itself that had placed them at a disadvantage.

Weiss Ferdl later wrote that he had "blown with the wind" as a popular entertainer, meaning that he had known how to adapt himself to the attitudes and sentiments of the public.[69] The following song, for example, expresses the frustration that common men and women felt over the inflation:

> It can't go on like this,
> Say the masons up on their scaffolds
> If you're drinking beer at lunch,
> The pleasure costs you four hundred marks.
> And if you want a slice of sausage,
> You don't get enough for a thousand marks.
> That's just what you pay for a small lunch,
> That's where having lunch has to stop.

> "A so kann's nimma weita gehn,
> Sag'n d'Maurer, die am Grust droben stehn.
> Trinkst zu der Brotzeit jetzt a Mass,
> Vierhundert Mark kost di der Gspass.
> An Leberkäs möchst aa dazu,
> Um Tausend Mark hast no net gnua.
> Dos bloss für die Brotzeit, da zahlst drauf,
> Da hört sich 's Brotzeitmacha auf."[70]

The complaint of this song is that it is unfair for masons to work so hard and then have to pay exorbitant prices for a simple lunch; there is an echo of Ferdinand Weisheitinger's old principle of just exchange. For "being good," these tradesmen should be better rewarded. In the early 1920s, it was imperative that Weiss Ferdl deal with the economic crisis on stage. His personality helped to determine how he did so.

Middle-class dissatisfaction with the Weimar Republic amounted to more than economic grievances. With Weiss Ferdl, the Platzl clientele returned to their old structure of social and political attitudes, ideas, and sentiments, from which they took a dim view of the new state. The salient points of this structure were: opposition to socialism, which took the form of opposition to the Republic once the danger of a left-wing takeover had passed; yearning for a traditional community; resentment of Jews; and steadfast loyalty to the fatherland, as it had been embodied by the defeated Empire.

Weiss Ferdl was closely associated with the counterrevolution in Munich; he even wrote the Einwohnerwehr's marching song. The Einwohnerwehr's purpose, according to the text, was to protect the property of Munich's citizens from the "do-nothing, the lazy guy, the have-not" who had tried once, and could try again, to take it away. But, in the refrain's words:

> Then came the Einwohnerwehr, our Einwohnerwehr—
> Right away it brings back peace to the country.
> Because the good man, who does his duty,
> Wants peace and quiet, and won't have it otherwise.
> Every man, whether lord or servant, observes the
>   rights of law—
> The Einwohnerwehr is seeing to it that no one takes
>   them away.[71]

Middle-class fears of losing property appear throughout this song, as does the tendency to cast the revolutionaries into the role of social "outsiders." Moreover, the Einwohnerwehr, which recruited heavily from among World War I veterans, gave its members a sense of victory to compensate for their sense of defeat; they had lost the war, but beaten the domestic enemy. When the Einwohnerwehr was outlawed by the government in Berlin in 1921, many of its antisocialist, battle-loving troops found their way into the ranks of the NSDAP.[72]

The rejection of socialism is evident in several aspects of Munich's popular culture. For example, the Oktoberfest, which had not been held during the war, became a symbol of the city's return to order. An entertainment booth owner named Carl Gabriel indicated this in a 21 January 1919 letter to the city police. He urged that the Oktoberfest be reintroduced the following autumn. Recounting how difficult the war had been on his profession, he offers another reason why the city should resume sponsoring the festival: "The largest part of the people would be held at a distance from revolutionary and seditious ideas by its reintroduction. Law and order in the father-land could be built up again." Two months after Gabriel wrote his letter, the city's Oktoberfest commission decided against holding the festival in 1919 because of the "food and apartment situations," but one year later decided to sponsor it in an abbreviated form, called the "Autumn Festival of 1920." In whatever way they planned to tone down the festival, they pleased some and displeased others. One Munich daily newspaper, the *Münchner Neueste Nachrichten,* hoped it would bring back "Munich's sense of humor and the old relaxed way of life," but a rival paper, the *Münchner Zeitung,* thought it would be a sham. The police had prepared themselves to preserve order, but in fact spent most of their time supervising the concession and entertainment stands, and running a "lost and found." Reflected one police inspector: "In spite of the enormous consumption of beer, riotous excesses did not arise. The beer gave the festival visitors a good disposition and all around one could hear: 'Now that we have a good mug of beer, politics doesn't matter to us' . . . It should not go unmentioned," he went on, "that the song, 'Deutschland, Deutschland über alles' was sung in two taverns on the last day of the festival just before the curfew began." Munich was orderly again, and the police breathed a sigh of relief.[73]

Weiss Ferdl fully appreciated the Oktoberfest's symbolization of Munich's new antileft mood. One of the first postwar festivals stimulated him to write one of his better-known songs, "Heut gehn ma auf die Wiesn" (Today We're Going to the Field), in reference to Theresa Field (Theresienwiese), on which the Oktoberfest was traditionally held. With his powerful voice adding to the song's conviction, Weiss Ferdl told how even small babies, carried on pillows, begin to love the Oktoberfest:

> Yes, it all starts on the field
> Even the revolution
> Although they were not many,
> There they overthrew a king,
> And when they want to call him back,
> It'll happen on the field.
>
> "Ja alles fängt auf der Wiesn an,
> Sogar die Revolution.

> Obwohl es warn ganz wenig,
> Dort habn sie gestürzt an König,
> Und wenn s' ihn rufen wieder aus,
> Geschiehts auf der Wiesn drauss."[74]

Weiss Ferdl saw the Revolution as an aberration in Bavaria, the work of a few, made possible by the confusion of the many. After the uncertain years of war and revolution, old traditions like "going to the field" were restoring people's sense of balance and identity.

From the Platzl stage, Weiss Ferdl continually hurled barbs of satire at the Revolution's political offspring, the Weimar Republic. "Wie soll ich wählen?" (How Should I Vote?) was a song aimed at the campaign advertising of the parties:

> Then you won't pay so many taxes,
> And your hens will lay more eggs—
> You'll get more milk from your cows,
> And have all the cattle you need.
> And your candidates in parliament, they'll
>   take care that royal Bavarian peace
>   and quiet comes back.
> So, forwards, backwards, upwards,
> Inflation, religion, reaction,
> Building up, taking down, stealing blind
> Right, left, and center, high and low,
>   phooey—
> All the time I ask, what is best for us?

> "Man zahlt nicht mehr so viel Steuer.
> Jede Henn legt dann mehr Eier,
> Die Küh geben viel mehr Milli,
> Rindviecher gibt's dann in Hülle und Fülle.
> Und Ihre Kandidaten im Reichstag, die schaun dann dazua,
> Dass wiederkehrt die königlich bayrische Ruah,
> Darum vorwärts, rückwärts, aufwärts,
> Inflation, Religion, Reaktion,
> Aufbau, Abbau, Raubbau,
> Rechts um, links um, Zentrum, hoch, nieder, pfui—
> Ich frag allweil, was ist zu unserem Heil."[75]

Weiss Ferdl was expressing the bewilderment felt by ordinary Germans in the face of the new political practices and institutions; he was also expressing their unwillingness to assume their new political responsibilities. The Platzl message was strongly antirepublican; Weiss Ferdl's popularity suggests that it was a message that people wanted to hear.

The monarchist themes that run through Weiss Ferdl's entertainment did not isolate the Platzl crowd from the radical right. Weiss Ferdl spelled out his attitude toward politics in the following terms: "Most of us have some work or activity and therefore no time to exercise the authority of government. A king could do that, because he had nothing else to do. He didn't have to stand, as we do, half a day at some office because some papers aren't right."[76] Weiss Ferdl favored restoring the monarchs, Hohenzollern and Wittelsbach, and even privately entertained members of the dethroned Wittelsbach family.[77] Platzl monarchism, however, did not predispose the public against National Socialism, or against other groups of the radical right wing. Hitler, it is important to note, did not begin claiming absolute political power for himself until after the putsch. In the early 1920s, he was the most prominent agitator in a loosely knit band of antirepublican groups.[78] Political issues were not being carefully defined at that time, nor were lines being carefully drawn. It was possible to join in this nostalgia for the Wittelsbachs and still admire and even support Hitler.

Nostalgia was basic to the Platzl spirit, not only with regard to the monarchy but especially with regard to "old Bavaria," the rolling farm districts of Lower Bavaria and the foothills of the Alps, from which nearly half the people of Munich had come. Among the music hall's specialties were "farm comedies" (Bauernpossen), lighthearted skits about life in the country, which were a trademark of Munich's popular stages. This country-centered humor both reflected and articulated an urban audience's yearning for a traditional, rural community. When Weiss Ferdl returned from World War I, he began to devote himself to this form of entertainment. After he became a codirector at Platzl in 1921, he wrote, staged, and published "farm comedies" and even some dramatizations of rural folk customs. Platzl, in the words of a 1928 newspaper article, was "one of the best places of care [Pflegestätten] for genuine old Bavarian, Munich folk art and for traditionally pleasant folk humor."[79] In an explanatory introduction to *In der Spinnstube* (In the Spinning Room),[80] subtitled "An Upper Bavarian Portrait with Song and Dance," Weiss Ferdl wrote: "The evening hours in which girls and boys [*Dirndeln und Burschen,* in traditional Bavarian] of the neighborhood come to visit a farmer are called spinning room, or *Gungl.* The girls bring their spinning wheels along; the boys sing, dance, and get all kinds of fun going." Thus Weiss Ferdl portrayed the "spinning room" as an occasion for folksongs and dances, and for good-natured conversation between the boys and girls: the country as it was, or as new city-dwellers wished it had been.

In *D'Scheidung* (The Divorce),[81] Weiss Ferdl appealed broadly to his audience's affection for their rural past. Set in the country and spoken in heavy Bavarian dialect, it surely delighted the crowd at Platzl. There are four stock characters: Jackl Hegmoser and his wife Kreszenz, a farm couple who have come to their priest, Sebastian Breitenlehner, because they want a divorce; and the priest's cook, Cilli Mollneder. Both the Hegmosers are hot tempered, hardheaded, and sharp-tongued, and they are furious with each other. Their complaints about the marriage are traditional, and meant to amuse; when the priest asks what is wrong, they simultaneously shout:

Kreszenz: Because the whole year long I let myself be o'pressed and plagued and he, that scoundrel, sits around in the tavern—
Hegmoser: Because that o'pressive devil, that miserable, doesn't give me any peace the whole year long—the nagging never quits.

"*Kreszenz:* Weil i' mi' 's ganz' Jahr schind'n und plag'n därfat und er, der Lump, hockt im Wirtshaus—
Hegmoser: Weil der Schindateufi, der elendi, 's ganze Jahr koa Ruah gibt, 's belfern net aufhört."

He values his drinking time with the men, and she feels overworked at home. They can both be quite insulting, but her rages are occasionally balanced by what must have been seen as typically feminine bursts of helpless, self-pitying tears.

The priest's cook, Cilli, is a skinny woman who constantly disturbs her employer about minor household affairs and stands behind his door to hear every detail of the problems brought before him. While the Hegmosers wait for the priest to see them, she offers to instruct them on how to best present their problem, but Jackl thwarts her:

Hegmoser: We'll go right to the smith [*Schmied*], and not to his kid [*Schmiedl*].
Cilli (offended): I would like to request that you speak of a priestly house with a little more respect.
Hegmoser: What did I say about the priestly house?
Cilli: The worthy sir [*der Hochwürdige Herr*] is not a smith. You may not speak so disrespectfully of a worthy man!
Hegmoser: I'm sure it's not because of a smith, but the smith's kid—that's disrespectful. Get it?

In this vein the exchange goes on.

Generally, the priest takes on the role of conciliator, but he is still "a man," as becomes clear at certain points. For example, the unpleasant Cilli interrupts the meeting again, and after she leaves, he says, "The skinny [cooks], thin as wire, those are the cheapest." Although he is a priest, his eyes are not closed to the way women look. Then, he nearly forgets himself when Kreszenz complains that all men stick together because they hear the same crude tavern talk about women:

Priest (energetically): Frau Hegmoser, I would like to energetically deny that. I have never sworn about women in the tavern, because I can't speak on that topic.
Kreszenz: But you listened and didn't say anything and even laughed along.
Priest (angry): Yes, lords, I can't plug up my ears because you women [*Weibsbilder*], you cursed [*vafluach*]—(He coughs.) That's also true. The men [*Mannsbilder*], when they come together, swear about the women, and the women, when they come together, swear about the men. It was always that way.

The priest's spirituality has not blinded him to the eternal battle of the sexes.

Most of *D'Scheidung* goes back and forth along these lines: the Hegmosers fight; the priest tries to calm them; Cilli listens in. In the

process, it reveals a great deal about popular Munich social attitudes. *D'Scheidung*'s standpoint is that of a Bavarian farm village.
For example, it comes out in one of Kreszenz's complaints that
Jackl "hoarded grain" at the time when food was so scarce, "when
the people stole money out of our pockets"—presumably during the
war, when government officials placed a ceiling on grain prices.
That he did this does not bother her nearly as much as the fact that
his name appeared in the local paper as an "unpatriotic grain
hoarder." It was in the country's interest to keep the grain—in his,
and in hers too, except for his having been caught and denounced.
The city's interest was to receive the grain. That such an obviously
rural attitude could be set inoffensively—and Weiss Ferdl wanted to
amuse, not offend—before a city audience indicates how deeply
rooted people in Platzl were in the Bavarian countryside.

The Hegmosers also see the possibility of obtaining a divorce
through country eyes. "That has to work," Jackl states. "In the city
you get divorced two or three times in a short while. It'll get that
way here too, I swear to God." It is true that divorces were becoming more frequent in Munich: in 1901 there were 2.8 per thousand in
the population, and in 1925 already 13.8 per thousand.[82] But it
sounds as though Jackl knows about these city happenings from a
country rumor, exaggerated and mostly wrong. Moreover, if divorce
is headed for the country, it will not arrive soon; the priest cleverly
tricks the Hegmosers out of it. He picks up a large book, supposedly
containing a ceremony of divorce, and begins to read aloud in Latin.
As though the book called for it, he periodically beats the Hegmosers with sticks. Realizing that the thick book probably calls for
more and more beatings, they agree to stay together. With a little in-
genuity, the priest has saved the institution of marriage and repulsed
the entry of this new, irreligious city custom into the country.

D'Scheidung, as an example of "old Bavarian" popular entertainment, gives striking testimony of the quite incomplete adaptation of
Munich's country-born newcomers to urban living. It beckoned the
Platzl crowd into a world of illusion, encouraging them to forget
their city experiences and to revel in their longing for the country. It
is remarkable that men and women who came to see Weiss Ferdl,
who were themselves probably contributing to the rise of divorce
statistics, could be made to laugh at divorce as an absurd and unnec-
essary invention of the city. It is no less remarkable that people who

had missed the grain that farmers hoarded or sold at illegal prices during the war could accept Jackl Hegmoser as a comic figure. No one in early twentieth-century Munich had a keener sense of what people wanted to see and hear, of what messages they wanted to receive, than Weiss Ferdl. His performances clearly indicate the popular yearning for a traditional, rural community. The attractive qualities in his depiction of "old Bavaria"—certainty of work and food on the farm, clearly defined masculine and feminine roles, religion as the basis of morality and behavior—were mirror images of what people lacked in the city. In the early 1920s, when *D'Scheidung* was performed, Munich's inhabitants had been struggling with economic hardships for a decade. Plagued by inflation and even by hunger, they looked back fondly upon times that they remembered or merely imagined to have been more stable. Munich was also confronting them with strange new patterns in the relationship between the sexes: courtships where neither the man nor the woman knew the other's family; divorce; prostitution; working women; homosexuality. Spiritually, people longed for a country priest who would guide them through difficult times. All told, men and women with a rural orientation felt unsettled in the city; it was a comfort, whether true or not, to believe that an easier life lay a generation or two in the past.

At one point in *D'Scheidung,* the Hegmosers grow exasperated with the priest; she threatens to become a Lutheran, and he threatens to become a Jew. The idea would not have been preposterous in Munich, where the religions and races mixed, but would have been inconceivable in the Bavarian countryside, where one could travel all day and find only Catholics. That was something else the Platzl audience missed: the social homogeneity of rural Bavaria. Munich's cosmopolitanism frightened them. They laughed as the Hegmosers threatened to become Lutherans and Jews because they had emotionally resumed places in a community that had no Lutherans and Jews. Weiss Ferdl had enabled them to feel that they belonged to a larger social body not by reconciling them to the society of the present but by transporting them back to the society of the past. This was an illusion, but it was the heart of the folksinger's message. Platzl retraced the time-honored lines between "outsiders" and "insiders" and reassured many of its customers that they were among the latter.

Industrialization, the long-term economic process against which the Platzl crowd was reacting, affected Munich in two ways that proved unfavorable to the young Weimar Republic. First, it threatened the income and status of middle-class groups. While owners of small businesses faced competition from factories and department stores, white-collar workers felt themselves slipping in relation to the working class, which grew in strength and numbers with each passing year.

Second, industrialization brought urbanization in its wake. Bavarian villagers and townspeople were moving into the cities, where industrial and commercial expansion had created opportunities for work. In rapidly growing population centers like Munich, they encountered a new range of problems for which they were unprepared: housing shortages, inadequate sanitation, traffic, noise, social heterogeneity, strange new secular codes of behavior, and so on. Indeed, the city's transformations were so dramatic that even its own natives could not always get accustomed to them. At Platzl, where a middle-class public assembled to enjoy the performances of folksingers like Weiss Ferdl, both sets of discontents are clearly in evidence: the one relating to economic pressure and the other to urban living. Weimar failed to help in both respects; it neither defended the middle class against the twin dangers of capitalism and socialism nor recreated the sense of community that unhappy city-dwellers missed.

Resentment of Jews also fed opposition to the new state. In Platzl's entertainment, Jewish stereotypes reinforced widely held prejudices that the Jews were materialistic, vulgar, and in any case, different. Weiss Ferdl's message articulated and confirmed the popular view of Jews as "outsiders" and thereby enabled thousands of non-Jews to feel like "insiders." Occasionally, the folksinger even received requests from the audience that he make fun of the Jews.[83] In a comic monologue of the early 1920s, he presented—and perhaps himself portrayed—"Herr Sali Kohn," a large-nosed, heavily accented Jewish peddler who defends Jews against the charge that they were responsible for losing the war. Reducing the war to a business calculation, Herr Kohn maintains that it could have been stopped earlier if Hindenburg had appealed to the enemy's financial interests: "You give a piece here, I give a piece there. We don't want to completely ruin a good deal." The audience surely laughed when they heard Herr Kohn imagining that these lines would come from Hindenburg's stoic mouth. The hilarity rises at the end of the monologue, as this Jew admits that whereas he formerly sold Hindenburg's picture, "it's not doing so well. Now I'm selling swastikas—they're going great."[84] Feeling superior to Herr Kohn was not difficult; he is an amusing character only because of his utter lack of dignity. Neither sensitive to the ideals for which Germany had gone to war nor principled enough to be outraged over Nazi anti-Semitism, he is wholly absorbed in petty considerations of profit and loss. Moreover, by claiming that the sale of swastikas has been profitable, he embodies the widespread belief that the Jews were continuing to prosper at times when most Germans were beset by economic hardships.

Compared to the statement that Hitler was shortly to make in *Mein Kampf* that the Jew "is and remains . . . a sponger who like a noxious bacillus keeps spreading as soon as a favorable medium invites him,"[85] Weiss Ferdl's portrayal of "Herr Sali Kohn" does not seem very severe. The National Socialist leader was a politician, of course, whereas Weiss Ferdl was an entertainer. Their difference of attitude lies deeper, however, than their difference of profession; they had fundamentally opposed views on whether to tolerate "outsiders." This is clear in a reply Weiss Ferdl made to the suggestion that he was anti-Prussian. Although he often joked at the Prussians' expense, he wrote, "I would be the unhappiest person if there were no Prussians."[86] That was no doubt true; he needed the Prussians as objects of satire. It even gratified him when Prussians were in the house at Platzl, because their presence added to the "old Bavarian" faithful's sense of group identity.[87] His attitude toward the Jews was similar. They were welcome at Platzl, and Weiss Ferdl later emphasized that a Jewish veterans' association once presented him with a wreath in appreciation of his entertainment.[88] As far as he was concerned, "outsiders" served to build up the confidence of "insiders"; there was no cause to physically exclude and much less to physically harm them. Nevertheless, a character like "Herr Sali Kohn" reflected and gave shape to the popular conception that Jews were self-seeking and unprincipled. In this way, the folksinger's comic treatment of the Jews formed part of the climate of middle-class prejudices that proved so stifling to the Weimar Republic.

Another theme of Weiss Ferdl's postwar entertainment, one that emerged in several songs, was patriotism. The folksinger deeply resented both Germany's defeat and what he considered to be her betrayal by the signers of the Versailles Treaty. In "Rings herum, Rings herum" (Surrounded, Surrounded), he calls upon Germans to engage in some form of counterattack and to ignore the Republic, which was conducting a foreign policy of moderation:

> Hand in hand, all together, away
>   with the parties
> The homeland, the homeland, the
>   fatherland is worth liberating!

> "Hand in Hand, all mit 'nand, weg mit den Parteien
> 's Heimatland, 's Heimatland, 's Vaterland gilt es zu befreien!"

Weiss Ferdl tended to see international politics in terms of simple moral precepts. Germany was a Christian nation of "law and honor," where people believed in "loving thy neighbor as thyself," but she was "surrounded" by unscrupulous, greedy, and vindictive neighbors:

Over in the east the Russian sits, brewing
    Bolshevism
The Pole and the Czech are watching if there's
    something they could steal.
England has covered up, just the way it wants
    to,
And wild France shows her teeth, would love
    to eat us up.
In a word, I'd say, an awkward situation.

"Im Osten drob'n der Russe sitzt, tut Bolschewismus brauen,
der Pole und der Tscheche spitzt, ob 's nicht was gibt zu klauen.
Old England hat sich eingedeckt nach eigenem Ermessen
und Frankreich wild die Zähne bleckt, möcht uns am liebsten fressen.
Mit einem Wort, ich sage, a' recht verzwickte Lage."[89]

"Rings herum" fails to ask whether Germany had in any way brought this situation upon herself. This omission is to be expected, however, because Weiss Ferdl had immersed himself in a German-

centered, and particularly Munich-centered world. The reasons behind English or French policy never occurred to him; he thought
only of their effects as he saw and felt them in Munich. And there
were plenty of these: perhaps 50,000 refugees from annexed territories like Alsace-Lorraine; children without fathers and wives
without husbands, since 13,600 Munich men—nearly one in twelve
between the ages of eighteen and fifty—had died because of the war;
and wounded veterans.[90] It is beyond doubt that this suffering
moved Weiss Ferdl. Like many Germans, he blamed the nation's
enemies and felt an urgent need for Germany to be strong again. He
helped by entertaining Munich's patriotic, paramilitary groups[91]
and by letting Platzl's audience feel the strength of their numbers
while he expressed the bitterness they had harbored since the defeat.

Although patriotism was a central attitude in Weiss Ferdl's entertainment, it did not preclude a deep attachment to the white
and blue colors of Bavaria. For example, the following song cast a
sarcastic light upon the province's relations with Berlin after the
Republican Defense Law had forced the disbanding of the Einwohnerwehr:

> We love all our German brothers—
> We want to emphasize it again.
> Send a lot of taxes up there all the time,
> Are filled with national joy.
> Know the Republican Defense Law quite well.
> Hollare Holaridurio
> And our little flag is white and blue.[92]

This was one of Bavaria's main grievances around 1922; for contributing to the Republic's treasury, she should have the right to defend herself against the forces of internal disorder. This song deals
with Bavaria's mistreatment by the federal German government in
much the same way that "Rings herum" deals with Germany's mistreatment by the other nations of Europe. In both cases, the folksinger's old principle of just exchange appears. Naturally, he presented the conflicts of this era as being between honorable victims,
with whom he identified, and callous villains. Regarding the Republican Defense Law, he cast the government in Berlin in the role
of the villain. Nevertheless, Weiss Ferdl never conceived of Bavaria

as an independent nation. Although he resented Prussia's predominance in the German nation and opposed the Republic after 1918, nothing he said on stage contradicts his later claim that "whereas I was a Bavarian through and through . . . like all good Bavarians I always felt myself to be also a German and was proud of my larger fatherland."[93] Of course, the fatherland he meant was the Empire. Nostalgia was part of the Platzl spirit; there was nothing peculiar about Weiss Ferdl seeing himself as the loyal subject of an empire that had ceased to exist, or of kings who had lost their thrones.

6

The Turn to National Socialism

Munich's late nineteenth- and early twentieth-century industrial and commercial growth affected the city's popular entertainment in two ways. First, it gave rise to fears of lost income and of lost status in the social group that made up the main part of the popular audience: the middle class. By dominating the public, these fears naturally commanded the attention of the performers. Folksingers Karl Valentin and Weiss Ferdl were free to address the fears in whatever terms they chose; had they failed to address them at all, their careers would have suffered. The widespread acclaim and affection that they enjoyed did not rest upon their talents alone, but rather upon their use of these talents to transmit messages of reassurance. People who worried that industrial forces were gradually turning them into "outsiders" by degrading them to the working class's level heard from the folksingers that their "insider" positions were secure.

Second, the economic changes of the period brought new forms of entertainment in their wake, forms that were already competing with the traditional folksingers in the 1920s: film, jazz, dance bands, and so on.[1] Indeed, it is appropriate to speak of an industrialization and commercialization of popular culture. The technological spirit that was rendering the productive methods of tradesmen's workshops obsolete had also produced the film; the lines of transport and communication that had opened Munich to international markets also opened it to jazz. With noticeable bitterness, Karl Valentin wrote in 1927 that "Munich is being 'Americanized.'" He proceeded to complain that "the modern American musical ruckus [Radaumusik]" was inspiring people to learn "perverse dances."[2] Weiss Ferdl viewed this with more equanimity. Platzl, he remarked confidently in 1933, "had survived the jazz racket [Jazz-Rummel]."[3] Despite their personal success, however, both folksingers would have realized that the new cultural trends posed a threat to their profession. Karl Valentin and Weiss Ferdl were not only among the best of the Munich folksingers but also among the last. No less than the disappointments of their early work lives, the fact that they were both masters of a declining trade sensitized them to the problems and concerns of their middle-class audience.

The recurrence of certain political and social themes in Karl Valentin's and Weiss Ferdl's Munich small-stage entertainment between around 1906 and 1923 points to the basic continuity of middle-class attitudes, sentiments, and ideas from the Empire to the early years of the Republic. This is not to suggest that neither folksinger underwent an artistic development. To the contrary, Valentin's skills at generating laughter reached the point that he was invited to display them in the legitimate theater in 1922, an honor that would have been practically unimaginable in the days of his "Russischer Salat." Weiss Ferdl's advance was even more clear-cut. In 1906, he was still a decade away from writing his own material; during World War I, the song leader became a songwriter.

Of greater relevance for this study is the treatment of political and social issues in the folksingers' acts. In this regard, the continuity of popular entertainment before and after the war is evident. The characters that Valentin portrayed in *Der Firmling* and *Das Christbaumbrettl* at the height of the economic crisis bear a strong resemblance to the "poor, skinny man" of 1907; Valentin's method of presenting these unfortunate buffoons to his audience and of endowing them with a social meaning essentially did not change. First, he would cleverly identify these figures with the social milieu of his public. Then, he would proceed to demonstrate that they no longer belonged to this milieu, that they had fallen into society's marginal spaces. He reassured the middle-class men and women of his audience by confronting them with an image of social failure and decline, and by letting them draw the conclusion that their hardships were small by comparison. Weiss Ferdl's much more overt social and political attitudes also exhibit a constancy between the prewar and postwar periods. The pronounced themes of the early 1920s—yearning for a traditional "old Bavarian" community, resentment of Jews, and patriotism—hark back to the entertainment for which Platzl had been well known prior to 1914. Antisocialism grew in importance and in emphasis after the war; it did not represent a new outlook, but rather expressed hatred for a revolution that had been led by Jews, that had threatened middle-class property, and that had offended German national feelings. When Weiss Ferdl voiced his opposition to Weimar from the Platzl stage, he was appealing to sentiments that he himself had been articulating for two decades.

Against this background of long-standing social and political attitudes, the support that the middle class gave the Revolution in late

1918 appears to have been a brief aberration in the historical course that links the pre-1914 world with the Weimar Republic. Tired of the war and of its unbearable hardships, middle-class men and women joined in the call for an end to the regime that had prosecuted it with such stubborn determination. It is hard to imagine how the Republic could have been more disillusioning for tradesmen, shopkeepers, white-collar workers, and their families. By elevating Jews into positions of leadership, by attacking the institution of private property, and by desecrating the national ideals that had survived the war, the new state fell abruptly in middle-class esteem. Rather than soothe insider and outsider anxieties, it aroused them.

IN THE EARLY 1920s, when Munich's middle class was providing folksingers Karl Valentin and Weiss Ferdl with an audience, it was also providing Adolf Hitler's National Socialist movement with supporters. What can be learned from these performers' acts about the middle class's reasons for turning to the NSDAP? In the case of Valentin, very little ties his entertainment to popular views on National Socialism. His *Die Raubritter vor München* even criticizes the militaristic trend with which the Nazis were associated and thus would appear to reveal his public's disapproval of Hitler, except that the play was given in a code that the public may not have understood. *Der Firmling* and *Das Christbaumbrettl* deal with the economic despair that made the middle class vulnerable to Hitler's appeals, but neither play goes on to indicate how the middle class responded to those appeals.

Weiss Ferdl's relationship to National Socialism bears more consideration. Antisocialism, yearning for a preindustrial community, prejudice against Jews, and patriotism: each of these middle-class attitudes found a voice at Platzl, each had antirepublican overtones, and each represented a potential connection between the middle class and the NSDAP. This was recognized by no less than Hitler himself, who not only had Weiss Ferdl invited to perform at party gatherings but also frequently led a small Nazi entourage to see the folksinger appear at Platzl.[4] Apparently, the Nazi leader left no record of his motives for doing so, but it is plain to see that being at the music hall afforded him some valuable public exposure.

If Weiss Ferdl had any reservations about his illustrious right-wing guest, they dissolved at the time of the Nazi putsch. Five weeks later, he figuratively but clearly expressed his support for its leaders in a letter to a local newspaper: "Berlin newspapers have maliciously reproached us for always conducting our politics of rebellion in beer halls," he wrote. "They do not know the situation. In Bavaria we need steam for politics. Without steam, the soul of the Bavarian people never boils."[5] He also voiced his sympathy for the Nazis on stage at Platzl.[6] Weiss Ferdl and the thousands of ordinary middle-class men and women for whom he spoke fervently appreciated the Nazis' deed and admired their courage.

This does not establish that "The Dachauers" or their middle-class Munich audience had backed or condoned National Socialism prior to 9 November 1923. Indeed, there is no record of Weiss Ferdl expressing himself about the Nazis or about any other group of the extreme right before the putsch. It would be mistaken to construe his support of the counterrevolutionary Einwohnerwehr before it was banned in 1921 as support for Hitler; no evidence shows that he followed the tide of many ex-Einwohnerwehr members who joined the NSDAP. Nor should one infer from his opposition to the Weimar Republic that he and the Platzl clientele adhered to National Socialist ideology; the middle class's rejection of Weimar was the climate within which the Hitler movement thrived, but this does not mean that those who rejected the new state inevitably became Hitler's supporters.

Weiss Ferdl's postwar entertainment indicates that many members of the middle class held the young Republic in contempt and approved of the Nazi putsch of 1923. But his performances fail to reveal the process by which the middle class came to accept Hitler. When did tradesmen, shopkeepers, and white-collar workers first become aware of the NSDAP? How did their perceptions of it change between 1919 and 1924? Which aspects of Nazi propaganda appealed to them most? How decisive was the putsch in the rise of Nazi support? Weiss Ferdl's acts do not contain answers to these questions.

An examination of the relationship between the Munich middle class and National Socialism would require a broader base of evidence than popular entertainment offers. It could include the following kinds of documents: newspapers and other periodicals that had wide middle-class readerships; middle-class occupational journals; and the Nazi press, in order to see how the NSDAP was being presented to the public. Interviews with people who were alive and old enough to respond to politics in the early 1920s would also be quite valuable, though the number of possible informants is naturally becoming quite small.

On the basis of this study of the Munich folksingers, three hypotheses appear worth pursuing. First, the atmosphere of political and economic crisis in the early 1920s may have disoriented middle-class people until they no longer cared about or even saw the lines that separated their social and political attitudes from National Socialist ideology. There was enough in common between their resentment over Versailles and the NSDAP's nationalistic fury, between their "old Bavarian" farm villages and the Nazi vision of a Germanic rural society, that the differences could be overlooked. Even the viciousness of Nazi anti-Semitism may not have alienated men and women who were themselves hostile toward Jews and suspicious of the Jewish influence in postwar Germany. In these turbulent years, the Nazis may have capitalized upon the inability of middle-class people to overcome their anxieties and focus upon the shadings of their political environment.

Second, it may have been the Nazis' determination to act more than their doctrines that generated middle-class interest and support in the early 1920s. Tradesmen, shopkeepers, white-collar workers, and their families saw themselves besieged by political and economic events. They embraced the NSDAP because it was poised for a counterattack upon the forces by which they felt threatened: industrialization; the modern city; the Jews; Versailles; and Marxist socialism. Perhaps Hitler succeeded at amassing support in postwar Munich less by converting people to his dogma than by stressing his readiness to fight in their behalf. He established himself as the "insider's" champion, the instrument of a great antisocialist, anti-industrial, and anti-Jewish national revival.

The third hypothesis emerges out of my conclusion that the social and political attitudes of the economically endangered middle class remained basically constant between the prewar and postwar periods, in a time of political upheaval. Further study should test the assumption that middle-class support for National Socialism, like middle-class opposition to the Weimar Republic, represented a continuation of pre-1914 views. The men and women who turned to Hitler may have been not only reacting against the Revolution of 1918–19 but also returning to the structure of attitudes within which they had felt secure before World War I.

Notes
Selected Bibliography
Index

ABBREVIATIONS

BAK   Bundesarchiv Koblenz

BHStAM   Bayerisches Hauptstaatsarchiv München

MSPD   Münchner Staatsarchiv/Polizeidirektion

ThMM   Theatermuseum München

StAM   Stadtarchiv München

VNK   "Karl-Valentin-Nachlass," Theatermuseum des Instituts für Theaterwissenschaft der Universität Köln

Notes

1. A City of Entertainment and a Sense of Decline

1. StAM, "Zeitungsausschnittsammlung—Weiss Ferdl," a 3 April 1924 article of the *Münchner-Augsburger Abend Zeitung.*

2. Weiss Ferdl, *Bayerische Schmankerln,* ed. Bertl Weiss (Munich: Süddeutscher Verlag, 1960), p. 34.

3. See Ludwig M. Schneider, *Die populäre Kritik an Staat und Gesellschaft in München, 1886–1914: Ein Beitrag zur Vorgeschichte der Münchner Revolution von 1918/19* (Munich: Stadtarchiv, 1975), pp. 4, 109–110; on the history of the Munich popular audience in the nineteenth century, see Thea Braatz, *Das Kleinbürgertum in München und seine Öffentlichkeit von 1830–1870: Ein Beitrag zur Mentalitätsforschung* (Munich: Stadtarchiv, 1972), pp. 93–95; and Eugen Weigl, *Die Münchner Volkstheater im 19. Jahrhundert, 1817–1900* (Munich: Stadtarchiv, 1961), pp. 85–86.

4. See Werner Maser, *Die Frühgeschichte der NSDAP* (Bonn and Frankfurt am Main: Athenäum Verlag, 1965); and Michael H. Kater, "Zur Soziographie der frühen NSDAP," *Vierteljahreshefte für Zeitgeschichte,* 19 (January 1971): 124–159. Citing Maser and Kater is not an attempt to brush aside the argument of Harold J. Gordon, Jr., that youth of all classes, radicalized by the war, became the central element of National Socialism. One can certainly ask, however, to what extent the war actually detached young people from their social backgrounds. Here, it is relevant to note that Gordon does not deny strong lower middle-class representation in the early Nazi party but only disputes its relative importance. See Harold J. Gordon, Jr., *Hitler and the Beer-Hall Putsch* (Princeton: Princeton University Press, 1972), pp. 7–15. An extremely useful synthesizing article is Hellmuth Auerbach, "Hitlers politische Lehrjahre und die Münchner Gesellschaft, 1919–23," *Vierteljahreshefte für Zeitgeschichte,* 25 (January 1977): 1–45.

5. See Karl Bosl, *München: Bürgerstadt-Residenz-heimliche Hauptstadt Deutschlands* (Stuttgart and Aalen: Konrad Theiss Verlag, 1971), p. 104; Carl Fritz, *München als Industriestadt* (Berlin: Puttkamer & Mühlbrecht Verlag, 1913), pp. 15–18; and Schneider, *Die populäre Kritik,* pp. 79–85. The following works are also useful on Munich's society and economy: Arthur Cohen and Edmund Simon, *Geschichte der Handelskammer München seit ihrer Gründung (1869): Bei-*

trag zur Wirtschaftsgeschichte der letzten Jahrzehnte (Munich: Industrie- und Handelskammer, 1926); and Wolfgang Zorn, "Bayerns Gewerbe, Handel und Verkehr, 1806–1970," in *Handbuch der bayerischen Geschichte,* vol. 4, pt. 2, ed. Max Spindler (Munich: C. H. Beck'sche Verlagsbuchhandlung, 1975), pp. 808–848. For a general perspective on the middle class throughout Germany, see Heinrich August Winkler, *Mittelstand, Demokratie und Nationalsozialismus* (Cologne: Kiepenheuer & Witsch Verlag, 1972), and "From Social Protectionism to National Socialism: The German Small-Business Movement in Comparative Perspective," *Journal of Modern History,* 48 (March 1976): 1–18; Robert Gellately, *The Politics of Economic Despair: Shopkeepers and German Politics 1890–1914* (London and Beverly Hills: SAGE Publications, 1974); and Herman Lebovics, *Social Conservatism and the Middle Classes in Germany, 1914–33* (Princeton: Princeton University Press, 1969), pp. 4–10.

6. See Schneider, *Die populäre Kritik,* pp. 85–89. On white-collar workers nationally, see Jürgen Kocka, *Klassengesellschaft im Kriege: Deutsche Sozialgeschichte 1914–18* (Göttingen: Vandenhoeck & Ruprecht, 1973), and "The First World War and the 'Mittelstand': German Artisans and White-Collar Workers," *Journal of Contemporary History,* 8 (January 1973): 101–123.

7. See Winkler, *Mittelstand, Demokratie und Nationalsozialismus;* Kocka, *Klassengesellschaft im Kriege;* and specifically on the war, Gerald D. Feldman, *Army, Industry, and Labor in Germany 1914–1918* (Princeton: Princeton University Press, 1966), pp. 464–473. On conditions in Munich, see Zorn, "Bayerns Gewerbe," pp. 821–826; and Cohen and Simon, *Geschichte der Handelskammer München,* pp. 385–527.

8. Thomas Mann, "Rede zur Eröffnung der 'Münchner Gesellschaft,' " in *Der Zwiebelfisch: Zeitschrift über Bücher, Kultur und Kunst,* 20 (1926–27): 3–5.

9. See Schneider, *Die populäre Kritik;* also, Karl Bosl, "Gesellschaft und Politik in Bayern vor dem Ende der Monarchie: Beiträge zu einer sozialen und politischen Strukturanalyse," *Zeitschrift für bayerische Landesgeschichte,* 28 (1965): 1–31; and Karl Möckl, "Gesellschaft und Politik während der Ära des Prinzregenten Luitpolds," in Karl Bosl, ed., *Bayern im Umbruch* (Munich and Vienna: Oldenbourg Verlag, 1969), pp. 5–36.

10. See, for example, Karl Valentin, *Karl Valentins Lachkabinett,* ed. Gerhard Pallmann (Munich: Piper Verlag, 1951), p. 6; and Arnolt Bronnen, *Begegnungen mit Schauspielern* (Berlin: Henschelverlag Kunst und Gesellschaft, 1967), pp. 126–127.

11. Henri Bergson, *Das Lachen* (Meisenheim am Glan: Westkulturverlag Anton Hain, 1948), pp. 11–17, 45–51, 107–109; Anton C. Zijderveld, *Humor und Gesellschaft, Eine Soziologie des Humors und des Lachens* (Graz, Vienna, and Cologne: Styria Verlag, 1976), pp. 56–58, 150–166, 174.

12. See Schneider, *Die populäre Kritik,* pp. 90–120.

13. "Die Komiker," *Münchner Stadtanzeiger,* 23 February 1951, p. 3; see also, Hermann Sinsheimer, *Gelebt im Paradies* (Munich: Richard Pflaum Verlag, 1953), p. 180.

14. On the terms, see *Münchner Woche: Vergnügungs- und Sportanzeiger,* vols. 1–2 (1919–20); see also Schneider, *Die populäre Kritik,* p. 103.

15. See Schneider, *Die populäre Kritik,* pp. 105–106, for an 1886 letter from

folksinger Johann Kögl to the Bavarian Prince Regent Luitpold, in which Kögl describes the typical audience as coming from the "middle and tradesman class," and then refers to the presence of "workers and tradesmen"; also MSPD 3813-II, "Apollo-Theater," for police reports from the years 1907, 1909, and 1915, which portray the audience as made up of young "workers and servants," "apprentices and children with adults" (1907), and of "soldiers" (1909), and then as "lower middle-class" (1915); see Bronnen, *Begegnungen mit Schauspielern,* pp. 126-127, where the author presents folksinger Karl Valentin's postwar audience as "lower middle-class"; and also Lion Feuchtwanger's literary reference to a folksinger's (Valentin's) "largely lower middle-class public," in Helmut Schwimmer, *Karl Valentin: Analyse zur Sprache und Literatur* (Munich: Oldenbourg Verlag, 1977), p. 131. Dr. Richard Lemp of the Munich City Library's manuscript collection helped in conversation to draw this social picture of the folksinger audience. See also Weiss Ferdl, *Bayerische Schmankerln,* p. 34; and Anton Sailer, also a folksinger, referring to a public of "common people" in "Zur Psychologie der Volkssänger," *Jugend,* 22 (Special Issue, 1935): 325.

16. See Schneider, *Die populäre Kritik,* pp. 77–78; on the cultural relationship between Munich's middle and working classes in the nineteenth century, see Werner K. Blessing, "Zur Analyse politischer Mentalität und Ideologie der Unterschichten im 19. Jahrhundert," *Zeitschrift für bayerische Landesgeschichte,* 34 (1971): 768–816. Lacking in Munich was a proletarian culture of the kind that Dieter Langewiesche has found in Vienna. See his "Arbeiterkultur in Österreich: Aspekte, Tendenzen und Thesen," in *Arbeiterkultur,* ed. Gerhard A. Ritter (Königstein im Taunus: Verlagsgruppe Athenäum, Hain, Scriptor, Hanstein, 1979), pp. 40–57.

17. See Bronnen, *Begegnungen mit Schauspielern,* pp. 126–127, for a description of the public waiting to see Valentin appear. On snobbish upper-class attitudes, see VNK, Album 2, an article of the *Münchner Neueste Nachrichten,* 16 July 1913; and Erwin and Elisabeth Münz, eds., *Geschriebenes von und an Karl Valentin* (Munich: Süddeutscher Verlag, 1978), pp. 56–59.

18. See Weiss Ferdl, *Weiss Ferdl erzählt sein Leben* (Munich: Richard Pflaum Verlag, 1953), p. 89; Kurt Horwitz, "Karl Valentin in einer anderen Zeit," in *Sturzflüge im Zuschauerraum der gesammelten Werke,* vol. 2 (Munich: Piper Verlag, 1969), p. 13; Schneider, *Die populäre Kritik,* p. 110; and, specifically raising the question of upper-class interest in popular entertainment, Weigl, *Die Münchner Volkstheater,* pp. 85–86.

19. For an example of the assumption that the folksingers' origins were strictly Bavarian, see Sinsheimer, *Gelebt im Paradies,* p. 178; Vienna tavern entertainment is discussed in Gerhard Eberstaller, *Zirkus und Varieté in Wien* (Vienna and Munich: Jugend und Volk Verlag, 1974), pp. 44–49; and in Josef Koller, *Das Wiener Volkssängertum in alter und neuer Zeit* (Vienna: Gerlach und Wiedling Verlag, 1931). Popular songs can be found in Rudolf Wolkan, *Wiener Volkslieder aus fünf Jahrhunderten* (Vienna: Wiener-Bibliophil Gesellschaft, 1920). On the theaters, see Eduard Bauernfeld, *Erinnerungen aus Alt-Wien,* ed. Josef Bindtner (Vienna: Wiener Druck, 1923), pp 56–57, 321–323; Erich Joachim May, *Wiener Volkskomödie im Vormärz* (Berlin: Henschelverlag, 1975); Otto Rommel, *Die Alt-Wiener Volkskomödie* (Vienna: Schroll Verlag, 1952), and *Jo-*

hann Nestroy: Ein Beitrag zur Geschichte der Wiener Volkskomödie (Vienna: Schroll Verlag, 1930); Johann Nestroy, *Ausgewählte Werke,* ed. Hans Weigel (Gütersloh: Sieg Mohn Verlag, 1962); Hartwin Gromes, "Vom Alt-Wiener Volksstück zur Wiener Operette" (Ph.D. diss., University of Munich, 1967), pp. 15–41; Weigl, *Die Münchner Volkstheater,* pp. 6–13, 19, 25–40; and Gudrun Kohl, *Vom Papa Geis bis Karl Valentin* (Munich: Wilhelm Unverhau Verlag, 1971), pp. 6–7.

20. Rommel, *Die Alt-Wiener-Volkstheater,* p. 994.

21. May, *Wiener Volkskomödie,* pp. 96–97. 227–228.

22. C. A. Riesel, "Der Volkssänger," *Jugend,* 22 (Special Issue, 1935): 338–340.

23. Werner K. Blessing, "Zur Analyse politischer Mentalität und Ideologie der Unterschichten im 19. Jahrhundert," *Zeitschrift für bayerische Landesgeschichte,* 34 (1971): 768–816.

24. Gregory H. Singleton, "Popular Culture or the Culture of the Populace?" *Journal of Popular Culture,* 11 (Summer 1977): 255; see also, Herbert J. Gans, *Popular Culture and High Culture: An Analysis and Evaluation of Taste* (New York: Basic Books, 1974), p. ix.

25. Valentin, *Karl Valentins Lachkabinett,* p. 6.

26. Ernst Hoferichter, *Vom Prinzregenten bis Karl Valentin* (Munich, Basel, and Vienna: Bayerischer Landwirtschaftsverlag, 1966), pp. 122–123.

27. René Prevot introducing Weiss Ferdl, *Weiss Ferdl guat troffa* (Munich: Hugendubel Verlag, 1933), p. 10.

28. Sinsheimer, *Gelebt im Paradies,* p. 179.

29. Rudolf Heberle, *From Democracy to Nazism: A Regional Case Study on Political Parties in Germany* (Baton Rouge: Louisiana State University Press, 1945).

30. See, for example, Winkler, *Mittelstand, Demokratie und Nationalsozialismus;* Gellately, *The Politics of Economic Despair;* and Kocka, *Klassengesellschaft im Kriege.*

31. See Anthony Nicholls, "Hitler and the Bavarian Background to German National Socialism," in *German Democracy and the Triumph of Hitler,* ed. Anthony Nicholls and Erich Matthias (London: George Allen & Unwin, 1971), pp. 100–101.

32. This criticism is meant for such works as the following: Gordon, *Hitler and the Beer-Hall Putsch;* Maser, *Die Frühgeschichte der NSDAP;* Albrecht Tyrell, *Vom "Trommler" zum "Führer": Der Wandel im Selbstverständnis Hitlers zwischen 1919 und 1924* (Munich: Wilhelm Fink Verlag, 1975); and Dietrich Orlow, *The History of the Nazi Party: 1919–33,* vol. 1 (Pittsburgh: University of Pittsburgh Press, 1969).

33. See Schneider, *Die populäre Kritik;* see also, Bosl, "Gesellschaft und Politik in Bayern"; and Möckl, "Gesellschaft und Politik während der Ära des Prinzregenten."

34. Karl-Ludwig Ay, *Die Entstehung einer Revolution: Die Volksstimmung in Bayern während des ersten Weltkrieges* (Berlin: Duncker & Humblot Verlag, 1968); Georg Kalmer, "Beamtenschaft und Revolution: Eine sozialgeschichtliche Studie über Voraussetzungen und Wirklichkeit des Problems," in Bosl, *Bayern im*

Umbruch, pp. 201–262; Willy Albrecht, *Landtag und Regierung in Bayern am Vorabend der Revolution von 1918* (Berlin: Duncker & Humblot Verlag, 1968); and Eberhard Kolb, "Geschichte und Vorgeschichte der Revolution von 1918/19 in Bayern," *Neue Politische Literatur,* 16 (1971): 383–394.

35. See Schneider, *Die populäre Kritik,* pp. 89, 390; Bosl, "Gesellschaft und Politik in Bayern," p. 2.

2. The Middle-Class Origins of Munich Entertainers Karl Valentin and Weiss Ferdl

1. For the statistics of Munich's population growth, see *1875–1975. 100 Jahre Städtestatistik in München: Statistisches Handbuch der Landeshauptstadt München* (Munich: Carl Gerber Verlag, 1975), p. 66; for official documents relating to the father's career, see Münz, *Geschriebenes von und an Karl Valentin,* pp. 20–27; on the Au, see *Au, Giesing, Haidhausen: 100 Jahre bei München 1854–1954* (Munich: Süddeutscher Verlag, 1954), pp. 20–23; an example of his references to furniture transport can be found in Karl Valentin, *Der Knabe Karl* (Berlin: Paul Steegemann Verlag, 1951), p. 1; this basic early family history is recounted by Valentin's daughter in Bertl Böheim-Valentin, *"Du bleibst da und zwar sofort!"* (Munich: Piper Verlag, 1971), pp. 10–13.

2. See Valentin, *Der Knabe Karl,* pp. 13, 16–17, 19, 22; and Böheim-Valentin, *Du bleibst da,* pp. 10–13.

3. Böheim-Valentin, *Du bleibst da,* pp. 12–13. Obviously, Valentin's daughter got most of her information from her grandmother, with whom she lived as a girl.

4. See Theo Riegler, *Das Liesl Karlstadt Buch* (Munich: Süddeutscher Verlag, 1961), pp. 31–32; Ernst Hoferichter, *Jahrmarkt meines Lebens* (Munich, Vienna, and Basel: BLV, 1963), pp. 138, 148.

5. Valentin, *Der Knabe Karl,* p. 6.

6. Ibid., pp. 5, 8–13, 18–21.

7. Böheim-Valentin, *Du bleibst da,* p. 12.

8. Ibid., p. 13; Valentin, *Der Knabe Karl,* pp. 13, 19, 16, 22.

9. Valentin, *Der Knabe Karl,* p. 8; see also, pp. 17–18.

10. Ibid., pp. 12, 26.

11. See Weigl, *Die Münchner Volkstheater,* p. 13; see also Braatz, *Das Kleinbürgertum in München,* pp. 93–95.

12. Michael Schulte, ed., *Karl Valentin in Selbstzeugnissen und Bilddokumenten* (Reinbek bei Hamburg: Rowohlt Verlag, 1968), p. 12; Valentin, *Karl Valentins Lachkabinett,* pp. 14–15; Ludwig Schrott, *Münchner Alltag in acht Jahrhunderten* (Munich: Hugendubel Verlag, 1975), p. 235.

13. See *Salvator-Saison 1909* (Munich: Selbstverlag der Paulanerbrauerei, 1909); and *Au, Giesing, Haidhausen,* pp. 44.

14. Karl Valentin, "Karl Valentin erzählt," in *Karl Valentins Lachkabinett,* p. 11.

15. Zorn, "Bayerns Gewerbe," p. 813.

16. Cited in Siegfried Obermeier, *Münchens goldene Jahre* (Munich: C. Bertelsmann Verlag, 1976), p. 108.

17. Andreas Welsch, *Münchner Volksleben in Lied und Wort,* vol. 2 (Munich: J. Kramer, 1887), p. 14.

18. For general remarks about the place of taverns in Munich society, see Schneider, *Die populäre Kritik,* pp. 100–101; and Obermeier, *Münchens goldene Jahre,* p. 109. Valentin describes his performance of the duty, against which he seems to have rebelled, in *Der Knabe Karl,* p. 20.

19. On Valentin, see *Der Knabe Karl,* pp. 21 and 12, respectively, on the interest in electricity and bicycles. For general information of this kind, see Ernst von Destouches, *Das Oktoberfest München 1810–1910* (Munich: J. Lindauersche Buchhandlung, 1910), pp. 38–44; Ludwig Hollweck, *München: von der Besiedlung der Münchner Gegend bis 1967 in Stichworten erzählt* (Munich: Wilhelm Unverhau Verlag, 1968), pp. 135–150; Schrott, *Münchner Alltag,* pp. 233–234.

20. Valentin, *Der Knabe Karl,* pp. 12, 16; see also, Karl Seybold, *Sechzig Jahre Tätigkeit im Münchner Feuerlöschwesen, 1866–1926* (Munich: Buchdruckerei Ph. L. Jung, 1926), pp. 29, 57, 61. Munich's first-aid units held a similar fascination. See *Der Knabe Karl,* p. 17; and generally, *100 Jahre Rotkreuzdienst in der Stadt und im Landkreis München* (Munich, 1975).

21. Valentin, *Der Knabe Karl,* p. 12.

22. Hannes König, "Versuch einer Charakteristik Karl Valentins," *Katalog des Valentin-Museums* (Munich: Werbedruck Rudolf Stepanek, 1960), p. 14; Ludwig Hollweck, "Bei Papa Geis im Oberpollinger," *Münchner Leben,* 15 (May 1970): 36.

23. Valentin, *Der Knabe Karl,* p. 26; on Maxstadt, see Joseph Maria Lutz, *Die Münchner Volkssänger* (Munich: Süddeutscher Verlag, 1956), pp. 30–31.

24. Valentin, *Der Knabe Karl,* p. 21.

25. Ibid.; and Valentin, "Karl Valentin erzählt," in *Karl Valentins Lachkabinett,* p. 12.

26. Valentin, *Der Knabe Karl,* pp. 11, 23; on the question of work-free Sundays, see Cohen and Simon, *Geschichte der Handelskammer München,* pp. 217, 287–288.

27. Böheim-Valentin, *Du bleibst da,* pp. 16–18.

28. Karl Valentin, "Wie ich Volkssänger wurde," *Bayerischer Hauskalender* (1928), p. 128.

29. Valentin, "Karl Valentin erzählt," in *Karl Valentins Lachkabinett,* pp. 14–15.

30. Valentin, *Der Knabe Karl,* p. 26; Böheim-Valentin, *Du bleibst da,* p. 15.

31. Schneider, *Die populäre Kritik,* p. 94.

32. Zorn, "Bayerns Gewerbe," pp. 811–812; Schneider, *Die populäre Kritik,* pp. 67, 79–82; Fritz, *München als Industriestadt;* and Emil Heberlein, *Das Kleingewerbe in Bayern vor dem Krieg 1914/15 und die Bestrebungen zu seiner Hebung* (Munich, Berlin, and Leipzig: J. Schweitzer Verlag, 1915), pp. 3–6.

33. Hoferichter, *Jahrmarkt meines Lebens,* p. 143. See also Böheim-Valentin, *Du bleibst da,* p. 23; Valentin, "Wie ich Volkssänger wurde," p. 128; and Münz, *Geschriebenes von und an Karl Valentin,* p. 32.

34. Schneider, *Die populäre Kritik,* p. 36.

35. In Karl Valentin, *Alles von Karl Valentin,* ed. Michael Schulte (Munich: Piper Verlag, 1978), pp. 174–177; see also Böheim-Valentin, *Du bleibst da,* pp. 19–21.

36. Valentin, *Der Knabe Karl,* p. 26.

37. The letter is in Böheim-Valentin, *Du bleibst da,* pp. 19–21; on the incomes, see Schrott, *Münchner Alltag.* Schrott presents the following figures: a young doctor at the beginning of his career, 80 marks a month; an assistant secondary school teacher, 135; a journeyman mason, working ten hours a day (Saturday included), 160–170.

38. Böheim-Valentin, *Du bleibst da,* p. 21.

39. Valentin, "Wie ich Volkssänger wurde," 128–129, and "Karl Valentin erzählt," in *Karl Valentins Lachkabinett,* pp. 12–13; and Münz, *Geschriebenes von und an Karl Valentin,* p. 32.

40. See VNK, Album 1, for the announcements, newspaper articles, and letters relating to appearances before private clubs, 1903–1907, especially before the music club Jung-München.

41. See Münz, *Geschriebenes von und an Karl Valentin,* pp. 32–33; VNK, Album 1, a 1906 advertisement for his apparatus, and the articles from unidentified newspapers about it; Böheim-Valentin, *Du bleibst da,* p. 23.

42. See VNK, Album 2, a 1907 program of the Hofjäger-Theater, Bernburg, a program of 16–18 March 1907 of Süssmilch's Walhalla Theater in Halle, and programs from both Landshut and Ingolstadt from 13 October and 27 December, 1907, respectively; Münz, *Geschriebenes von und an Karl Valentin,* p. 32; Böheim-Valentin, *Du bleibst da,* pp. 22–23; Valentin, "Wie ich Volkssänger wurde," p. 128, and "Karl Valentin erzählt," in *Karl Valentins Lachkabinett,* p. 13.

43. Valentin, "Karl Valentin erzählt," in *Karl Valentins Lachkabinett,* pp. 13–14; Böheim-Valentin, *Du bleibst da,* p. 23; Valentin, *Der Knabe Karl,* p. 26; Hoferichter, *Jahrmarkt meines Lebens,* p. 143; and Valentin, "Wie ich Volkssänger wurde," p. 129.

44. Valentin, *Der Knabe Karl,* p. 26; Valentin, "Karl Valentin erzählt," in *Karl Valentins Lachkabinett,* p. 14; Münz, *Geschriebenes von und an Karl Valentin,* p. 32.

45. Valentin, "Karl Valentin erzählt," in *Karl Valentins Lachkabinett,* p. 14; Böheim-Valentin, *Du bleibst da,* pp. 24–27; Valentin, *Der Knabe Karl,* p. 28, and "Wie ich Volkssänger wurde," p. 129.

46. Valentin, *Alles von Karl Valentin,* pp. 13–14.

47. Valentin, "Wie ich Volkssänger wurde," p. 129.

48. Schneider, *Die populäre Kritik,* pp. 5, 206–220; Fritz, *München als Industriestadt,* pp. 7, 18–25; and *1875–1975. 100 Jahre Städtestatistik,* pp. 66–67.

49. Weiss Ferdl, *Weiss Ferdl erzählt,* pp. 8–9; *Weiss Ferdl guat troffa,* pp. 13–15; and *Ich bin kein Intellektueller* (Munich: Paul Hugendubel Verlag, 1941), pp. 7–8.

50. Weiss Ferdl, *Weiss Ferdl erzählt,* p. 9; *Ich bin kein Intellektueller,* pp. 7–9; and *Weiss Ferdl guat troffa,* p. 15.

51. Weiss Ferdl, *Weiss Ferdl erzählt,* p. 9.

52. Ibid., p. 17; and *Weiss Ferdl guat troffa,* p. 16.

53. Weiss Ferdl, *Weiss Ferdl erzählt,* pp. 17–20.

54. Ibid., pp. 11–16; *Weiss Ferdl guat troffa,* p. 19; and *Ich bin kein Intellektueller,* pp. 13–14.

55. Weiss Ferdl, *Ich bin kein Intellektueller,* p. 14; and *Weiss Ferdl erzählt,* p. 26.

56. Fritz, *München als Industriestadt*, pp. 24–25; Schneider, *Die populäre Kritik*, pp. 19–31.

57. Weiss Ferdl, *Ich bin kein Intellektueller*, p. 14; and *Weiss Ferdl erzählt*, pp. 26–31.

58. Weiss Ferdl, *Weiss Ferdl erzählt*, pp. 33–38.

59. Ibid., pp. 39–51; and *Ich bin kein Intellektueller*, pp. 16–18.

60. Weiss Ferdl, *Weiss Ferdl erzählt*, pp. 54–55.

61. Ibid., p. 53.

62. Weiss Ferdl, *Weiss Ferdl guat troffa*, pp. 40–42.

3. The Folksingers and Their Audiences Before World War I

1. For an excellent recent overview, see Hans-Ulrich Wehler, *Das deutsche Kaiserreich, 1871–1918* (Göttingen: Vandenhoeck & Ruprecht, 1977). A succinct treatment can be found in Gerhard A. Ritter's introduction to *Das deutsche Kaiserreich, 1871–1914* 3rd ed. (Göttingen: Vandenhoeck & Ruprecht, 1977), pp. 9–23.

2. Otto Falckenberg, *Mein Leben—Mein Theater,* ed. Wolfgang Petzet (Munich, Vienna, and Leipzig: Zinnen Verlag, 1944), pp. 95–99; on the expressions of protest in Munich, see also MSPD 2401, "Goethe Bund"; and MSPD 2057-1, "Die elf Scharfrichter."

3. Generally, on censorship in Munich, and on the Munich advisory council, see Herbert Lehnert and Wolf Segebrecht, "Thomas Mann im Münchner Zensurbeirat (1912/13): Ein Beitrag zum Verhältnis Thomas Mann zum Frank Wedekind," *Jahrbuch der deutschen Schillergesellschaft,* 7 (1963): 190–200; and R. J. V. Lenman, "Art, Society, and the Law in Wilhelmine Germany: The Lex Heinze," *Oxford German Studies,* 8 (1973): 86–113. For the documents, see MSPD 4342, I-IV, "Zensurbeirat bei der Kgl. Polizeidirektion München."

4. BHStAM, II 1936 A.V. MA92423, "Das Prinz-Regenten-Theater in München," "Prolog" for "Eröffnung des Prinz-Regenten-Theater in München," 20 August 1901.

5. Lehnert and Segebrecht, "Thomas Mann im Münchner Zensurbeirat." See also Artur Kutscher, *Wedekind: Leben und Werk,* ed. Karl Ude (Munich: List Verlag, 1964), pp. 178–194, 275–278; Frank Wedekind, *Prosa: Erzählungen, Aufsätze, Selbstzeugnisse, Briefe,* ed. Manfred Hahn (Berlin and Weimar: Aufbau Verlag, 1969), p. 209. For the documents of Wedekind's controversies, see BHStAM, Abt. II. 1936 A.V. MA92415, "Frank Wedekind"; MSPD 4342, I-IV, "Zensurbeirat bei der Kgl. Polizeidirektion München"; MSPD 4593, "Schloss Wetterstein."

6. See MSPD 3804-7, "Kleines Theater," especially the "police directive" of 18 October 1907. Evidence about the practice of censorship with regard to popular and other small stages can be found in the same f)'d; in MSPD 3811-IV, "Colosseum"; in MSPD 3812-III, "Blumensäle"; and in MSPD 3809-I, "Cabaret der sieben Tantenmörder."

7. Weiss Ferdl, *Bayerische Schmankerln*, pp. 88–89.

8. Christian Schütze, ed., *Facsimile Querschnitt durch den Simplicissimus* (Bern, Stuttgart, and Vienna: Scherz Verlag, 1963), p. 94.

9. MSPD 3804-7, "Das Kleine Theater," especially an article of the *Allgemeine Rundschau,* 22 August 1908, and an article of the *Münchner Neueste Nachrichten,* 13 January 1909, describing the court trial. For more about Munich's "decency" campaigners, see BHStAM, Abt. II, 1936 A.V., MA92786, "Bekämpfung unzüchtiger Bilder, Schriften."

10. Max Hochdorf, *Die deutsche Bühnengenossenschaft* (Potsdam: Gustav Kiepenheuer Verlag, 1921), p. 184; Aloys Kaufmann, "Die sozialen Leistungen der deutschen Bühnengenossenschaft," (Ph.D. diss., University of Erlangen, 1931), pp. 30–31.

11. Georg Assmann, "Die Verträge des Künstlers im Theater-, Konzert- und Kabarettleben" (Ph.D. diss., University of Königsberg, 1928), pp. 40–42; Hochdorf, *Die deutsche Bühnengenossenschaft,* p. 179.

12. Gerhard Brückner, "Die rechtliche Stellung der Bühnenkünstler in geschichtlicher Entwicklung" (Ph.D. diss., University of Göttingen, 1930), pp. 56–59; for a polemical version, see ThMM 4°1119, *Stenographischer Bericht über die Verhandlungen des provisorischen Nationalrates des Volksstaates Bayern: Neunte öffentliche Sitzung,* 3 January 1919, the speech of Florath entitled, "Besserung der Lage aller künstlerischen Berufe," pp. 265–268.

13. E. Koschmieder, *Die Altersversorgung der deutschen Bühnenkünstler* (Esslingen: Wilhelm Langguth Verlag, 1929), pp. 21–29; Aloys Kaufmann, "Die sozialen Leistungen," pp. 62–63.

14. Gustav Assmann, *Die gesetzliche Unfallversicherung der Bühnenangehörigen* (Berlin: Verlag der Genossenschaft Deutscher Bühnenangehörige, 1928), p. 3.

15. *Münchner Neuigkeits-Blatt,* 8 March 1912, p. 2.

16. Hochdorf, *Die deutsche Bühnengenossenschaft,* pp. 184–185; and Kaufmann, "Die sozialen Leistungen," p. 18.

17. Georg Assmann, "Die Verträge des Künstlers im Theater-, Konzert- und Kabarettleben," pp. 55–56. See also Ernst Toller's remarks before the Provisional National Council of the Bavarian People's State, ThMM 4°1119, pp. 280–281.

18. Joachim Ringelnatz, *Mein Leben bis zum Kriege* (Berlin: Ernst Rowohlt Verlag, 1931), p. 250.

19. Johannes Gotta, *Der Kabarettkünstler* (Leipzig: Hermann Beyer Verlag, 1925), pp. 43–44.

20. *Der Neue Weg (Deutsche Bühnengenossenschaft),* 41 (12 October 1912): 1205.

21. MSPD 2941, "Verband zur Wahrung der Interessen der Münchner Volkssänger," the 16 March 1914 letter to the police; and Erwin Münz, "Die Münchner Volkssänger-Verband," in *Katalog des Valentin-Museums* (Munich: Werbedruck Rudolf Stepanek, 1960), p. 41.

22. ThMM 4°1119, Ernst Toller, pp. 80–81.

23. Frau Weiss Ferdl in conversation, September 1978.

24. From Weiss Ferdl's private "salary book" (*Gagebuch*), it is clear that he was earning much more than a typesetter would have by late 1907, when he received 231 marks in one month. His income rose steadily thereafter, until

300–400 marks was normal for a month in 1912. Special acknowledgment to Frau Weiss Ferdl for making this document available. There are no such figures for Valentin, but letters of his, recently published, show that he made money before the war not only by delivering songs and monologues but also by having them printed and selling them. See Münz, *Geschriebenes von und an Karl Valentin,* pp. 42–46.

25. "Platzl Texte von Liedern," text no. 47, lyrics by Franz Blumenberg, 1909. The "Platzl Texte" can be found in the Monacensia-Sammlung of Munich's City Library (Stadtbibliothek).

26. Ibid., no. 7, lyrics by M. Simon.

27. Weiss Ferdl, *Weiss Ferdl erzählt,* pp. 84–89.

28. "Platzl Texte," "Grüsse an die Heimat," lyrics by Karl Krommer.

29. Weiss Ferdl, *Weiss Ferdl erzählt,* p. 89.

30. "Platzl Texte," "Der Jäger Abschied," "Bauern-Hymne," "Tegernsee-lied," and no. 8, "Lied aus unseren bayerischen Bergen."

31. Hollweck, *München,* p. 142.

32. "Platzl Texte," "Weibi, Weibi!" lyrics by Edmund Skurawy.

33. BHStAM MInn 20 66545, "Sittenpolizei, 1909–15," *Münchner Neuigkeits-Blatt,* ed. Wilhelm Kraemer, 9 (7 August 1912); the 1912 and 1913 issues of the *Münchner Humoristische Blätter* are filled with comments on the subject of divorce. Documents pertaining to the public outcry against "perversion" can be found in BHStAM, Abteilung II, 1936 A.V., Staatsministerium des Äussern, MA 92786, "Bekämpfung unzüchtiger Bilder, Schriften."

34. "Platzl Texte," "Der Alte Peter."

35. Ibid., no. 33.

36. Schneider, *Die populäre Kritik,* p. 190.

37. "Platzl Texte," no. 7, "Das deutsche Flaggenlied," lyrics by Richard Thiele, and "Nur Infanterie allein," lyrics by Paul R. Lehnhard.

38. Ibid., no. 37, "Altes Soldatenlied."

39. Frau Weiss Ferdl, in conversation, September 1978; also, Weiss Ferdl, *Weiss Ferdl erzählt,* p. 84.

40. Valentin, *Alles von Karl Valentin,* pp. 14–15.

41. Schneider, *Die populäre Kritik,* pp. 15–16; for the food costs and on how they were borne, see Schrott, *Münchner Alltag,* pp. 246–247.

42. Böheim-Valentin, *Du bleibst da,* p. 25.

43. Ibid., p. 64.

44. Münz, *Geschriebenes von und an Karl Valentin,* p. 45. Ludwig M. Schneider tended to ignore the Platzl-like attitudes in his study; see Schneider, *Die populäre Kritik,* pp. 304–312.

45. Schneider, *Die populäre Kritik,* pp. 115–117; Schneider's work suggests that there never was an attempt to silence the "popular critique"; censorship should rather be seen as an inhibiting force, ready to move against anything that went too far.

46. Valentin, *Alles von Karl Valentin,* pp. 16–17.

47. Schneider, *Die populäre Kritik,* pp. 242–250.

48. Ibid., pp. 304–312.

49. "Hoch Zeppelin!" lyrics by Roland, *Salvator-Saison 1909* (Munich: Selbstverlag der Paulanerbrauerei, 1909), p. 6.

50. See Theo Riegler, *Das Liesl Karlstadt Buch* (Munich: Süddeutscher Verlag, 1961), pp. 30–36; Böheim-Valentin, *Du bleibst da,* pp. 57–58; Valentin, *Der Knabe Karl,* p. 30.

51. Valentin, *Alles von Karl Valentin,* pp. 279–284.

52. See Michael Schulte's footnote in *Alles von Karl Valentin,* p. 283.

53. VNK, Albums 1 and 2. See programs, newspaper articles, and other documents relating to the popular cabaret and beer-hall appearances.

54. See "Karl Valentin erzählt," in Valentin, *Karl Valentins Lachkabinett,* p. 15.

55. VNK, Album 1, "Programm zum Ehren-Abend für Herrn A. Maier, Direktor der Dachauer-Bauern-Kapelle"; see also Valentin, "Karl Valentin erzählt," pp. 17–18.

56. Riegler, *Das Liesl Karlstadt Buch,* p. 24.

57. On Valentin's use of the label to describe himself, see "Wie ich Volkssänger wurde," *Bayerischer Hauskalender* (1928), pp. 128–130. Indeed, he even became a kind of chronicler of the folksinger tradition. See ThMM 00923, Karl Valentin, "Verzeichnis der Namen des Volkssänger-Albums in München von 1780–1928."

58. Michael Schulte, ed., *Karl Valentin in Selbstzeugnissen und Bilddokumenten* (Reinbek bei Hamburg: Rowohlt Verlag, 1968), p. 37.

59. See VNK, Album 1, 1909, "Programm des Kochelbräu-Märzenbier-Ausschanks." This same album gives a good idea of Valentin's appearances before such gatherings. On Weiss Ferdl, see his *Weiss Ferdl erzählt,* p. 94.

4. The Wartime Munich Stage and Middle-Class Hardships

1. See Schrott, *Münchner Alltag,* p. 248; Georg August Baumgärtner, *Zehn Jahre Münchner Hilfstätigkeit: Ein Kapitel vaterländischen Opfersinns in Kriegs- und Nachkriegszeit* (Munich: Knorr & Hirth Verlag, 1924), pp. 32–34; Weiss Ferdl, *Weiss Ferdl erzählt,* pp. 59–60; and for a particularly propagandistic account by a Munich writer, see Lena Christ, *Unser Bayern Anno 14/15,* pt. 1 (Munich: Albert Langen Verlag, 1914–15), p. 3.

2. See Wedekind, *Prosa,* pp. 259, 260–264, and 620–631; Kutscher, *Wedekind,* p. 317; and Wolfgang Petzet, *Die Münchner Kammerspiele, 1911–72* (Munich, Vienna, and Basel: Verlag Kurt Desch, 1973), p. 71. Wedekind is only one case: others, equally unexpected, are Hugo Ball, Erich Mühsam, and Ludwig Thoma. See Hugo Ball, *Briefe 1911–27* (Einsiedeln, Zurich, and Cologne: Benziger Verlag, 1957), pp. 34–35; Gerhard Edward Steinke, *The Life and Work of Hugo Ball, Founder of Dadism* (The Hague and Paris: Mouton Press, 1967), p. 220; Heinz Hug, *Erich Mühsam: Untersuchungen zum Leben und Werk* (Glashütten im Taunus: Verlag Detlev Auvermann KG, 1974), pp. 35–37; Ludwig Thoma, *Ein Leben in Briefen, 1875–1921* (Munich: Piper Verlag, 1963), pp. 263–267. For insightful comments on the motives behind some of these conversions, see Kurt Martens, *Schonungslose Lebenschronik,* pt. 2 (Vienna, Berlin, Leipzig, and Munich: Rikola Verlag, 1924), p. 144.

3. Robert Kothe, *Saitenspiel des Lebens* (Munich: Knorr & Hirth Verlag, 1944), p. 180.

4. VNK, unnumbered album, *35 Jahre Benz;* Album 1, letters dated 18 November 1914 and 21 September 1914, thanking Valentin for appearing; BHStAM, Abt. IV (Kriegsarchiv), Stellvertretendes Sanitätsamt, I.A.K., Bund 46, "Veranstaltungen," the advertisement "200. Führungswoche für die Verwundeten."

5. Paul Busse, *Geschichte des Gärtnerplatztheaters in München* (Munich: Druck und Verlag A. Waldbaur, 1924), p. 43.

6. Weiss Ferdl, *Weiss Ferdl guat troffa,* pp. 27, 30–31, and *Weiss Ferdl erzählt,* pp. 60–61; see also BHStAM, Abt. IV (Kriegsarchiv), 1. bayerische Reserve-Division Feld-Intendantur, Bund 40, Akt 7, "Soldatenheime, Kinos, Singspieltrupps, usw., 1917–18," military documents pertaining to the organization of entertainment at the front.

7. See "Vaterländische Lieder," printed in Munich by M. Müller & Sohn, generously provided from Weiss Ferdl's private documents by Frau Weiss Ferdl, September 1978.

8. Weiss Ferdl, *Weiss Ferdl guat troffa,* p. 28, and also, *Weiss Ferdl erzählt,* pp. 62–63.

9. Weiss Ferdl, *Weiss Ferdl guat troffa,* p. 116.

10. Frau Weiss Ferdl in conversation, September 1978; Weiss Ferdl, *Weiss Ferdl guat troffa,* pp. 31–32, and *Weiss Ferdl erzählt,* pp. 67–70.

11. Weiss Ferdl, *Weiss Ferdl guat troffa,* pp. 118–124. Weiss Ferdl personally knew the soldiers' fear that wives or lovers would be unfaithful to them. A love poem written to his young wife on 9 June 1917, entitled "Precious Berta," ends: "After a sweet word of love / Do you maybe have someone else?" Thanks to Frau Weiss Ferdl for showing me this poem that means so much to her.

12. Frau Weiss Ferdl in conversation, September 1978; Weiss Ferdl, *Weiss Ferdl guat troffa,* p. 33.

13. VNK, unnumbered album, *35 Jahre Benz.* Valentin himself did not go into the army; one suspects that the induction officers took at least some of his chronic health complaints seriously.

14. MSPD 2941, "Verband zur Wahrung der Interessen der Münchner Volkssänger," 1927 police document.

15. MSPD 3811-V, "Colosseum," "engaged artist" lists of 4 October 1916, 19 October 1916, 3 November 1916, and so on, and a program for the period 16–31 December 1917.

16. Anton Sailer, "Grau war Schwabing, und schön dazu," in *Denk ich an München: Ein Buch der Erinnerungen,* ed. Hermann Proebst and Karl Ude (Munich: Grade & Unzer Verlag, 1966), p. 129; see also, Hug, *Erich Mühsam,* pp. 36–37.

17. BHStAM MInn 20 (Innenministerium) 66272, "Schutzhaft, 1915–24, Bd. 1," a 29 July 1915 letter from the Bavarian Ministry of Justice to the Bavarian Ministry of War; 66276, "Spionage, 1913–14," a 12 November 1914 letter from the Munich police department to the chief of the general staff of the Army III b. in Berlin; 66277, "Spionage, 1915–16," 9 August 1915 letter from the Ministry of War to the general commands of Armies I, II, and III; 66278, "Spionage, 1916–17," a police report, entitled "Erfahrungen auf dem Gebiete der Spionageabwehr während des Krieges," pp. 59-62.

18. See *Almanach für die Spieljahre 1910–21, Kgl. Hof- und Nationaltheater und Kgl. Residenztheater* (Munich, 1910–1921).

19. See Petzet, *Die Münchner Kammerspiele,* pp. 73–74; and MSPD 2503, "Verband zur Förderung deutscher Theaterkultur," an article by Dr. Paul Lerch of Berlin, printed in the *Augsburger Volkszeitung,* 17 September 1916.

20. Richard Riess, "Kabarett im Kriege," *Der Zwiebelfisch,* 7 (1915): 96.

21. MSPD 3810-III, "Colosseum," some 1909 "engaged artist" lists, presented by the "Colosseum" to the police, which demonstrate the international birthplaces of performers before the war; 3811-IV, "Colosseum," an article from the *Münchner Zeitung,* 20 October 1914, and a "Colosseum Program mit dem Spielplan," for the week of 24 November 1914; 3811-V, "Colosseum," programs and lists of "engaged artists," 1915–1917, and articles in the *Münchner Zeitung,* 5 October 1915 and 5 April 1916; 3811-VI, "Colosseum," programs and "engaged artists" lists. These "engaged artists" lists were turned in even during the early years of the Republic, and only in the mid-1920s do they reflect the return of performers from nations that had opposed Germany in the war.

22. Riess, "Kabarett im Kriege," p. 96; see also MSPD 3811-V, "Colosseum," a 4 July 1916 letter from the Labor Board (Arbeiter-Sekretariat) of Munich to the General Command of the First Army Corps.

23. VNK, *35 Jahre Benz.*

24. Böheim-Valentin, *Du bleibst da,* p. 149.

25. For example, see MSPD 3811-V, "Colosseum," a 2 March 1916 letter from director Max Allfeld to the police.

26. MSPD 2503, "Verband zur Förderung deutscher Theaterkultur," an article from *Volkswart* (Cologne), 10 (January-February 1917): 19, 22, and an article from *Münchner Neueste Nachrichten,* 30 August 1916.

27. MSPD 3811-V, "Colosseum," police letters of instruction entitled "local police permission."

28. MSPD 4589, "Frühlings Erwachen," advertisements of the Chamber of Plays, for 5 September 1915 and 2 January 1917, and an article (with no date listed in the file) from the *Allgemeine Rundschau,* no. 37.

29. MSPD 4342-III, "Zensurbeirat bei der Kgl. Polizei Direktion München," 21 December 1916, police report on a session of the advisory council; MSPD 4342-IV, *Zensurbeirat Journal, 1915-18.*

30. MSPD 4593, "Schloss Wetterstein," Martens's 22 May 1916 letter to the police, and their 1 June reply.

31. Wedekind, *Prosa,* pp. 623–624.

32. MSPD 3813-II, "Apollo-Theater," a police report of 10 December 1915. The assumption that the officer was plain-clothed is based partially on the common sense that a uniform would alert the management to leave out uncensored acts, and partially on the knowledge that the city did use plainclothesmen in other cases; on the latter, see MSPD 3535, "Universalbund." And on Karl Valentin, see Schwimmer, *Karl Valentin,* pp. 125–126.

33. BHStAM MK 7 (Unterricht und Kultus) 40 900, "Schriftsteller, Dichter, 1914–39," a 20 September 1914 letter to the Ministry; see also, Oskar Maria Graf, *Gelächter von Aussen* (Munich: Verlag Kurt Desch, 1966), p. 43; and Martens, *Schonungslose Lebenschronik,* p. 144.

34. MSPD 4043, "Oktoberfest 1913," a 7 August 1914 directive from the Ministry of the Interior to the police.

35. See Hollweck, *München*, p. 171.

36. See Busse, *Gärtnerplatztheater*, p. 35.

37. See Kaufmann, "Die sozialen Leistungen," pp. 42–44, 116; see also Hochdorf, *Die deutsche Bühnengenossenschaft*, pp. 232–237.

38. MSPD 3811-V, a letter of 4 July 1916 from the Labor Board of Munich to the General Command of the First Army Corps, and the General Command's 13 July reply.

39. Crown Prince Ruprecht, in a 17 July 1917 letter to Chancellor Hertling, cited in Feldman, *Army, Industry, and Labor*, p. 422.

40. Ibid., pp. 422–424, 464–477; Ay, *Die Entstehung einer Revolution*, p. 99.

41. Feldman, *Army, Industry, and Labor*, pp. 472–473.

42. Ibid., pp. 464–468; Ay, *Die Entstehung einer Revolution*, pp. 97–100; and Kocka, *Klassengesellschaft im Kriege*, pp. 73–74, 82.

43. *Verbands-Zeitschrift der staatlichen Büro-Angestellten*, Special Edition, (November 1919): 2–3.

44. See *Bericht über die Massnahmen der Stadtgemeinde München zur Bekämpfung der Wohnungsnot und über die Tätigkeit des Wohnungsamtes vom 1. April 1919 bis 1. April 1920* (Munich: G. J. Manz Verlag, 1920), p. 8; *Die Beseitigung der Wohnungsnot in München: Denkschrift und Anträge des städtischen Wohnungsreferenten* (Munich, 1927), pp. 16–17.

45. Liesl Karlstadt, *Original-Vorträge von Karl Valentin* (Munich: Verlag Max Hieber, 1926), p. 23.

46. Schrott, *Münchner Alltag*, p. 248.

47. Cohen and Simon, *Geschichte der Handelskammer München*, pp. 392–393.

48. Josef Benno Sailer, "Ärztliche Gutachten zur Kriegs-Ernährung," in his *O Kommunal Verband!* (Munich: Grossmünchen Verlag, 1920), pp. 26–27.

49. On the food crisis, see Ay, *Die Entstehung einer Revolution*, pp. 29–33; Hollweck, *München*, p. 171; and Zorn, "Bayerns Gewerbe," pp. 820–821.

50. See BHStAM MInn 20 (Innenministerium) 65614, "Aufsicht auf die Presse, 1915–16," an article of the *Münchner Neueste Nachrichten*, May 1916. On the admissibility of articles like this in the wartime press, see the same file for the 10 January 1916 resolution of the Reichstag budget committee, no. 203, and the speech of SPD deputy Dittmann during the 18 January 1916 session of the Reichstag; see MInn 20 65615, "Aufsicht auf die Presse, 1916–17," a 26 November 1916 directive from the Ministry of War to Bavarian editors, a 15 January 1917 letter from the Ministry of War to the Ministry of the Interior, and a 20 March 1917 letter from the Ministry of the Interior to the War Minister.

51. Sailer, "Hamster-Hymne," *O Kommunal Verband!* p. 25.

52. See Ay, *Die Entstehung einer Revolution*, pp. 26–27; Willy Albrecht, *Landtag und Regierung in Bayern am Vorabend der Revolution*, pp. 429–430; and the review essay of Eberhard Kolb, "Geschichte und Vorgeschichte der Revolution von 1918/19 in Bayern," *Neue Politische Literatur*, 16 (1971): 385.

53. Quoted in Ay, *Die Entstehung einer Revolution*, p. 71.

54. Oskar Maria Graf, *Prisoners All!* trans. Margaret Green (New York: Knopf, 1928), p. 258.

55. Sailer, "Hamster-Hymne, " p. 25.

56. Josef Benno Sailer, *Des Bayernkönigs Revolutionstage* (Munich: Verlag Carl Durk, 1919), p. 4; see also Graf, *Prisoners All!* p. 258.

57. Valentin, *Alles von Karl Valentin,* pp. 67–70. In this collection of Valentin's routines, the story about the cook appears as part of another monologue, entitled *Kreszenz Hiagelgwimpft.* Elsewhere it is included in *Die Frau Funktionär.* See Valentin, *Gesammelte Werke* (Munich: Piper Verlag, 1961), pp. 57–59.

58. ThMM 1358, "Absolvierte Engagements von Karl Valentin und Liesl Karlstadt, 1915–35," p. 2.

59. Mentioning this woman conductor without mentioning that women had been at this job only since the second year of the war, 1915, reveals an acceptance of what must have been a startling wartime change. See Hollweck, *München,* p. 170.

60. See Ay, *Die Entstehung einer Revolution;* and Albrecht, *Landtag und Regierung.*

61. See Schwimmer, *Karl Valentin,* pp. 125–126.

62. Valentin, *Alles von Karl Valentin,* pp. 284–291; see VNK, Album 2, a 1916 advertisement "Aus der guten alten Zeit," and a 1916 or 1917 advertisement of the Annenhof, where Valentin was appearing.

63. This quotation is from the wartime letters of Bavarian writer Ludwig Thoma, who swung in 1914 from a critically satirical attitude toward the German military to all-out nationalism. See his *Ein Leben in Briefen,* pp. 263–267.

64. Graf, *Prisoners All!* pp. 257–258.

65. The play did indeed appear. See VNK, Album 2, for a 1916 advertisement.

66. "Absolvierte Engagements," pp. 1–2. Valentin and Karlstadt appeared at the Hotel Wagner's Wien-München, at the Annenhof, and at Serenissimus during the war.

67. See, for example, VNK, Album 2, an article of the *Münchner Neueste Nachrichten,* 3 June 1915, and an unidentified article about a Serenissimus evening, probably from 1917.

5. The Middle Class Against Weimar

1. For a detailed study of the Revolution's leaders and main events, see Allan Mitchell, *Revolution in Bavaria 1918–19: The Eisner Regime and the Soviet Republic* (Princeton: Princeton University Press, 1969). The leaders have been the subject of several studies: Sterling Fishman, "Prophets, Poets, and Priests: A Study of the Men and Ideas that Made the Munich Revolution of 1918–19" (Ph.D. diss., University of Wisconsin, 1960); Franz Schade, *Kurt Eisner und die bayerische Sozialdemokratie* (Hannover: Verlag für Literatur und Zeitgeschehen, 1961); Falk Wiesemann, "Kurt Eisner, Studie zu einer politischen Biographie," in Bosl, *Bayern im Umbruch,* pp. 387–426; and Hug, *Erich Mühsam.* An excellent description of the impression Eisner made as a politician is to be found in Karl

Alexander von Müller, *Mars und Venus: Erinnerungen, 1914–19* (Stuttgart: Gustav Klipper Verlag, 1954), p. 273. See also Ernst Toller, *Eine Jugend in Deutschland* (Amsterdam: Querido Verlag, 1933).

2. Professor Karl Bosl of the University of Munich called for new research into the Bavarian Revolution in an important article in 1965: "Gesellschaft und Politik in Bayern vor dem Ende der Monarchie: Beiträge zu einer sozialen und politischen Strukturanalyse," *Zeitschrift für bayerische Landesgeschichte*, 28 (1965): 1–31. Results began to appear in 1968–69: Ay, *Die Entstehung einer Revolution;* Peter Kritzer, *Die bayerische Sozialdemokratie und die bayerische Politik in den Jahren 1918 bis 1923* (Munich: Stadtarchiv, 1969); Albrecht, *Landtag und Regierung in Bayern;* and Bosl, *Bayern im Umbruch.* This last work, a collection of essays, contains pieces by Ay and Kritzer which summarize their work and, of special importance, Georg Kalmer's "Beamtenschaft und Revolution: Eine sozialgeschichtliche Studie über Voraussetzungen und Wirklichkeit des Problems," pp. 201–262, and Heinrich Hillmayr's "München und die Revolution von 1918–19," pp. 453–504.

Together, these works place the Revolution's leaders and followers into the same picture and thereby amount to a revision of earlier historical understanding. They take aim, often, at Allan Mitchell's *Revolution in Bavaria* for underestimating the popular energy that fed the Revolution.

For two excellent summary articles, see Eberhard Kolb, "Geschichte und Vorgeschichte der Revolution von 1918–19 in Bayern," *Neue Politische Literatur*, 16 (1971): 383–394; and Georg Kalmer, "Die 'Massen' in der Revolution von 1918–19 in Bayern: Die Unterschichten als Problem der bayerischen Revolutionsforschung," *Zeitschrift für bayerische Landesgeschichte*, 34 (1971): 316–357.

The revisionists also offer a fine collection of documents, Karl-Ludwig Ay's *Appelle einer Revolution: Dokumente aus Bayern zum Jahr 1918/19* (Munich: Süddeutscher Verlag, 1968).

Specifically on the hardships of the Revolution, see Mitchell, *Revolution in Bavaria*, pp. 231–241; Ay, *Appelle*, unit 84, and pp. 35–37; and Cohen and Simon, *Geschichte der Handelskammer München*, pp. 464–470; *Bericht über die Massnahmen der Stadtgemeinde München zur Bekämpfung der Wohnungsnot und über die Tätigkeit des Münchner Wohnungsamtes vom 1. April 1919 bis 1. April 1920* (Munich: G. J. Manz Verlag, 1920), p. 8; *Bericht über die Tätigkeit des Münchner Wohnungsamtes vom 1. April 1918 bis 1. April 1919* (Munich: G. J. Manz Verlag, 1919), p. 32.

3. VNK, Album 1, 4 January 1919, "Programm zu der Empfangsfeier unserer vom Felde zurückgekehrten Kameraden," and 18 January 1919, "Begrüssungsfeier für die vom Felde heimgekehrten Kameraden der Münchner Berufs-Feuerwehr"; ThMM 1358, "Absolvierte Engagements von Karl Valentin und Liesl Karlstadt, 1915–35," pp. 2–3; on Serenissimus, see Bronnen, *Begegnungen mit Schauspielern*, pp. 126–127.

4. Weiss Ferdl, *Weiss Ferdl erzählt*, pp. 75–77, and *Weiss Ferdl guat troffa*, pp. 37–39; and the entries of 26 October–15 November 1918, from Weiss Ferdl's unpublished "Tagebuch," generously provided by Frau Weiss Ferdl, September 1978. For a contemporary testimony on how Munich was still, during the war, drawing in new inhabitants from the surrounding country, see *Die Beseitigung der*

Wohnungsnot in München: Denkschrift und Anträge des städtischen Wohnungsreferenten (Munich, 1927), p. 17.

5. See Ay, *Die Entstehung einer Revolution,* and Albrecht, *Landtag und Regierung in Bayern.*

6. ThMM 1119, *Stenographischer Bericht über die Verhandlungen des provisorischen Nationalrates des Volksstaates Bayern, Neunte öffentliche Sitzung,* 3 January 1919, pp. 273–277; Martens, *Schonungslose Lebenschronik,* pp. 175–176.

7. BHStAM, Abt. II, 1936 A.V., MA 92225, "Der Rat der bildenden Künstler," particularly a 21 December 1918 letter to the Foreign Ministry, a 12 December 1918 letter from the Ministry of Education and Culture to other ministries, and a 21 February 1919 letter from the Ministry of Education and Culture to the Council.

8. *Stenographischer Bericht,* pp. 265–273; MSPD 3547, "Künstlergewerkschaft Bayerns," a government proclamation of the *Bayerische Staatszeitung,* 4 April 1919, a 27 December 1918 letter from the Ministry of Social Welfare to the Artists' Union, and a January 1919 statement of purpose; Martens, *Schonungslose Lebenschronik,* p. 175; BHStAM, MA I, Arbeiter- und Soldatenrat 23, "Kulturelle Veranstaltungen," the announcement of 28 December 1918 entitled "Vordringliche Wünsche der bildenden Künstler."

9. BHStAM, MA I, Arbeiter- und Soldatenrat 28, "Pressebüro," a 7 February 1919 letter from the Artists' Union to the Ministry of Social Welfare.

10. Martens, *Schonungslose Lebenschronik,* p. 176; MSPD 3547, "Künstlergewerkschaft Bayerns," an 8 May 1920 proclamation of the Ministries of Social Welfare and of Commerce, Industry, and Business, the *Satzungen* of 2 March 1920, and an article from the *Münchner Zeitung,* 16 February 1921.

11. BHStAM, MAI, Arbeiter- und Soldatenrat 23, "Kulturelle Veranstaltungen," the *Vertrag zwischen dem Aktionsausschuss der Arbeiter-, Soldaten- und Bauernräte und der Leitung des Neuen Theaters Münchens,* and a memorandum of the Artists' Union entitled *Die Deutsche Volksbühne.*

12. BHStAM, MAI, Arbeiter- und Soldatenrat 23, "Kulturelle Veranstaltungen," *Die Deutsche Volksbühne; Almanache für die Spieljahre 1910–21, Kgl. Hof- und Nationaltheater und Residenztheater* (Munich, 1910–1921); Paul Busse, *Geschichte des Gärtnerplatztheaters in München,* p. 45; *Münchner Volksbühne,* August 1920, "Generalversammlung des Vereins Münchner Volksbühne," pp. 89–90.

13. *Stenographischer Bericht,* pp. 280–281.

14. Hochdorf, *Die deutsche Bühnengenossenschaft,* pp. 242–243; Assman, "Die Verträge des Künstlers," pp. 43, 55–56; Bruckner, "Die rechtliche Stellung der Bühnenkünstler," pp. 62–63; Heinz Glang, "Das Recht des Arbeitnehmers, insbesondere des Bühnenkünstlers, auf Beschäftigung" (Ph.D. diss., University of Kiel, 1933), p. 16.

15. Schrott, *Münchner Alltag,* p. 260.

16. Michael Gasteiger, *Die Not in München* (Munich: Verlag der Reichszentrale für Heimatdienst, 1923).

17. Ibid., p. 23.

18. Ibid., p. 6. Actually, Gasteiger reported a population rise of roughly 8 percent, but statistics presented in Hollweck's *München,* pp. 169, 182, indicate the

smaller figure. A good recent article on the economic burdens that the Versailles Treaty placed upon Germany is Peter Krüger's "Das Reparationsproblem der Weimarer Republik in fragwürdiger Sicht," *Vierteljahreshefte für Zeitgeschichte,* 29 (January 1981): 21–47.

19. Hollweck, *München,* p. 178; see also, Schneider, *Die populäre Kritik,* pp. 52–56; *Die Beseitigung der Wohnungsnot in München; Bericht über die Tätigkeit des Münchner Wohnungsamtes; Bericht über die Massnahmen der Stadtgemeinde München zur Bekämpfung der Wohnungsnot;* and Gasteiger, *Die Not in München,* pp. 18–19.

20. Gasteiger, *Die Not in München,* pp. 8–9; on the development of the coal shortage, stressing the damage done to Munich's economy by the revolutionary government, see the Chamber of Commerce's commissioned history, Cohen and Simon, *Geschichte der Handelskammer München,* p. 465; on the wartime shortage of coal in Bavaria, see Feldman, *Army, Industry, and Labor,* pp. 422-424; and Zorn, "Bayerns Gewerbe," p. 821.

21. Gasteiger, *Die Not in München,* pp. 14–16.

22. *Der Bayerische Mittelstand* (Munich), 1 (October 1919): 1, 4.

23. Ibid., 2–3 (December 1919): 13.

24. Cohen and Simon, *Geschichte der Handelskammer München,* p. 525; see also Lebovics, *Social Conservatism,* pp. 4–5.

25. Lebovics, *Social Conservatism,* p. 10.

26. Gasteiger, *Die Not in München,* p. 10.

27. Zorn, "Bayerns Gewerbe," p. 826.

28. Winkler, *Mittelstand, Demokratie und Nationalsozialismus,* pp. 28–35.

29. See Lebovics, *Social Conservatism,* pp. vii, 6–7; Gasteiger, *Die Not in München,* p. 9.

30. *Auszug aus dem Jahresbericht und Rechnungsabschluss für das Rechnungsjahr 1920 (31. Vereinsjahr): Hilfsverein der Lehrerinnen in München* (Munich, 1921). Presumably, the "hospital fees" were monthly.

31. Gasteiger, *Die Not in München,* pp. 17–18.

32. Cohen and Simon, *Geschichte der Handelskammer München,* p. 496; Gasteiger, *Die Not in München,* p. 10.

33. BHStAM MK7 (Unterricht und Kultus) 40850, "Die Notlage der deutschen Kunst, 1919–20."

34. People's Stage chairman Georg Mauerer, an untitled speech, in "General-Versammlung des Vereins Münchner Volksbühne," *Münchner Volksbühne: Blätter für Theater und Musik,* 12 (August 1920): 89–90.

35. E. Koschmieder, *Die Altersversorgung der deutschen Bühnenkünstler* (Esslingen: Wilhelm Langguth Verlag, 1929), p. 28; see also Otto Hellmer, "Alters-, Invaliden- und Hinterbliebenen Fürsorge der Bühnenangehörigen in Deutschland" (Ph.D. diss., University of Munich, 1924), pp. 64–65.

36. Lutz, *Die Münchner Volkssänger,* pp. 48–51.

37. Weiss Ferdl, *Weiss Ferdl erzählt,* p. 79.

38. Frau Weiss Ferdl in conversation, September 1978.

39. Valentin, *Karl Valentins Lachkabinett,* p. 23.

40. Both can be found in Valentin, *Alles von Karl Valentin: Das Christbaumbrettl,* pp. 322–329; *Der Firmling,* pp. 330–337. Direct evidence of *Der Firmling*'s

1922 premier can be found in VNK, Album 2, an advertisement of the Germania-Brettl from 1922. Evidently this took place on 9 December 1922. The play remained upon the program until 28 February 1923. *Das Christbaumbrettl* premiered on the same stage on 1 July 1922; see Valentin, *Karl Valentins Lachkabinett*, p. 198.

41. Liesl Karlstadt in Valentin, *Karl Valentins Lachkabinett*, p. 82.

42. *Berichte aus Berliner Zeitungen über Karl Valentin und Liesl Karlstadt* (1929).

43. Josef Benno Sailer, "Ärztliches Gutachten zur Kriegs-Ernährung," *O Kommunal Verband!* (Munich: Grossmünchen Verlag, 1920), pp. 26–27.

44. J. Specter, "Die Theaterskandale und die Zensurfrage," *Münchner Volksbühne,* 7 (March 1921): 49–50.

45. BHStAM, Abt. II: MK 7 (Kultus und Unterricht) 41007, "National-theater in München," vol. 1, 28 May 1923 letter from the artistic director of the Bavarian State Theater to Dr. Matt, Bavarian Minister of Instruction and Culture; see also MSPD 4350, "Theaterskandale," *Bayrische Kurier,* 11 May 1923, as well as a police document of 6 February 1921 describing such incidents at the performance of a play by Schnitzler, and an article in the *Frankfurter Zeitung,* 16 June 1921, describing them at a dramatized reading of some Heinrich Heine poems.

46. Arnolt Bronnen, *Tage mit Bertolt Brecht* (Darmstadt: Luchterhand Verlag, 1976), pp. 128, 171–172.

47. BHStAM, Abt. II: MA 1943 (Äussern) 100 403, "Antisemitische Agitationen und Versammlungen," ministry document of 27 October 1921.

48. Ursula Haass, "Die Kulturpolitik des bayerischen Landtages in der Zeit der Weimarer Republik, 1918–33" (Ph.D. diss., University of Munich, 1967), p. 131.

49. MSPD 4350, "Theater-Skandale," a police document of 6 February 1921, as well as *Münchner Neueste Nachrichten,* 15 January 1920, and the police document, signed by Commissioner Pöhner, of 23 December 1919; see also Petzet, *Die Münchner Kammerspiele,* p. 168, and Hermann Essweis, "Bericht des Kunstbeirates der Münchner Volksbühne," *Münchner Volksbühne,* 1 (September 1919): 6–7, and "Theaterskandale," 35–36.

50. Hochdorf, *Die deutsche Bühnengenossenschaft,* p. 254.

51. "Der Bürger-General oder die sicherheitsgefährliche Volksbühne," *Münchner Volksbühne,* April 1920: 57, and Mauerer's speech, "General-Versammlung des Vereins Münchner Volksbühne," August 1920: 89–90.

52. ThMM 1358, "Absolvierte Engagements von Karl Valentin und Liesl Karlstadt, 1915–35," p. 3.

53. Theo Prosel, *Freistaat Schwabing: Erinnerungen des Simplwirts* (Munich: Süddeutscher Verlag, 1951), pp. 113–114.

54. VNK, Album 1, announcement "Festabend der Einwohnerwehr München des 26. Stadtbezirkes am 2. Dezember 1919 im grossen Saal des Löwenbräukellers," and a 12 September 1919 "Kameradschaftsabend— Bayerische Schützenbrigade 21." See further VNK, Album 1, a 24 September 1919 announcement for the "Reichsbund der Kriegsbeschädigten, Kriegsteilnehmer und Hinterbliebenen: Bezirksgruppe Au-Giesing," "Weihnachtsfeier

Bürgerbräu Keller" on 11 December 1920, "Künstler-Sommerfest mit Ball," at the Hotel Wagner on 23 July 1922, and "Zu Gunsten des Deutschen Hilfswerkes für Kriegs- und Zivilgefangene," at the Kindl-Keller on 31 July 1922; and "Absolvierte Engagements," pp. 3-5.

55. Handschriftenabteilung der Stadtbibliothek München: "1946 Fragebogen des Schutzverbandes deutscher Schriftsteller."

56. Karl Valentin, *Originalvorträge* (Munich: G. Franz'sche Buchdruckerei, 1926), pp. 4, 11-12.

57. Kurt Horwitz, "Karl Valentin in einer anderen Zeit," *Sturzflüge im Zuschauerraum der Gesammelten Werke,* vol. 2 (Munich: Piper Verlag, 1969), p. 11.

58. Viktor Mann, in Michael Schulte, *Das grosse Karl Valentin Buch* (Munich and Zurich: Piper Verlag, 1973), p. 27.

59. StAM "Zeitungsausschnittsammlung—Karl Valentin," *Die Weltbühne,* December 1922.

60. Valentin, *Originalvorträge,* p. 9.

61. Valentin, *Alles von Karl Valentin,* pp. 352-371.

62. Sinsheimer, *Gelebt im Paradies,* p. 182.

63. Hermann Hesse, in Schulte, *Das grosse Karl Valentin Buch,* p. 136.

64. "Absolvierte Engagements," p. 5.

65. Ibid., pp. 4-5; Valentin's activities can be followed in the documents of VNK, Albums 1, 2, and 3.

66. Münz, *Geschriebenes von und an Karl Valentin,* pp. 59-60; Riegler, *Das Liesl Karlstadt Buch,* p. 37; Petzet, *Die Münchner Kammerspiele,* pp. 154-155.

67. "Absolvierte Engagements," pp. 5-6; VNK, Albums 2 and 3.

68. Weiss Ferdl, *Münchner Humor* (Munich: Verlag Münchner Humor, 1924-25).

69. Weiss Ferdl, *Bayrische Schmankerln,* pp. 94-95.

70. Ibid., p. 93.

71. StAM "Zeitungsausschnittsammlung—Weiss Ferdl," "Einwohnerwehr Marschlied, Text von Weiss Ferdl," July 1919.

72. Auerbach, "Hitlers politische Lehrjahre," p. 18.

73. MSPD 4043, "Oktoberfest 1913"; MSPD 4044, "Oktoberfest 1915"; MSPD 4047, "Oktoberfest 1920"; MSPD 4049, "Oktoberfest 1921—Vorverhandlungen."

74. Weiss Ferdl, *Gemütliches München,* ed. Bertl Weiss (Munich: Süddeutscher Verlag, 1961), p. 111; special thanks to Frau Weiss Ferdl, who played for me a cherished phonograph recording of her husband singing this song.

75. Weiss Ferdl, *Gemütliches München,* pp. 97-98.

76. Ibid., pp. 157-158.

77. Frau Weiss Ferdl in conversation, September 1978.

78. See Albrecht Tyrell, *Vom "Trommler" zum "Führer": Der Wandel von Hitlers Selbstverständnis zwischen 1919 und 1924* (Munich: Wilhelm Fink Verlag, 1975).

79. StAM "Zeitungsausschnittsammlung—Weiss Ferdl," an article of the *Münchner Zeitung,* 20 April 1928.

80. The works here mentioned were published at Weiss Ferdl's Verlag Münchner Humor on Hildegardestrasse. In a September 1978 conversation, Frau

Weiss Ferdl recalled that the press was established there in 1925, and moved in 1930. City telephone directories bear her out as to the first date, and confirm that the press moved—to Linderallee—no later than July 1933. I name two works from a collection of eleven, eight of which had been published by 1930, located in the Theatermuseum München. See Weiss Ferdl, *Szenen und Possen* (Munich: Verlag Münchner Humor).

81. Weiss Ferdl, *Szenen und Possen.*

82. *1875–1975. 100 Jahre Städtestatistik in München* (Munich: Carl Gerber Verlag, 1975), p. 164.

83. Weiss Ferdl, *Weiss Ferdl guat troffa*, p. 24.

84. "Verschiedene Ansichten," in *Münchner Humor* (Munich: Verlag Münchner Humor, 1924–25).

85. Adolf Hitler, *Mein Kampf*, trans. Ralph Manheim (Boston: Houghton Mifflin, 1943), p. 305.

86. StAM "Zeitungsausschnittsammlung—Weiss Ferdl," an article of 1928.

87. Weiss Ferdl, *Weiss Ferdl erzählt*, p. 89.

88. Ibid., pp. 96–97, and *Weiss Ferdl guat troffa*, p. 24; Frau Weiss Ferdl in conversation, September 1978.

89. Special thanks to Frau Weiss Ferdl for presenting me with a copy of "Rings herum's" sheet music as a gift.

90. Gasteiger, *Die Not in München*, p. 6; see also, *Die wichtigsten Wohlfahrts- und Fürsorge-Einrichtungen Münchens: Verein für Fraueninteresse und Frauenarbeit* (Munich: Ernst Reinhardt Verlag, 1920).

91. Georg August Baumgärtner, *Zehn Jahre Hilfstätigkeit: Ein Kapitel vaterländischen Opfersinns in Kriegs- und Nachkriegszeit* (Munich: Knorr & Hirth Verlag, 1924), p. 155 aumgärtner mentaons an "Evening of Greeting for Munich's Volunteers" at the Bürgerbräukeller on 29 April 1920. Weiss Ferdl was on the program along with "patriotic speeches."

92. WeissDdrdl, "Far306hnelein weiss und blau," *Weiss Ferdl guat troffa*, pp. 127–128.

93. Weiss Ferdl, *Weiss Ferdl erzählt*, pp. 95–96.

6. The Turn to National Socialism

1. There were already seventy film theaters in Munich in 1929. See *Wohlfahrts- und Jugendamt der Landeshauptstadt München nach dem Weltkriege*, ed. Städtisches Wohlfahrts- und Jugendamt München (Munich: Druck und Buchbinderarbeit, Gebrüder Paulus A.G., 1929), p. 175.

2. See "München als Kunst- und Kulturstadt," in *Der Zwiebelfisch: Zeitschrift über Bücher, Kunst und Kultur*, 20 (1926-27): 47.

3. Weiss Ferdl, *Weiss Ferdl guat troffa*, p. 23.

4. Ibid., p. 150.

5. StAM "Zeitungsausschnittsammlung—Weiss Ferdl," "München voran," by Weiss Ferdl, *Münchner-Augsburger Abend-Zeitung*, 16 December 1923.

6. StAM "Zeitungsausschnittsammlung—Weiss Ferdl," *Münchner-Augsburger Abendzeitung*, 3 April 1924. The contents of this newspaper article are described in the first paragraph of chapter 1.

Selected
Bibliography

Archives

Bayerisches Hauptstaatsarchiv München, Abteilung II

1936 A.V. Staatsministerium des Äussern

MA 92225, "Der Rat der bildenden Künstler (1918/19)"
MA 92415, "Frank Wedekind"
MA 92423, "Das Prinz-Regenten Theater in München"
MA 92786, "Bekämpfung unzüchtiger Bilder, Schriften"

Staatsministerium des Innern 20

65614-6, "Aufsicht auf die Presse, 1915–18"
66252-3, "Öffentliche Sittlichkeit, Bd. I-II"
66269, "Revolution 1918"
66272, "Schutzhaft, 1915–24, Bd. I"
66276-9, "Spionage, 1913–23"
66283, "Politische Unruhe"
66545, "Sittenpolizei, 1909–25"

MK7, Ministerium für Unterricht und Kultus

40 850, "Die Notlage der deutschen Kunst, 1919–20"
40 900, "Schriftsteller, Dichter. 1914–1939"
41 007, "Nationaltheater in München, Bd. I"

MA1, Ministerium des Äussern

991, "Wissenschaft und Kunst, 1918–19"
Arbeiter- und Soldatenrat 23, "Kulturelle Veranstaltungen"
Arbeiter- und Soldatenrat 28, "Pressebüro"

MA 1943, Ministerium des Äussern

100 403, "Antisemitische Agitationen und Versammlungen"

Münchner Staatsarchiv

Polizeidirektion

2057 I-III, "Die elf Scharfrichter"
2401, "Goethe Bund"
2503, "Verband zur Förderung deutscher Theaterkultur"
2941, "Verband zur Wahrung der Interessen der Münchner Volkssänger"
3535, "Universalbund"
3537, "Bund deutscher Gelehrter und Künstler"
3547, "Künstlergewerkschaft Bayerns"
3652, "Münchner Künstlergewerkschaft 1927 e.V."
3804-7, "Kleines Theater"
3809 I-III, "Münchner Künstler-Cabaret"
3810 III, "Colosseum"
3811 IV-VII, "Colosseum"
3812 I-IV, "Blumensäle"
3813 I-II, "Apollo-Theater"
4043, "Oktoberfest 1913"
4044, "Oktoberfest 1915"
4047, "Oktoberfest 1920"
4049, "Oktoberfest 1921—Vorverhandlungen"
4050, "Oktoberfest 1921"
4342 I-IV, "Zensurbeirat bei der kgl. PolDir München"
4350, "Theater-Skandale"
4589, "Frühlings Erwachen"
4593, "Schloss Wetterstein"

Staatsanwaltschaft München I

1735, "Hugo Ball: 'Der Henker' Prozess"
1769, "1914 Simplicissimus Majestätsbeleidigung"
1816, "1916 Lena Christ wegen Ehrenbeleidigung"
1955, "Hochverrat gegen Alfred Blumcke, Kunstmaler und Student"
2038, "1919 Hochverrat gegen Karl Haussmann, Volkssänger"
2057, "Hochverrat gegen Robert Holstein, Maler"
2075, "Beihilfe zum Hochverrat gegen Johann Kister, Humorist"

Theatermuseum München

1119, "Stenographischer Bericht über die Verhandlungen des provisorischen Nationalrates des Volksstaates Bayern"
1358, "Absolvierte Engagements von Karl Valentin und Liesl Karlstadt, 1915-35"
462, Johann Weil, "Notenbuch (im Varieté Bamberger Hof um 1880)"
577, Josef Mittlerer, "Das Münchner Colosseum" (printed copy: Munich, 1932)
7478, "Satzungen des Münchner Bühnen-Club E.V., Clubhaus Kanalstrasse 42" (Munich: J. Schön, 1916)

6444, "Kolosseum München"
923, Karl Valentin, "Verzeichnis der Bildertafeln"
0923, Karl Valentin, "Verzeichnis der Namen des Volkssänger-Albums in München von 1780–1928"

Bayerisches Hauptstaatsarchiv München, Abteilung IV, Kriegsarchiv

"Stellvertretendes Sanitätsamt, I.A.K. Band 46"
"1. Bayer. Reserve-Division. Feld-Intendantur. Band 40, Akt 7"

Münchner Stadtarchiv-Zeitungsausschnittsammlung

Dietrich Eckart
Weiss Ferdl
Oskar Maria Graf
Kathi Kobus
Erich Mühsam
Joachim Ringelnatz
Ludwig Thoma
Karl Valentin

Monacensia Sammlung der Stadtbibliothek, München

Handschriften-Abteilung

Alois Hönle
Karl Lindermaier
Karl Valentin

Kartei-Katalog

"Platzl Texte von Lieder"
"Gast- und Vergnügungsstätte Platzl: Programmhefte um 1927"

Theatermuseum des Instituts für Theaterwissenschaft der Universität Köln

Karl-Valentin-Nachlass

Other Works

Albrecht, Willy. *Landtag und Regierung in Bayern am Vorabend der Revolution von 1918*. Berlin: Duncker & Humblot Verlag, 1968.
Almanache für die Spieljahre 1910–21: Kgl. Hof- und Nationaltheater und Kgl. Residenztheater. Munich, 1910–1921.
Arens, Hanns. *Unsterbliches München*. Munich and Esslingen: Bechtle Verlag, 1968.

Assmann, Gustav. *Die gesetzliche Unfallversicherung der Bühnenangehörigen.* Berlin: Verlag der Genossenschaft deutscher Bühnenangehöriger, 1929.
—— "Die Verträge des Künstlers im Theater-, Konzert- und Kabarettleben." Ph.D. diss., University of Königsberg, 1928.
Au, Giesing, Haidhausen: 100 Jahre bei München, 1854–1954. Munich: Süddeutscher Verlag, 1954.
Auerbach, Helmut. "Hitlers Politische Lehrjahre und die Münchner Gesellschaft, 1919–23." *Vierteljahreshefte für Zeitgeschichte,* 25 (January 1977): 1–45.
Auszug aus dem Jahresbericht und Rechnungsabschluss für das Rechnungsjahr 1920 (31. Vereinsjahr): Hilfsverein der Lehrerinnen in München. Munich, 1921.
Ay, Karl-Ludwig. *Appelle einer Revolution: Dokumente aus Bayern zum Jahre 1918/19.* Munich: Süddeutscher Verlag, 1968.
—— *Die Entstehung einer Revolution: Die Volksstimmung in Bayern während des ersten Weltkrieges.* Berlin: Duncker & Humblot Verlag, 1968.
Ball, Hugo. *Briefe, 1911–27.* Einsiedeln, Zurich, and Cologne: Benziger Verlag, 1957.
Bauernfeld, Eduard. *Erinnerungen aus Alt-Wien,* ed. Josef Bindtner. Vienna: Wiener Drucke, 1923.
Baumgärtner, Georg August. *Zehn Jahre Münchner Hilfstätigkeit: Ein Kapitel vaterländischen Opfersinns in Kriegs- und Nachkriegszeit.* Munich: Knorr und Hirth Verlag, 1924.
Bergson, Henri. *Das Lachen.* Meisenheim am Glan: Westkultur Verlag Anton Hain, 1948.
Bericht über die Massnahmen der Stadtgemeinde München zur Bekämpfung der Wohnungsnot und über die Tätigkeit des Münchner Wohnungsamtes vom 1. April 1919 bis 1. April 1920. Munich: G. J. Manz Verlag, 1920.
Bericht über die Tätigkeit des Münchner Wohnungsamtes vom 1. April 1918 bis 1. April 1919. Munich: G. J. Manz Verlag, 1919.
Berichte aus Berliner Zeitungen über Karl Valentin und Liesl Karlstadt. 1929.
Die Beseitigung der Wohnungsnot in München: Denkschrift und Anträge des Städtischen Wohnungsreferenten. Munich, 1927.
Beyer, Hans. *Von der Novemberrevolution zur Räterepublik in München.* Berlin: Rutten & Hoening Verlag, 1957.
Bischoff, William. "Artists, Intellectuals, and Revolution: Munich, 1918–19." Ph.D. diss., Harvard University, 1970.
Blei, Franz. *Schriften in Auswahl.* Munich: Biederstein Verlag, 1960.
Blessing, Werner K. "Zur Analyse politischer Mentalität und Ideologie der Unterschichten im 19. Jahrhundert." *Zeitschrift für bayerische Landesgeschichte,* 34 (1971): 768–816.
Böheim-Valentin, Bertl, *"Du bleibst da und zwar sofort!"* Munich: Piper Verlag, 1971.
Bosl, Karl, ed. *Bayern im Umbruch.* Munich and Vienna: Oldenbourg Verlag, 1969.
—— "Gesellschaft und Politik in Bayern vor dem Ende der Monarchie: Beiträge zu einer sozialen and politischen Strukturanalyse." *Zeitschrift für bayerische Landesgeschichte,* 28 (1965): 1–31.

———— *München: Bürgerstadt-Residenz-heimliche Hauptstadt Deutschlands*. Stuttgart and Aalen: Konrad Theiss Verlag, 1971.

Braatz, Thea. *Das Kleinbürgertum in München und seine Öffentlichkeit von 1830–1870: Ein Beitrag zur Mentalitätsforschung*. Munich: Stadtarchiv, 1972.

Bracher, Karl Dietrich. *Die deutsche Diktatur: Entstehung, Struktur, Folgen des Nationalsozialismus*, 5th rev. ed. Cologne and Berlin: Verlag Kiepenheuer & Witsch, 1969.

Brandenburg, Hans. *Im Feuer unserer Liebe*. Munich: Verlag Herbert Nenner, 1956.

Brecht, Bertolt. *Tagebücher 1920–22: Autobiographische Aufzeichnungen 1920–54*. Frankfurt am Main: Suhrkamp Verlag, 1975.

Brehm, Friedl. *Ludwig Thoma und der Simplicissimus*. Feldafing/Oberbayern: Friedl Brehm, 1966.

Bronnen, Arnolt. *Begegnungen mit Schauspielern*. Berlin: Henschelverlag Kunst und Gesellschaft, 1967.

———— *Tage mit Bertolt Brecht*. Darmstadt: Luchterhand Verlag, 1976.

Bruckner, Gerhard. "Die rechtliche Stellung der Bühnenkünstler in geschichtlicher Entwicklung." Ph.D. diss., University of Göttingen, 1930.

Budzinski, Klaus. *Die Muse mit der scharfen Zunge*. Munich: Paul List Verlag, 1961.

Busse, Paul. *Geschichte des Gärtnerplatztheaters in München*. Munich: A. Waldbaur Verlag, 1924.

Christ, Lena. *Unser Bayern Anno 14/15*. Munich: Albert Langen Verlag, 1914–15.

Cohen, Arthur, and Edmund Simon. *Geschichte der Handelskammer München seit ihrer Gründung (1869): Beitrag zur Wirtschaftsgeschichte der letzten Jahrzehnte*. Munich: Industrie- und Handelskammer, 1926.

Craig, Gordon A. *Germany 1866–1945*. Oxford: Clarendon Press, 1978.

Destouches, Ernst von. *Das Oktoberfest in München 1810–1910*. Munich: J. Lindauersche Buchhandlung, 1910.

Dombart, Theodor. *Schwabing: Münchens älteste und schönste Tochter*. Munich: Hanns Lindner Verlag, 1967.

Dreher, Conrad. *Münchner Originale*. Stuttgart, Leipzig, Vienna, and Berlin: Deutsche Verlags Anstalt.

Eber, Hans. "Münchner Originale." *Illustrierte Fremdenzeitung*, 29 August 1925, pp. 749–750.

Eberstaller, Gerhard. *Zirkus und Varieté in Wien*. Vienna and Munich: Jugend und Volk Verlag, 1974.

100 Jahre Rotkreuzdienst in der Stadt und im Landkreis München. Munich, 1975.

1875–1975. Einhundert Jahre Städtestatistik in München: Statistisches Handbuch der Landeshauptstadt München. Munich: Carl Gerber Verlag, 1975.

"Erinnerung an Andreas Welsch." *Münchner Anzeiger*, 9 March 1956, p. 4.

Falckenberg, Otto. *Mein Leben—Mein Theater*, ed. Wolfgang Petzet. Munich, Vienna, and Leipzig: Zinnen Verlag, 1944.

Feldman, Gerald D. *Army, Industry, and Labor in Germany 1914–1918*. Princeton: Princeton University Press, 1966.

Fishman, Sterling, "Prophets, Poets, and Priests: A Study of the Men and Ideas

That Made the Munich Revolution of 1918–19." Ph. D. diss., University of Wisconsin, 1960.

Franz, Georg. "Munich: Birthplace and Center of the National Socialist German Workers' Party." *Journal of Modern History,* 29 (December 1957): 319–334.

Fritz, Carl. *München als Industriestadt.* Berlin: Puttkamer und Mühlbrecht Verlag, 1913.

Gasteiger, Michael (Stadtrat). *Die Not in München.* Munich: Reichszentrale für Heimatdienst, 1923.

Gay, Peter. *Freud, Jews, and Other Germans: Masters and Victims in Modernist Culture.* Oxford: Oxford University Press, 1978.

——— *Weimar Culture: The Outsider as Insider.* New York and Evanston, Ill.: Harper & Row, 1968.

Geis, Jacob. *Münchner Original Couplets.* Leipzig: Frank Dietrich Verlag.

Gellately, Robert. *The Politics of Economic Despair: Shopkeepers and German Politics 1890–1914.* London and Beverly Hills: SAGE Publications, 1974.

Glang, Heinz. "Das Recht des Arbeitnehmers, insbesondere des Bühnenkünstlers auf Beschäftigung." Ph.D. diss., University of Kiel, 1933.

Glossy, Blanks, and Robert Haas, eds. *Wiener Comödienlieder aus drei Jahrhunderten.* Vienna: Anton Schroll Verlag, 1924.

Gordon, Harold J., Jr. *Hitler and the Beer-Hall Putsch.* Princeton: Princeton University Press, 1972.

Gotta, Johannes, *Der Kabarettkünstler.* Leipzig: Hermann Beyer Verlag, 1925.

Graf, Oskar Maria. *Gelächter von Aussen.* Munich: Kurt Desch Verlag, 1966.

——— *Prisoners All,* trans. Margaret Green. New York: Knopf, 1928

Greul, Heinz, *Bretter die die Zeit bedeuten: Die Kulturgeschichte des Kabaretts.* Cologne and Berlin: Kiepenheuer & Witsch Verlag, 1969.

Gromes, Martin. "Vom Alt-Wiener Volksstück zur Wiener Operette." Ph.D. diss., University of Munich, 1967.

Haas, Ursula, "Die Kulturpolitik des bayerischen Landtages in der Zeit der Weimarer Republik, 1918–33." Ph.D. diss., University of Munich, 1967.

Hausenstein, Wilhelm. *Die Masken des Komikers Karl Valentin.* Munich: Karl Alber Verlag, 1948.

Heberlein, Emil. *Das Kleingewerbe in Bayern vor dem Kriege 1914/15 und die Bestrebungen zu seiner Hebung.* Munich, Berlin, and Leipzig: J. Schweitzer Verlag, 1915.

Hellmer, Otto. "Alters-, Invaliden-, Hinterbliebenen Fürsorge der Bühnenangehörigen in Deutschland." Ph.D. diss., University of Munich, 1928.

Helmstätt, Carl, *Siebzig Jahre aus meinem Leben 1834–1904.* Munich: Pössenbacher'sche Buchdruckerei, 1904.

Hentschel, Volker. *Weimars letzte Monate: Hitler und der Untergang der Republik,* 2nd ed. Düsseldorf: Droste Verlag, 1979.

Hochdorf, Max. *Die deutsche Bühnengenossenschaft.* Potsdam: Gustav Kiepenheuer Verlag, 1921.

Hoferichter, Ernst, *Jahrmarkt meines Lebens.* Munich, Vienna, and Basel: Bayerischer Landwirtschaftsverlag, 1963.

——— *Vom Prinzregenten bis Karl Valentin.* Munich, Basel, and Vienna: Bayerischer Landwirtschaftsverlag, 1966.

Holborn, Hajo. *A History of Modern Germany, 1840-1945,* vol. 3. New York: Alfred A. Knopf, 1969.

Hollweck, Ludwig. "Bei Papa Geis im Oberpollinger." *Münchener Leben,* 15 (May 1970): 36–37.

—— "Erinnerungen an Karl Valentin." *Bayerland* (March 1969): 19–26.

—— *Karikaturen: Von den fliegenden Blättern zum Simplicissimus, 1844 bis 1914.* Munich: Süddeutscher Verlag, 1973.

—— *München: von der Besiedlung der Münchner Gegend bis 1967 in Stichworten erzählt.* Munich: Wilhelm Unverhau Verlag, 1968.

Huber, Gerdi. *Das Klassische Schwabing: München als Zentrum der intellektuellen Zeit- und Gesellschaftskritik an der Wende des 19. zum 20. Jahrhunderts.* Munich: Wolfe Verlag, 1973.

Hug, Heinz. *Erich Mühsam: Untersuchungen zum Leben und Werk.* Glashütten im Taunus: Detlev Auvermann KG, 1974.

Jansen, Reinhard. *Georg von Vollmar: Eine politische Biographie.* Düsseldorf: Droste Verlag, 1958.

Jones, Gareth Stadman. "Working-Class Culture and Working-Class Politics in London, 1870–1900: Notes on the Remaking of a Working Class." *Journal of Social History,* 7 (Summer 1974): 460–508.

Kalmer, Georg. "Die 'Massen' in der Revolution 1918/19: Die Unterschichten als Problem der bayerischen Revolutionsforschung." *Zeitschrift für Bayerische Landesgeschichte,* 34 (1971): 316–357.

Karl, Willibald. *Jugend, Gesellschaft und Politik im Zeitraum des ersten Weltkrieges.* Munich: Stadtarchiv, 1973.

Das Karl Valentin Buch. Munich: Knorr & Hirth Verlag, 1932.

Karlstadt, Liesl. *Original-Vorträge von Karl Valentin.* Munich: Max Hieber Verlag, 1926.

Katalog des Valentin-Museums. Munich: Werbedruck Rudolf Stephanek, 1960.

Kater, Michael H. "Zur Soziographie der frühen NSDAP." *Vierteljahreshefte für Zeitgeschichte,* 19 (January 1971): 124–159.

Kaufmann, Aloys. "Die sozialen Leistungen der deutschen Bühnengenossenschaft." Ph.D. diss., University of Erlangen, 1931.

Keilhacker, Martin. *Jugendpflege und Jugendbewegung in München: Von den Befreiungskriegen bis zur Gegenwart.* Munich: Bayerland Verlag, 1926.

Kocka, Jürgen. "The First World War and the 'Mittelstand': German Artisans and White-Collar Workers." *Journal of Contemporary* History, 8 (January 1973): 101–123.

—— *Klassengesellschaft im Krieg: Deutsche Sozialgeschichte 1914–1918.* Göttingen: Vandenhoeck & Ruprecht, 1973.

Kohl, Gudrun, *Von Papa Geis bis Karl Valentin.* Munich: Wilhelm Unverhau Verlag, 1971.

Kolb, Eberhard. "Geschichte und Vorgeschichte der Revolution von 1918/19 in Bayern." *Neue Politische Literatur,* 16 (1971): 383–394.

Koller, Josef. *Das Wiener Volkssängertum in alter und neuer Zeit.* Vienna: Gerlach und Wiedling Verlag, 1931.

"Die Komiker." *Münchner Stadtanzeiger,* 23 February 1951, p. 3.

König, Hannes. "Das Genius des Unzulänglichen." *Bayerland* (March 1969): 6–18.

Koschmeider, E. *Die Altersversorgung des deutschen Bühnenkünstler.* Esslingen: Wilhelm Langhuth Verlag, 1929.

Kothe, Robert. *Saitenspiel des Lebens.* Munich: Knorr & Hirth Verlag. 1944.

Kritzer, Peter. *Die bayerische Sozialdemokratie und die bayerische Politik in den Jahren 1918 bis 1923.* Munich: Stadtarchiv, 1969.

Kronegg, Ferdinand. *Münchner Volksschauspiel: Szenen und Bilder aus Bayerns Geschichte.* Munich: Seitz & Schauer Verlag, 1898.

Krüger, Peter. "Das Reparationsproblem der Weimarer Republik in fragwürdiger Sicht: Kritische Überlegungen zur neuesten Forschung." *Vierteljahreshefte für Zeitgeschichte,* 29 (January 1981): 2–47.

Kutscher, Artur. *Wedekind: Leben und Werk,* ed. Karl Ude, rev. ed. Munich: List Verlag, 1964.

Landauer, Carl. 'lvhe Bavapian Problem in the Weimar Republic." *Journal of Modern History,* 16 (September and June 1944): 93–115, 201–223.

Laqueur, Walter. "The Role of the Intelligentsia in the Weimar Republic." *Social Research,* 39 (Summer 1972): 213–22.

────── *Weimap: A Cultural History, 1918–33.* New York: G. P. Putnam's Sons, 1974.

────── *Young Germany: A History of the German Youth Movement.* New York: Basic Books, 1972.

────── and George Mosse, eds. *Literature and Politics in the Twentieth Century.* New York and Evanston, Ill.: Harper & Row, 1967.

Lebovics, Hermann, *Social Conservatism and the Middle Classes in Germany, 1914–33.* Princeton: Princeton University Press, 1969.

Lehnert, Herbert, and Wulf Segebrecht. "Thomas Mann im Münchner Zensurbeirat (1912/13): Ein Beitrag zum Verhältnis Thomas Mann zu Frank Wedekind." *Jahrbuch der deutschen Schillergesellschaft,* 7 (1963): 190–200.

Lenman, R. J. V. "Art, Society, and the Law in Wilhelmine Germany: The Lex Heinze." *Oxford German Studies,* 8 (1973): 86–113.

Lutz, Josef Maria. *Die Münchner Volkssänger.* Munich: Süddeutscher Verlag, 1956.

Malcolmson, Robert W. "Popular Culture and Social Change." *Journal of Popular Culture,* 4 (Spring 1971): 1039–1044.

Mann, Golo. *Deutsche Geschichte des 19. und 20. Jahrhunderts.* Frankfurt am Main: Samuel Fischer Verlag, 1966.

Martens, Kurt. *Schonungslose Lebenschronik,* pt. 2. Vienna, Berlin, Leipzig, and Munich: Rikola Verlag, 1924.

Maser, Werner. *Die Frühgeschichte der NSDAP.* Bonn and Frankfurt am Main: Athenäum Verlag, 1965.

May, Erich Joachim. *Wiener Volkskomödie und Vormärz.* Berlin: Henschelverlag, 1975.

Mayer, Arno J. "The Lower Middle Classes as an Historical Problem." *Journal of Modern History,* 47 (September 1975): 409–436.

Millowitsch, Willy, ed. *Da bleibt kein Auge trocken.* Munich: Lichtenberg Verlag, 1966.

Mitchell, Allan. *Revolution in Bavaria, 1918-19: The Eisner Regime and the Soviet Republic.* Princeton: Princeton University Press, 1965.

Möckl, Karl. *Die Prinzregentenzeit: Gesellschaft und Politik während der Ära des Prinzregenten Luitpold von Bayern.* Munich and Vienna: Oldenbourg Verlag, 1972.

Mosse, George. *The Crisis of German Ideology.* New York: Howard Fertig Press, 1966.

―――― *Germans and Jews: The Right, the Left, and the Search for a "Third Force" in Pre-Nazi Germany.* New York: Howard Fertig Press, 1970.

―――― *The Nationalization of the Masses.* New York: Howard Fertig Press, 1975.

Mühsam, Erich. *Fanal: Aufsätze und Gedichte 1905-32,* ed. Kurt Kreiler. Berlin: Klaus Wagenbach Verlag, 1977.

―――― *Unpolitische Erinnerungen.* Leipzig: Volk und Buch Verlag, 1949.

Müller, Karl Alexander von. *Im Wandel einer Welt: Erinnerungen.* Munich: Süddeutscher Verlag, 1966.

―――― *Mars und Venus: Erinnerungen, 1914/19.* Stuttgart: Gustav Klipper Verlag, 1954.

"Münchner Volkssänger." *Jugend,* 22 (Special Issue, 1935).

Münsterer, Hans Otto. *Erinnerungen aus den Jahren 1917-22.* Zurich: Verlag der Arche, 1962.

Münz, Erwin and Elisabeth Münz, eds. *Geschriebenes von und an Karl Valentin.* Munich: Süddeutscher Verlag, 1978.

Nestroy, Johann. *Ausgewählte Werke,* ed. Hans Weigel. Gütersloh: Sigbert Mohn Verlag, 1962.

―――― *Gesammelte Briefe (1831-62),* ed. Fritz Brukner. Vienna: Wallishausser Verlag, 1938.

Neubauer, Helmut. *München und Moskau 1918/19: Zur Geschichte der Rätebewegung in Bayern.* Munich: Isar Verlag, 1958.

Nicholls, Anthony, and Erich Matthias, eds. *German Democracy and the Triumph of Hitler.* London: George Allen & Unwin, 1971.

Nipperdey, Thomas. *Gesellschaft, Kultur, Theorie: Gesammelte Aufsätze zur neueren Geschichte.* Göttingen: Vandenhoeck & Ruprecht, 1976.

Obermeier, Siegfried. *Münchens goldene Jahre.* Munich: C. Bertelsmann Verlag, 1976.

Orlow, Dietrich. *The History of the Nazi Party: 1919-33,* vol. 1. Pittsburgh: University of Pittsburgh Press, 1969.

Perktold, K. "Der Weiss Ferdl lebt im 'Platzl' weiter." *Münchner Stadtzeitung,* 15 March 1956, p. 3.

Petzet, Wolfgang. *Die Münchner Kammerspiele, 1911-72.* Munich, Vienna, and Basel: Verlag Kurt Desch, 1973.

Phelps, Reginald H. "Before Hitler Came: Thule Society and Germanen Orden." *Journal of Modern History,* 35 (September 1963): 245-261.

Piper, Reinhold. *Mein Leben als Verleger.* Munich: Piper Verlag, 1964.

Plewnia, Margarete. *Auf dem Weg zu Hitler: Der "völkische Publizist" Dietrich Eckart.* Bremen: Schunemann-Universitäts-Verlag, 1970.

Prevot, René. "Papa Geis und sein Kabarett bleiben unvergessen." *Münchner Merkur,* 9 February 1953, p. 4.

Proebst, Hermann, and Karl Ude, eds. *Denk ich an München: Ein Buch der Erinnerungen.* Munich: Gräfe und Unzer Verlag, 1966.

Prosel, Theo. *Freistaat Schwabing: Erinnerungen des Simplwirts.* Munich: Süddeutscher Verlag, 1951.

Raupach, Ernst. *Der Müller und sein Kind.* Leipzig: Phillip Reclam Verlag.

Riegler, Theo. *Das Liesl Karlstadt Buch.* Munich: Süddeutscher Verlag, 1961.

Riess, Richard. "Kabarett im Kriege." *Der Zwiebelfisch,* 7 (1915): 96–97.

Ringelnatz, Joachim. *Mein Leben bis zum Kriege.* Berlin: Ernst Rowohlt Verlag, 1931.

———— *Simplicissimus Künstlerkneipe und Kathi Kobus.* Munich.

Ringer, Fritz. *The Decline of the German Mandarins: The German Academic Community, 1890–1933.* Cambridge: Harvard University Press, 1969.

Ritter, Gerhard A., ed. *Arbeiterkultur,* Königstein/Taunus: Verlagsgruppe Athenäum, Hain, Scriptor, Haustein, 1979.

———— ed. *Das deutsche Kaiserreich, 1871–1914,* 3rd ed. Göttingen: Vandenhoeck & Ruprecht, 1977.

Rohrbach, Paul. *Deutsches Leben: Wurzeln und Wandlungen.* Wiesbaden: Eberhard Brockhaus Verlag, 1948.

Rommel, Otto. *Die Alt-Wiener Volkskomödie.* Vienna: Schroll Verlag, 1952.

———— *Johann Nestroy: Ein Beitrag zur Geschichte der Wiener Volkskomik.* Vienna: Schroll Verlag, 1930.

Sailer, Josef Benno. *Des Bayernkönigs Revolutionstage.* Munich: Carl Durk Verlag, 1919.

———— "Gesangshumoristen Karl Maxstadt." *Faschingszeitung,* 1931, p. 5.

———— *O Kommunal Verband!* Munich: Grossmünchen Verlag, 1920.

Salvator-Saison 1909. Munich: Selbstverlag der Paulanerbrauerei, 1909.

Sauer, Wolfgang, "Weimar Culture: Experiments in Modernism." *Social Research,* 39 (Summer 1972): 254–284.

Schade, Franz. *Kurt Eisner und die bayerische Sozialdemokratie.* Hannover: Verlag für Literatur und Zeitgeschehen, 1961.

Schmidt, Erwin. *Die Geschichte der Stadt Wien.* Vienna and Munich: Jugend und Volk Verlag, 1978.

Schneider, Ludwig M. *Die populäre Kritik an Staat und Gesellschaft in München, 1886–1914: Ein Beitrag zur Vorgeschichte der Münchner Revolution von 1918/19.* Munich: Stadtarchiv, 1975.

Schnorbus, Axel. *Arbeit und Sozialordnung in Bayern vor dem ersten Weltkrieg (1890–1914).* Munich: Stadtarchiv, 1969.

Schrott, Ludwig. *Münchner Alltag in acht Jahrhunderten.* Munich: Hugendubel Verlag, 1975.

Schrumpf, Ernst. *Das Münchner Volkstheater.* Munich, 1913.

Schulte, Michael, ed. *Das grosse Karl Valentin Buch.* Munich and Zurich: Piper Verlag, 1973.

———— ed. *Karl Valentin in Selbstzeugnissen und Bilddokumenten.* Reinbek bei Hamburg: Rowohlt Verlag, 1968.

Schütze, Christian, ed. *Facsimile Querschnitt durch den Simplicissimus.* Bern, Stuttgart, and Vienna: Scherz Verlag, 1963.

Schwimmer, Helmut. *Karl Valentin: Analyse zur Sprache und Literatur.* Munich: Oldenbourg Verlag, 1977.

Seybold, Karl. *Sechzig Jahre Tätigkeit im Münchner Feuerlöschwesen, 1866–1926.* Munich: Buchdruckerei Ph. L. Jung, 1926.

Sieczynski, Rudolf. *Altwiener Volkskomiker.* Vienna: Wiener Verlag, 1947.

Simplicissimus Künstler-Kneipe. Munich: Künstlerkneipe Simplicissimus.

Singleton, Gregory H. "Popular Culture or the Culture of the Populace?" *Journal of Popular Culture,* 11 (Summer 1977): 254–266.

Sinsheimer, Hermann. *Gelebt im Paradies.* Munich: Richard Pflaum Verlag, 1953.

Spindler, Max, ed. *Handbuch der Bayerischen Geschichte,* vol. 4, pt. 2, *Das Neue Bayern 1800–1970.* Munich: C. H. Beck'sche Verlagsbuchhandlung, 1975.

Steinke, Gerhardt Edward. *The Life and Work of Hugo Ball, Founder of Dadaism.* The Hague and Paris: Mouton Verlag, 1967.

Stern, Fritz. *The Politics of Cultural Despair: A Study in the Rise of the Germanic Ideology.* Berkeley and Los Angeles: University of California Press, 1963.

Thoma, Ludwig, *Ein Leben in Briefen.* Munich: Piper Verlag, 1963.

Tränhardt, Dietrich. *Wahlen und politische Strukturen in Bayern 1848–1953: Historisch-soziologische Untersuchungen zum Entstehen und zur Neuerrichtung eines Parteisystems.* Düsseldorf: Droste Verlag, 1973.

Toller, Ernst. *Eine Jugend in Deutschland.* Amsterdam: Querido Verlag, 1933.

Tyrell, Albrecht. *Vom "Trommler" zum "Führer": Der Wandel von Hitlers Selbstverständnis zwischen 1919 und 1924.* Munich: Wilhelm Fink Verlag, 1975.

Ude, Karl. *Frank Wedekind.* Mühlacker: Stieglitz Verlag, 1966.

Valentin, Karl. *Alles von Karl Valentin,* ed. Michael Schulte. Munich: Piper Verlag, 1978.

——— *Gesammelte Werke.* Munich: Piper Verlag, 1961.

——— *Karl Valentins Lachkabinett,* ed. Gerhard Pallmann. Munich: Piper Verlag, 1951.

——— *Der Knabe Karl.* Berlin: Paul Steegemann Verlag, 1951.

——— *Original-Vorträge.* Munich: G. Franz'sche Buchdruckerei, 1926.

——— *Original-Vorträge.* Munich: F. P. Erlacher.

——— *Original-Vorträge.* Munich: Karl Valentin.

——— *Sturzflüge im Zuschauerraum der Gesammelten Werke,* vol. 2. Munich: Piper Verlag, 1969.

——— "Wie ich Volkssänger wurde." *Bayerischer Hauskalender* (1928).

Valentin-Zeitung, ed. *Valentinisartorausstellungsturmausschuss.* Munich: Piper Verlag, 1971.

Vicinus, Martha. *The Industrial Muse: A Study of Nineteenth Century British Working-Class Literature.* New York: Harper & row, 1974.

Waite, Robert G. L. *Vanguard of Nazism: The Free Corps Movement in Postwar Germany, 1918–23.* Cambridge: Harvard University Press, 1952.

Walker, Mack. *German Home Towns: Community, State, and General Estate 1648–1871.* Ithaca and London: Cornell University Press, 1971.

Wedekind, Frank. *Prosa: Erzählungen, Aufsätze, Selbstzeugnisse, Briefe.* Berlin and Weimar: Aufbau Verlag, 1969.

Wehler, Hans-Ulrich. *Das Deutsche Kaiserreich, 1871–1918.* Göttingen: Vanden-hoeck & Ruprecht, 1977.

Weigl, Eugen. *Die Münchner Volkstheater im 19. Jahrhundert 1817–1900.* Munich: Stadtarchiv, 1961.

Weiss Ferdl. *Bayerische Schmankerln,* ed. Bertl Weiss. Munich: Süddeutscher Verlag, 1960.

———— *Gemütliches München,* ed. Bertl Weiss. Munich: Süddeutscher Verlag, 1961.

———— *Ich bin kein Intellektueller.* Munich: Paul Hugendubel Verlag, 1941.

———— *Münchner Humor.* Munich: Verlag Münchner Humor, 1924–25.

———— "So wurde ich Münchner Volkssänger." *Münchner Merkur,* 29–30 December 1951, p. 5.

———— *Szenen und Possen.* Munich: Verlag Münchner Humor.

———— *Weiss Ferdl erzählt sein Leben.* Munich: Richard Pflaum Verlag, 1953.

———— *Weiss Ferdl guat troffa.* Munich: H. Hugendubel Verlag, 1933.

———— *Weissblaues Welttheater.* Freiburg-im-Breisgau: Hyperion Verlag, 1960.

Welsch, Andreas. *Münchner Volksleben in Lied und Wort.* Munich: Kramer Ver-lag.

———— *Süddeutsche Couplets und Solo-Vorträge.* Munich: Kramer Verlag.

Die wichtigsten Wohlfahrts- und Fürsorge-Einrichtungen Münchens: Verein für Fraueninteressen und Frauenarbeit. Munich: Ernst Reinhardt Verlag, 1920.

Willett, John. *Art and Politics in the Weimar Period: The New Sobriety, 1917–33.* New York: Pantheon Books, 1978.

Winkler, Heinrich August. "From Social Protectionism to National Socialism: The German Small-Business Movement in Comparative Perspective." *Journal of Modern History,* 48 (March 1976): 1–18.

———— *Mittelstand, Demokratie und Nationalsozialismus.* Cologne: Kiepenheuer & Witsch Verlag, 1972.

Wohlfahrts- und Jugendamt der Landeshauptstadt München nach dem yeltkriege, ed. Städtisches Wohlfahrts- und Jugendamt München. Munich: Gebrüder Parcus A-G, 1929.

Wolkan, Rudolf. *Wiener Volkslieder aus fünf Jahrhunderten,* vol. 2. Vienna: Wie-ner Bibliophilengesellschaft, 1920.

Wolter, Karl Kurt. *Karl Valentin—privat.* Munich and Cologne: Günter Olzog Verlag, 1958.

Zijderveld, Anton C. *Humor und Gesellschaft: Eine Soziologie des Humors und des Lachens.* Graz, Vienna, and Cologne: Styria Verlag, 1976.

Index

DATE DUE

JUN 01 1999			
GAYLORD			PRINT